SELF-HEALING

Ancient Wisdom Applied to Today`s World

by Bruce Taylor

Disclaimers

The author is not a medical practitioner and does not dispense medical advice. The healing information in this book is intended solely to augment, and not replace in any way, medical advice and treatment by your medical doctor. The author assumes no responsibility for the way an individual chooses to interpret and use the information presented in this book.

With Gratitude

This book would not exist without the support and guidance of everyone with whom I have shared time during this journey through life. There are too many to name here. Please know that I am deeply grateful to all of you.

I would particularly like to thank His Holiness Lungtuk Tenpai Nyima for guiding me in relearning the nature of mind, Devageet for imparting his wisdom on the world of healing, John Milton for guiding me in gaining experiential knowledge of the human experience, and Javier Regueiro for his friendship and support in diving deep into my shadow side.

I would also like to thank the participants at the many gatherings, workshops, and retreats that I have facilitated over the past few years. Your insights, feedback, and presence have played a major role in shaping the contents of this book in a way that will hopefully make it more accessible to the reader.

Lastly, I would like to thank my wife, Carie, for her patience, Love, and support throughout the journey of creating both this book and 'The Way Home'.

I Love you all. Thank you.

Table of Contents

Contents

"At the center of your being you have the answer; you know what you are and you know what you want."

— Lao Tzu

Introduction

Welcome to an alternative view of healing. This perspective combines esoteric knowledge of the human experience with ancient healing wisdom to provide a way for everyone to become their own self-healer.

In this model of the healing arts, physical and mental ailments are seen as messengers to be heard rather than things to be cured. Your ailments are indicators that you have barriers inside yourself to your being able to experience life from the essence of who you really are. The process of becoming a self-healer involves learning how to hear those messages and to then remove the underlying barriers.

Others can guide you through this healing process but only you can actually remove the barriers inside you. You have to become your own self-healer.

Embarking upon the journey of healing yourself is not something to be undertaken lightly. That journey will ask you to delve deep inside yourself in order to remove all the barriers inside you that you have built against Love. It will dissolve away the illusions that you hold about yourself, will reveal the essence of who you really are, and will have a profound effect on your understanding of both healing and the human experience. It is not for the faint of heart.

If you feel ready to embark upon that inner journey then welcome. All that you will need to bring with you is an open mind and a fierce determination to heal yourself. You will face many challenges and pitfalls along the way. However, the rewards are immeasurable. Not only will it increase your level of health, it will also provide you with the opportunity to: awaken to who you really are; take back your life from those who have told you how you 'should' live it; cultivate a sense of inner peace; and, become Love.

However, please don't believe me. In fact, please don't believe anything that you read in this book. I am going to present a perspective on the human experience that may be substantially different from your current beliefs. It may be challenging for you to have your beliefs questioned in this way. I am not asking you to blindly believe anything. Our journey together is not about creating a new belief system. It is about providing you with the tools to experientially discover for yourself whether or not you can become your own self-healer.

All that I ask is that you remain open to the possibility that what you read may be true for you. With that openness, you can then choose to take the insights that you glean from this book and apply them to your own healing journey. You will be able to see for yourself if there is anything in this perspective on healing that is of value to you.

I found out for myself. I grew up in Canada and was raised to 'believe' that healing was solely about 'fixing' any physical or mental problems that arose in the body and mind. I also believed in the 'Canadian Dream' that material success would bring me an abundance of happiness. I spent the first twenty years of my adult life achieving that dream. I made it. I became 'successful' and had everything that was supposed to make me happy. Unfortunately, it didn't work; at least not for me. I was miserable.

I had become highly 'successful' and struggled each morning to get up and face the day. I sank ever deeper into despair until it eventually became so intolerable that I chose to walk away from that life. I left everything behind and set out on 'safari'. I travelled the world for twelve years. I was searching for a way to be happy and for a form of love that resonated with me. During that time, a close friend of mine was diagnosed with terminal cancer and I also began to search for a cure. Yup, I was a dreamer.

Shortly after setting out, I found myself in a Tibetan monastery where I studied the 'nature of mind' under the guidance of an enlightened master. He opened my eyes to what the human experience is all about. The experiential knowledge that I gained from him triggered me to go on an inner journey of self-discovery. I soon felt drawn to leave the monastic world and began to wander the globe. I didn't actually know what I was doing or where I was going. I simply felt determined to find another way of living, or should I say being, and went looking for it. During that journey, I:

- made the practice of mindful awareness be my normal waking state;

- connected to my inner guide and learned to trust it;

- cultivated self-Love;

- did a great deal of inner healing work;

- studied past life regression;

- was exposed to a number of indigenous cultures;

- explored a number of religions and learned the difference between religion and spirituality;

- undertook shamanic initiation in Peru; and,

- discovered a form of healing that worked for me.

It was a beautiful and challenging journey. It gifted me with an experiential understanding of the human experience that went far beyond the prevailing view of my society. I found the Love that I had been searching for and a deep sense of inner peace and joy arose from inside me. My desire for any fleeting happiness dissolved away. I also discovered a perspective on healing that changed my entire view of what healing was really all about.

This book focuses specifically on what I discovered about healing. It describes a healing modality that anyone can use for becoming a self-healer. I used it to heal myself and also witnessed others use it to heal themselves of both minor and potentially terminal ailments. I invite you, the reader, to explore it for yourself.

I also invite you to expand upon it. I feel that this healing modality is a starting point for taking healing to a whole new level. I envision that our understanding of healing will expand and grow as more and more people add their own healing insights.

Enjoy the ride. I know I did.

"Love is not a thing to understand. Love is not a thing to feel. Love is not a thing to give and receive. Love is a thing only to become and eternally be." (1)

— Sri Chinmoy

1. The Human Experience

The process for becoming a self-healer that we are going to explore in this book will ask you to open yourself up to the possibility that you are more than just a mind and body. Doing that will shift you into a way of being that will enable you to both heal yourself and discover the essence of who you really are.

Thus, before we dive deeper into self-healing, we are first going to explore what this journey through life is all about. We will explore what it means to be a human being and will introduce a form of Love that goes far beyond the prevailing understanding of the word love.

****

What is a Human Being?

We will begin with the question, 'What is a human being?'

Are we just a body? Are we a body that also has a mind with its associated thoughts and feelings? Do we also have a soul that is inhabiting that body and mind?

I am not going to presume to be able to give you a definitive answer to these questions. There have been many attempts made to do so in the past and those attempts have invariably led to the creation of one belief system or another. My intention is not to seed a new belief system. My intention is to point you towards something and then provide you with tools that will allow you to answer these questions for yourself. I will go into detail on those tools in the subsequent chapters.

In this chapter, I am going to present an interpretation of the human experience. There is a Buddhist expression, 'The finger points at the moon but the finger is not the moon'. The interpretation provided in this chapter is pointing at something but it is not that something. Please remember that the information presented in this chapter is only a pointer and that it is not to be taken as gospel.

All I ask is that you remain open to the possibility that it will point you toward something that you can experientially discover for yourself.

I travelled the world in search of my own answers to life's mysteries and was gifted with the opportunity to work with a number of enlightened masters. They invited me to discover the essence of who I am and gave me guidance in doing so. The result was an experiential knowledge of the human experience. I discovered that, at least for me, there was indeed 'something else'; something beyond my mind and body.

During my travels, I was also able to study a wide variety of belief systems and cultures. I found that all of those belief systems were fundamentally pointing at the same thing; that the human experience is more than simply a journey of the mind and body. There is something else – a soul, witnessing consciousness, bit of God, or higher self – that is functioning in tandem with the mind and body.

I attempted many times to describe the human experience to those who asked. Eventually, I began to draw a pictorial image of my experience of being human for those who wanted to know. A friend then asked if I could map a variety of belief systems onto that image. The result is shown in *'Diagram 1 – The Human Being'*.

Before I describe the diagram, I invite you NOT to believe anything that I say. This diagram is simply one interpretation of the human experience. It has been created with the sole intention of pointing you towards the possibility that you are more than your body and mind. It is not intended to accurately define what is beyond your body and mind. It is the finger not the moon. Please don't get lost in rationalizing the validity of the image or the mapping. All that I ask is that you be open to the possibility that there is something to point at.

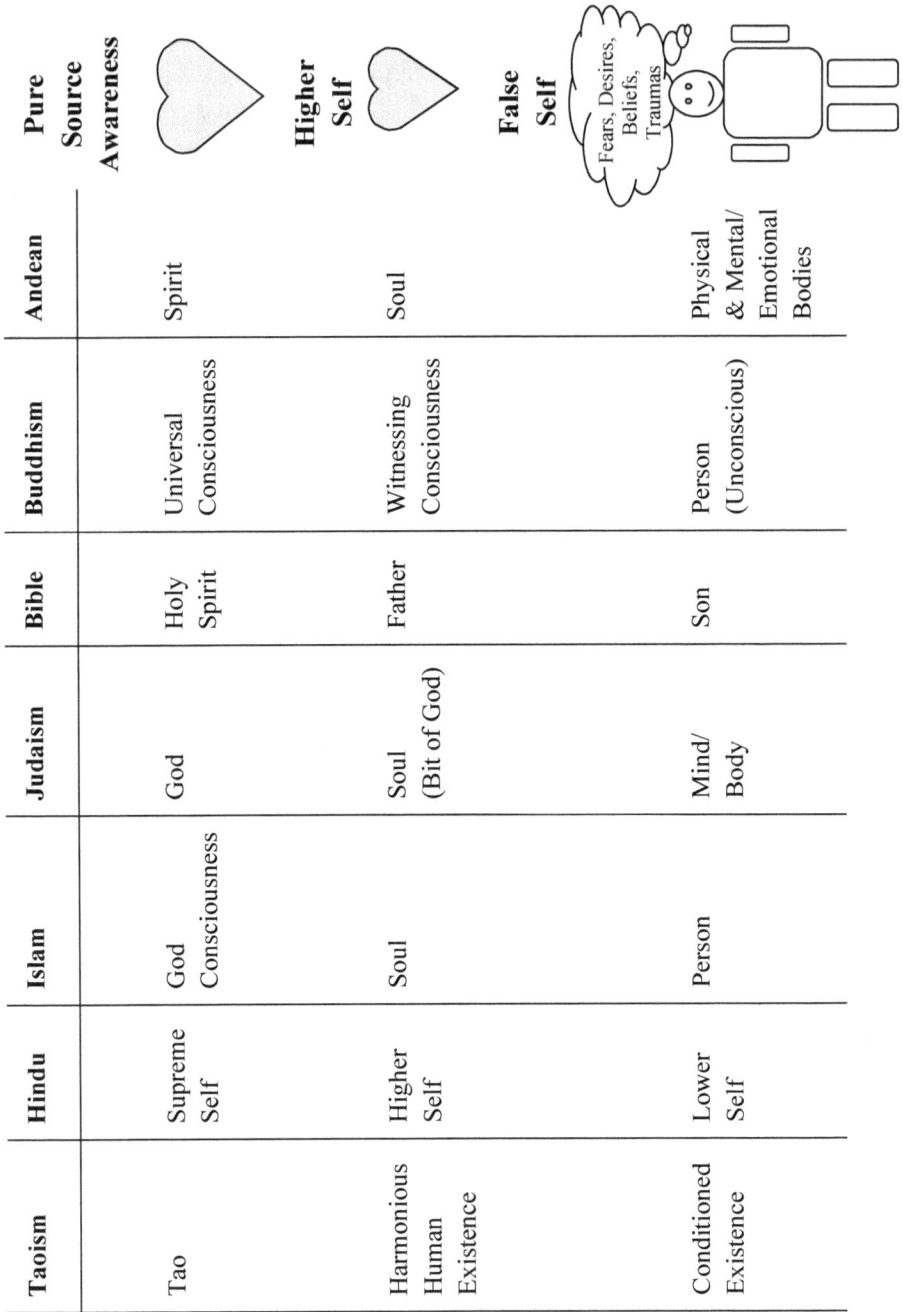

	Taoism	Hindu	Islam	Judaism	Bible	Buddhism	Andean
Pure Source Awareness	Tao	Supreme Self	God Consciousness	God	Holy Spirit	Universal Consciousness	Spirit
Higher Self	Harmonious Human Existence	Higher Self	Soul	Soul (Bit of God)	Father	Witnessing Consciousness	Soul
False Self	Conditioned Existence	Lower Self	Person	Mind/Body	Son	Person (Unconscious)	Physical & Mental/Emotional Bodies

False Self thought bubble: Fears, Desires, Beliefs, Traumas

Diagram 1 – The Human Being

The image in diagram 1 shows a person with a cloud above their head. The person represents the body and the cloud represents the mind. Inside the mind is the ego which, for the purposes of this book, is simply a set of fears, beliefs, desires, and emotional traumas. The mind, with the ego inside it, and the body are together referred to as the false self. That false self may feel very real to a person who is identified with it, yet it is still false.

At the top of the diagram is a large heart with the words 'Pure Source Awareness' written above it. It is known simply as Source and it is a field of awareness that infuses everything in this world of form. The energy of Source is Divine Love.

Below the large heart, and above the body and mind, is another heart with the words 'Higher Self' written above it. The Higher Self is also known as the soul. All souls are seeded out of Source and all carry the same energy of Divine Love. There is one Source and many souls.

What is a person? The prevailing understanding of a person is someone who has a mind and body. A human being is far more than that. A human being includes the person, with its mind and body, as well as a soul.

****

The Human Being and Various Belief Systems

In diagram 1, there are seven columns that show the mapping of a few existing belief systems onto this interpretation of the Human Being. This is a highly simplified mapping and I apologize in advance for any misinterpretations that may exist. My intention is simply to highlight that many different belief systems are all pointing at there being something to the human journey that goes beyond the mind and body.

The column closest to the image in Diagram 1 maps the Andean Spiritual Tradition's interpretation of the human experience. It describes the human being as having four bodies:

The **Physical** body that we can see and feel;

The **Mental / Emotional** body that contains all of our thoughts and emotions;

The **Soul** which is the eternal part of ourselves that was seeded out of Source and reincarnates over and over again; and,

The **Spirit** which is the pure Source Awareness out of which all souls are created.

The other columns in diagram 1 show how each of Buddhism, Christianity, Judaism, Islam, Hinduism, and Taoism can also be mapped onto the same graphic.

It does not matter which, if any, of these models of the human being are accurate. To me, they are all simply fingers pointing at the moon, they are not the moon. What is intriguing to me is that they all indicate the possibility that there is a higher self (a.k.a. witnessing consciousness, Father, Soul, or harmonious human existence) that we can all return to if only we would let go of identifying with the false self.

****

What is Love?

We have now opened up the possibility that the human being is more than just an ego-mind and body. That opens the door to self-healing and you can step through that door by expanding your understanding of the word 'Love' to being something that you become not something you give or receive.

Humanity has created a complex relationship with the word love because of a misunderstanding as to its source. For the remainder of this book, we will be differentiating between 'love' and 'Love'.

We invite you to be open to the possibility that there is a field of energy that underlies everything in this world of form. That field has been referred to by different belief systems as the Holy Spirit, Tao, God, the Universal Consciousness, pure Source awareness, and many other terms. We will be referring to it as Source and we will be referring to the energy of Source as Divine Love; or Love for short. Love is the essence of who we are.

We invite you to also be open to the possibility that you have a soul, an individuated aspect of Source. From my own experience, I know that I have a soul and that you do as well. Our souls are seeded from Source and they also carry the energy of Divine Love. In this way, Love is available to everyone because it is constantly flowing from their Soul into their minds and bodies. However, please do not believe me. Instead, find out for yourself if there is an aspect of you that exists beyond your mind and body. We will give you techniques for doing so later in this book.

Unfortunately, people have forgotten about this form of Love. People have become identified with the false self; the mind and body. At that point, they are lost. They are disconnected from their soul and from the energy of Divine Love. They are functioning from their ego-minds and there is no Love in their thoughts, words, and deeds.

Despite this forgetting, most people are subconsciously thirsting for Love and so they have created alternative forms of love; mind-based love and heart-based love. These two forms of love are ego-based and there is no Love in them.

Mind-based love is the form of love that we are referring to when we say things such as: I love chocolate because it tastes good; I love hockey because I enjoy the rush that I get when my team wins; or I love you because you make me happy. Mind-based love is all about what your ego gains from having what it wants. There is no Love and no healing power in this form of love.

Heart-based love is other centered. It is all about wanting what's best for another person. You are practicing heart-based love when, in essence, you say, 'I love you and I know what is best for you so do what I say'. This form of love is all about imposing your ego's beliefs of what is best for others on them. There is no Love and no healing power in this form of love.

People are typically living their lives in a futile search for Divine Love in the one place that it does not exist; the world of ego-based love. The result is a life of fleeting moments of sensory satisfaction amidst a sea of endless suffering.

This difference between love and Love is what Sri Chinmoy is alluding in the following statement.

"Love is not a thing to understand. Love is not a thing to feel. Love is not a thing to give and receive. Love is a thing only to become and eternally be." (1)

Both mind-based love and heart-based love are games of the ego. They are not Love. They are given and received, and have no healing energy associated with them. They have nothing to do with Divine Love. Divine Love is the Love that you become. You become it when your mind falls silent and you drop your identification with the ego-mind and body. It is Divine Love that people are actually seeking and it is Divine Love that will heal.

For the remainder of this book, we will be using upper case Love to refer to Divine Love and lower case love to refer to ego-based love.

Understanding, and then living, this distinction is key to your becoming a self-healer.

We will also be using the terms Higher Self, inner guide, and soul interchangeably to refer to the aspect of you that lies beyond the body and mind. Finally, we will be using the terms Source and pure Source awareness to refer to the field of energy that infuses everything in this world of form. All of these terms are defined in the glossary at the back of this book. Please substitute your own terms as you see fit.

****

Life is a School in which to Learn your Soul Lessons.

In order to understand the world of self-healing, we must first explore what life is really all about.

Is life simply a playground for exploring the games of the ego or is it more than that?

The answer to that question depends entirely on you. If you are identified with the false self (the mind and body), and see no value in going beyond the false, then your life will be a game of the ego. You will be cast adrift amidst the emotions and thoughts that are triggered by your false self. You will be seeking ego-based gratification and will be trying to both protect and strengthen your ego. In essence, you will be a prisoner of your ego.

On the other hand, if you are open to the possibility that you are more than a body and mind then a whole world of possibilities opens up to you. Life becomes a school in which you are able to learn the lessons of your soul's journey. Everything that comes into your life is then an opportunity to learn something about your ability to remain as Love while existing in this world of form.

Self-healing is about removing everything that causes you to become disconnected from the eternal being of Love that you are. And, the only things that can disconnect you are the various aspects of your own ego. Essentially, it is only when you are triggered into functioning in the world from your ego that you are disconnected from Love.

So, the core question underlying the journey of becoming a self-healer is, 'what triggers you into functioning from your ego rather than from Love?'

The answer is the fears, beliefs, emotional traumas, and desires that make up your ego. You cannot be functioning from fear and be Love.

You cannot be espousing or defending a belief and be Love. You cannot be caught up in the emotions and thoughts of an emotional trauma and be Love. You cannot be pursuing a desire and be Love. In essence, you cannot be functioning from your ego and be Love.

For this reason, these four components of your ego are known as the 'Barriers to Love'. Life is fundamentally about learning your soul lessons and removing your Barriers to Love so that you can exist as who you really are; Love. Life is then Love in action. Removing those barriers to Love is the self-healing journey and, once completed, you will be free from disease.

Whether you realize it or not, your Higher Self (also known as your inner guide) is constantly creating situations in your life that will provide you with opportunities to learn your soul lessons. That is why you will find recurring patterns in your life. If you miss the lesson from a given life situation then your inner guide will create a similar situation in order to give you another chance to learn that same lesson. That cycle will keep on recurring until you learn the lesson.

How do you learn your lessons?

You find and remove the Barriers to Love that are causing you to react to life events from your ego rather than from Love. For example, if you become angry then you can either lash out at the world from that anger or you can delve inside to find the part of your ego that you are trying to defend by becoming angry. If you can find and remove the Barrier to Love underlying your anger then you will be free of that source of anger. You will then be able to respond to similar situations in your life with Love rather than with anger.

Under this perspective on life, there are no good or bad events. Every event that comes into your life is providing you with the opportunity to learn your lessons; regardless of whether your ego thinks that the situation is good or bad. In the words of Rumi,

"Out beyond the ideas of rightdoing and wrongdoing, there is a field. I'll meet you there."

I invite you to drop all ideas of right and wrong and to step out into that field. You can do that by treating life as a school in which to learn your soul lessons.

By accepting the possibilities that you are more than the mind and body and that life is about learning your soul lessons, you will have opened the door to self-healing.

*"Your task is not to seek for Love, but merely to seek and find all the
barriers within yourself that you have built against it."*
— Jalal ad Din Muhammad Rumi

2. What is Healing?

The answer to this question begins by first developing a clearer
understanding of disease. We cannot begin to heal something until we
know what it is that we are trying to heal. Thus, the first question to be
asked in exploring the world of healing is,

What is disease?

I was raised to believe that disease was something to be cured by the
medical community. A pill was to be taken or a scalpel was to be used to
get rid of it. When I set out on my own inner journey, I had no idea that
there was any other way of looking at disease. I was a rather naive person.

I soon found out that there was another perspective on disease. In many
parts of the world, disease is seen as something to be heard rather than
something to be cured.

Under this alternative perspective, every physical and psychological
ailment has an energetic source. Basically, when a disturbance is created
in a person's life force energy then an illness, pain, or psychological
problem will eventually manifest. In essence, a pain or illness is simply a
messenger indicating that there is an energetic disturbance in your energy
body. If you are able to release that disturbance then your energy will
begin to flow freely and your body will heal itself. The body is a self-
healing mechanism.

****

Healing involves removing Energetic Disturbances

Healing essentially involves removing the energetic disturbances that are the root cause of all pain and illness. Energetic disturbances are created in your energy body whenever you either take on a false belief or have a misalignment in your life.

We take on false beliefs whenever we:

- become *fearful* of something;

- accept the *conditioned beliefs* of others as our own;

- *desire* something; or,

- experience an *emotionally traumatic event* that we are unable to process at the time it occurs.

We then get lost in reacting to life's events from those false beliefs rather than allowing our energy to flow freely and responding to life from Love.

These four sources of our taking on false beliefs – *fears, conditioned beliefs, desires, and emotional traumas* – are the four components of our ego. They are our barriers to Love. Removing your barriers to Love will release the energetic disturbances from your energy body that are causing your pains and illnesses. The body will then heal itself.

Rumi was referring to this process when he said that:

"Your task is not to seek for love, but merely to seek and find all the barriers within yourself that you have built against it."

Energetic disturbances are also created in our energy body when we use 'Free Will' to choose a life that is out of alignment with the life that our soul incarnated to live. In this case, you are using 'Free Will' to try and satisfy the whims of your ego. That choice can result in your living a life that is misaligned with the essence of who you are. This kind of choice will create an energetic disturbance in your energy body. Again, that disturbance will eventually lead to a pain or illness if not released.

You can release this type of energetic disturbance by changing your life choices to bring your life into alignment with the life that you incarnated to live. The body will then heal itself.

In summary, healing involves releasing the energetic disturbances caused by your fears, desires, beliefs, emotional traumas, and by living a life that is in alignment with the life you incarnated to live.

****

Healing Yourself Will Dissolve your Ego

The journey of becoming a self-healer will profoundly affect your experience of being human. It is full of challenges and pitfalls that will shake you to the core. It will destroy all of the illusions that you hold about yourself and will dissolve away your ego.

Why would you want to do that?

Because the rewards of undertaking such a journey are limitless. You will have a healthy body and mind, an ever-increasing sense of inner peace, have remembered who you really are, and be living a life that is in alignment with who you are. You will have also opened the door to returning home to Source.

Why are the rewards so vast?

Going back to the image in diagram 1, the cloud above your head contains your fears, desires, beliefs, and traumas, and they will all disappear. Your mind will become a clear vessel and you will have access to the energy of Divine Love that is flowing to you from your soul. You will have awakened from the misconception that you are the body and mind, and will have become the eternal being of Love that you have always been. Life for you then becomes Love in action.

Please don't believe me. You can discover all of this for yourself using the process for becoming a self-healer that is described in this book. All that you need to do is to remain open to the possibility that you are more than just the body and mind and then embark upon your own self-healing journey.

****

Not all Diseases are meant to be Healed

There are two instances that I am aware of in which there is no healing to be done, despite the presence of a disease or illness. The first occurs when a soul has completed their incarnation and chooses to use a disease as its way to leave the body. The second arises when there are soul lessons to be learned from a person having a debilitating illness, disease, or injury.

An example of the former was my mother. She passed away from cancer and I spent the last two months of her live assisting my father in caring for her. At the time, I looked at the message behind her disease and it was simply that she was finished here and that it was time for her to go. There was nothing to be done except to Love and support her as she crossed over.

Examples of the latter are commonplace. For example, a child may be born with Down's syndrome in order to teach the people around them lessons around Love, compassion, and humility. A person may have a debilitating disease or injury in order to learn lessons around receiving Love and activating gifts and abilities that they may not have otherwise accessed.

Even in these cases where an illness or injury is not meant to be healed, there is still a message to be gleaned. However, these instances are the exception rather than the norm. For the most part, all illnesses can be healed using this self-healing process.

****

How far do you want to go?

This self-healing process can be used for both healing existing ailments and preventing future ones. It is your choice as to how far you wish to go on the self-healing journey. You can focus:

- solely on removing the barriers to Love underlying your existing pains and illnesses; or,

- on removing all of your barriers to Love so that you can prevent future disease and become Love.

You do not have to remove all of your barriers to Love in order to heal your existing ailments. Every barrier to Love inside you does create an energetic disturbance and those disturbances will eventually manifest as physical and psychological ailments if not released. However, the key word in that last sentence is 'eventually'. Some of your barriers to Love will have manifested as ailments and many others will not; at least not yet.

If you choose to focus solely on healing your existing ailments then you will be removing some, but not all, of your barriers to Love. Your body will be healthy but the source of future ailments will still exist inside you. Your mind will also be full of thoughts and emotions stemming from your unresolved barriers to Love. You will be functioning in the world from those thoughts and emotions, and will continue to suffer the turmoil of a life lived at the whims of your ego.

That said, you will have a healthy body and will be able to keep it healthy by removing the barriers to Love underlying any new ailments that arise. That may be enough for you.

However, this process for becoming a self-healer can also be used to remove all of your barriers to Love; not just the ones underlying your existing ailments. You can use it to find and remove the barriers to Love that have not yet manifested as ailments. This has the effect of performing preventative maintenance on your body. It will also result in your dissolving your ego completely and returning 'home' to the being of Love that you have always been.

It is even possible that illness could become a thing of the past for you. If you remove all of your barriers to Love then there will be nothing inside you that could create an illness.

The Q'ero of Peru are an indigenous people who live high up in the Andes. They have a prophecy that humanity is on the cusp of moving into a golden age called the Taripay Pacha. In that age, we will '*remember who we are*' and disease will be a thing of the past. How do we remember who we are? We drop our identification with the false, by removing the barriers to Love that make up the false self, and thereby awaken to the eternal beings of Divine Love that we are. Disease will then be a thing of the past.

I feel that humanity does have the opportunity to move into this kind of golden age. All we have to do is to have each person turn inwards and heal themselves.

This book is an invitation for you to become a self-healer. It is also an invitation for you to awaken.

It is your choice how far you wish to take your healing journey. You may find that the healing of one particular health issue is enough for you or you may feel drawn to return all the way 'home' to the being of Love that you are. You may even find that a point in between the two resonates with you. It is your healing journey. Only you can walk your path and it is entirely up to you as to how far you take it.

I simply recommend that you set out. Begin by healing your existing ailments and see where that leads you.

"If a man must move the world, he must first move himself."

— Socrates

3. The Skeptic's View

Before we explore self-healing at a deeper level, I would first like to introduce my skeptical side.

I did not blindly believe that this healing modality would work for me. I was a devout skeptic. I had once been told a definition of stupidity that very much resonated with me. It defined stupidity as *'blindly believing anything that you read or are told'*. I liked that definition.

I felt like I had spent the first forty years of my life being 'stupid'. I had bought into my society's definition of 'success' hook, line, and sinker. That moment of blind belief had cost me over twenty-five years of my life. I was not going to blindly believe anyone or anything again. Instead, I was going to remain open to anything as being possible and then find out for myself whether or not it had any truth for me.

That is how I approached this new, at least for me, healing paradigm. I was openly skeptical. I was both open to the possibility that it had merit and skeptical that healing could be achieved in this way.

****

Stories of Healing

I then began to explore this healing modality for myself. I began to use it on my own journey and also observed how it was being used by others around me. I was pleasantly surprised to discover that it could explain some of the stranger healing experiences that I had encountered.

For example, a sick woman was brought in to the Tibetan monastery where I was studying with an enlightened master. She had a high fever and the doctors in the nearby hospital had not been able to help her. Her husband and son had brought her to the monastery in the hopes that the master could help. They had carried her into his office and she had walked out on her own just a little while later.

At the time, I had been rather confused about what he had done. As far as I knew, he had no medicine in his office. How had he healed her? I asked a monk what His Holiness had done and the monk said that he had driven a dark energy out of her. That didn't make any sense to me and so I had just smiled and nodded. I was also told that the woman's illness had returned a few days later.

I really didn't have an explanation for how that woman could have walked out of the monastery under her own power. It seemed that she had been healed, albeit temporarily.

It wasn't until I came across this alternative view of healing that I had a possible explanation. Had His Holiness released an energetic disturbance from her life force energy?

I had a feeling that he had done exactly that. He may have removed an energetic disturbance from her body and seemingly healed her. With the energetic disturbance removed, the body would have healed itself. However, if the underlying barrier to Love that had created the energetic disturbance in the first place was not also been removed, then the energetic disturbance would have been recreated and the disease would have returned.

At best, removing an energetic disturbance from another person will only provide temporary relief from a disease. It is only when the barrier to Love that is creating the energetic disturbance is removed that any lasting healing will occur.

Had the master really temporarily healed her by removing an energetic disturbance? I cannot say for sure. All I really know is that she had been healed and then the illness had returned. I feel that it is at least possible that this all happened because he removed the energetic disturbance but not the underlying barrier to Love.

I received further evidence that this healing modality may have some merit from a man in India that I studied with. He had created his own healing technique based on this perspective of healing. Using that technique, he would guide people into a meditative state and then ask their inner guide to reveal the source of their ailment. I witnessed him use this technique successfully a number of times. He also shared two rather intriguing stories with me.

In the first, a woman with cancer had come to see him. He put her into a meditative state and discovered that the energetic disturbance underlying her cancer came from her believing that she had to accept a verbally abusive relationship with her father. If she would move to another town, and live away from her father, then the disturbance would be released. She did this and the cancer did disappear from her body.

In the second story, a woman came to him with an extreme fear of being in crowds. It had gotten to the point where she could not be in a room with more than three people. This fear was drastically affecting her life. She had previously sought out psychological help but no one had been able to help her. She was desperate when she came to see the man I studied with in India.

He guided her into a meditative state and helped her to recall a traumatic event that had occurred when she was a baby. She had been lying in a pram when her brother had peered into the pram while wearing a Halloween mask. She had been petrified and had thought that a demon was coming for her. That experience had cemented a false belief inside her that demons were trying to get her. Once she realized that it had only been her brother in a mask, she was able to let go of the false belief about demons and the fear was gone. She was no longer afraid of being in a crowd.

A more dramatic, and personal, example came while I was working with a shaman in Peru. A friend of mine had been diagnosed with cancer and western medicine had not been able to heal him. The doctors had tried radiation and chemotherapy but neither had worked. They had then told him that there was nothing more they could do and that he had two months to live. He had refused to give up and had decided to try taking Ayahuasca with the shaman I knew.

I was in the ceremony when he did so. I watched as he accessed a deep emotional trauma and went through many hours of emotional turmoil. He allowed all of the emotional pain that was inside him to surface and then spent the next two weeks healing the emotional traumas underlying that pain. He then returned to see his doctor and the cancer was shrinking. Within a few months, it was gone.

In this latter case, I feel that the Ayahuasca had not healed him. He had healed himself. The role of the Ayahuasca had been to help him access the deep emotional pain that he had been holding inside himself. He had then healed the emotional traumas that lay at the root of his emotional pain and his body had healed itself.

Another story that I would like to share involved one of my best friends. She was diagnosed with terminal cancer at the age of 32. She was initially given two months to live and lasted for fifteen. She was my primary inspiration for seeking an alternative healing modality. I Loved her and badly wanted to find a way to help her. That desire left me feeling open to exploring any form of healing that came my way.

After discovering this alternative approach to healing, I had returned to Vancouver in order to be with her. Shortly after I arrived, she was moved into a palliative care ward in a downtown hospital. I spent a great deal of time with her in that hospital and one night she agreed to try this approach to healing with me.

I had activated my clairvoyant sense by that time and, with her permission, was observing her energy body while guiding her into a meditative state. We had only been doing this for a few minutes when I 'saw' an incident from her childhood that was horrendous. I was shocked. I stopped what I was doing and simply looked into her eyes.

She was gazing back at me softly and said, *"I know why I have cancer"*. She had seen it too. I simply nodded. I also knew why she had cancer.

I then asked her if she wanted to do anything about it and she replied, *"No, I can't do that to my family"*.

There was nothing more to say. I understood her choice and accepted it. I do feel that she could have healed herself of cancer but that would have required exposing an emotional trauma that she did not want to face. She knew that her options were to either face it or leave the body. She chose to leave. From that point forward, I spent as much time as I could with her. I did my best to Love her and was with her when she passed. I felt both deep sadness for the loss of my friend and relief that her suffering was over.

This perspective on healing applies to all pains and illnesses not just terminal ones. For example, I participated in a two-week intensive healing program that included doing an active meditation at six o'clock every morning. One stage of that meditation involved jumping up and down on the spot for ten minutes while holding one's arms up in the air. I found this stage to be absolutely exhausting and my left hamstring began to hurt more and more each day.

It eventually became excruciatingly painful and I asked one of the people facilitating the program if she could do something for me. She simply replied with, *"What is it trying to tell you?"* I was surprised by her answer and didn't know what to say. She looked at me for a few moments and then turned and walked away.

I decided to see if I could find out what this pain was trying to tell me. I went into a meditation and asked to be shown the message that this pain was bringing me. The message was that it was only my mind that was holding me back from being able to do the active meditation. My body would have no trouble doing it but my mind was telling me that it was too hard. In effect, my mind was literally 'hamstringing' me. I decided to drop this false belief and the next day I was able to do the meditation without any trouble. The pain was gone and my body was indeed quite capable of doing it.

That little episode showed me a great deal about how I was limiting the body's capabilities with my mind. I began to watch how often I did that in my life.

That two-week program helped me to break through to a few of my more deeply held emotional traumas and to heal them. It was two of the most challenging and beautiful weeks of my life. After the two weeks were over, I left the program and spent the next month gradually making my way back to India. I eventually returned to the ashram in India where I had first been introduced to the possibility that pain and illness were messengers.

During that month, I lost 25 pounds in body weight. I didn't change my exercise program or eating habits in any way during that time. The weight simply fell away. I was rather surprised by this and was more than a little curious as to why it had happened.

I told a few people at the ashram about my weight loss and they weren't surprised. They all gave me a similar reason for my sudden weight loss. They basically told me that people often hold emotional pain in their bodies in the form of excess weight and that the weight falls away when the pain is released. I wondered if that could actually be true.

I then began to monitor my weight closely. Low and behold, I found that I would indeed gain weight when I was in resistance to either facing an emotional issue that was surfacing or making a change in my life that I was feeling drawn to make. Once I stopped resisting, and either faced myself or made the change, my weight would return to its 'normal' state. I now treat fluctuations in my weight as signs that I needed to delve inside and find whatever it is that I am resisting.

Through these experiences, and many others like them, I was able to accept that this healing modality did have merit for me. I was able to verify that all of my pains and illnesses were indeed messengers and that my body would heal itself once I responded to those messages. I soon began to use this healing process for every ailment that arose in my body and mind. I even began to proactively remove my barriers to Love so that their underlying energetic disturbances would not lead to any future physical or psychological ailments.

I became my own self-healer.

Life is awareness experiencing itself through form.

4. Becoming a Self-Healer

We now embark upon the journey of becoming a self-healer. We have already opened the door to the possibility that energetic disturbances are at the root of your pains and illnesses. We are now going to explore a way to walk through that door.

There are a number of tools and techniques that you will need in order to find and remove the barriers to Love underlying your ailments. In this chapter, we will present those tools along with a process that you can use to heal yourself of any pain and illness.

I developed this process by walking my own path. As I did so, I began to see patterns in the healing journey that I was undergoing. Those patterns led me to develop a set of tools and techniques that I was able to use effectively on myself. I then began to guide others in removing the barriers to Love underlying their own physical and psychological ailments. This enabled me to expand the process that I had created for healing myself into a process that could be applied to anyone's self-healing journey.

Everyone has their own unique healing journey to follow. You have your own unique set of barriers to Love to remove and only you can remove them. No one can walk your healing journey for you. You have to walk it yourself.

However, you do not have to walk it alone and you do not have to walk it blindly. Others can support you by pointing you in a direction, showing you what to look for along the way, and providing Loving support as you follow your own unique path.

Self-healing is more of an art than a science. The set of fears, beliefs, desires, and emotional traumas that you have inside you are going to be different from the ones that are inside me. For example, the sources of your feelings of guilt, anger, or lack of self-worth are going to be different from the sources of mine. The similarities in our journeys are in the process for self-healing but not in the content of the individual healing we each undertake during our journeys.

Thus, you can become your own self-healer by taking the process that I am going to outline here and applying it to your own life situations. Others have done so before you. I guided people through this process while facilitating retreats on removing the barriers to Love. That enabled me to refine the process further and I now feel that it is ready to be gifted to all those who are interested in becoming their own self-healer.

****

A Process for Becoming a Self-Healer

This process can be used both to heal yourself of any existing physical or psychological ailment and to proactively remove your energetic disturbances before they manifest as ailments.

The process consists of three steps:

1. Look in the Mirror (to observe your signposts; pain, emotion, fear, and non-Loving motivation)

2. Find the Barrier to Love (underlying the signpost).

3. Remove the Barrier to Love.

The first two steps are summarized in diagram 2.

BECOMING A SELF-HEALER (PART ONE)

USE AWARENESS TO **FIND** your **BARRIERS TO LOVE**

1. Begin by **"LOOKING IN THE MIRROR"**

Use MINDFUL AWARENESS (with **HONESTY, INTEGRITY,** and **ACCEPTANCE**) to OBSERVE your INNER REACTION to LIFE'S EVENTS.

If your **INNER REACTION** is either **FEAR, ANGER** (or any other EMOTION), **PAIN,** OR A **NON-LOVING MOTIVATION,** then you are being shown a **SIGNPOST** indicating that HEALING is needed.

HEALING is initiated by FINDING and REMOVING **THE BARRIER TO LOVE** (Fear, Belief, Emotional Trauma, or Desire) that triggered the **SIGNPOST**.

2. Find **THE BARRIER TO LOVE** using:

- ♥ SELF-LOVE (*) - Which is ACCEPTANCE
- ♥ INSIGHT MEDITATION - While FEELING the SIGNPOST
- ♥ TRUST – That you will be shown THE SOURCE inside you of the SIGNPOST

YOU WILL BE SHOWN 1 OF 2 THINGS:

   i.   A BARRIER TO LOVE

- Simply becoming AWARE of a BARRIER TO LOVE heals **90%** of them.
- For the other **10%,** see step '3. REMOVE THE BARRIER TO LOVE'

   ii.   A MISALIGNMENT between your LIFE and your SOUL'S JOURNEY

- Find and remove the BARRIERS TO LOVE underlying any fear or resistance you have to changing your life and then bring your life into ALIGNMENT.

  * SELF-LOVE is a Flame of Transformation or Sacred Fire.
    It burns away all the illusions that you hold about yourself.

Diagram 2 – Becoming a Self-Healer (Part One)

Step One: Begin by Looking in the Mirror.

Looking in the Mirror' means to become aware of your inner reaction to life's events. You do that by observing what is going on inside your body and mind in reaction to what is happening outside.

Mindful Awareness

This practice of observing your inner reactions to life's events is called **Mindful Awareness**. It enables you to connect to your witnessing consciousness, or Higher Self, and to respond to life rather than react to it. You are able to observe the emotions and thoughts that arise in the body and mind without becoming lost in them. That ability to observe your inner world gives you the space to choose how to respond to external events rather than simply reacting to them from whatever thoughts or emotions have been triggered.

Note: One way to cultivate mindful awareness is to take a ten day Vipassana retreat. Vipassana is a form of meditation. It is known as Gautama Buddha's gift to the world. It is the practice of observing one's inner world while remaining connected to the witnessing consciousness or Higher Self.

Own your Emotions

In order to become a self-healer it is necessary to **own your emotions** and to stop blaming others for the way you feel. Owning your emotions means to accept that every emotion is sourced from a barrier to Love inside you and is not being caused by an external event. It is only by owning your emotions that you can delve inside and heal the barrier to Love inside you that is triggering them. Other people may act as triggers for you but they do not cause you to feel the way you do. Your unhealed barriers to Love do that. If you want to blame others for the way you feel then self-healing is not for you.

The Four Signposts

The combination of **mindful awareness** and **owning your emotions** enables you to find the *Signposts* indicating that healing is required. A signpost is a symptom that arises inside you when a barrier to Love has been triggered. By bringing honesty, integrity, and acceptance to what is going on in your inner world, you can use mindful awareness to observe when one of the signposts has arisen inside you. There are four signposts:

- *Pain* – A physical pain, illness, or psychological ailment is an indicator that healing is needed. An energetic disturbance in your energy body has been left in place long enough for that disturbance to manifest physically or psychologically.

- *Anger* (or any other emotion) – Anger is one of your greatest allies on the healing journey. The only way that you can become angry is by having an unhealed barrier to Love inside you. No one else can cause you to become angry. If you feel anger arising in you then it is an opportunity to delve inside and heal the underlying barrier to Love. You can even remove that barrier to Love before the energetic disturbance that it has created manifests as a disease.

  It is for this reason that a person who triggers your anger is actually doing you a favor. They are showing you that you have an unresolved Barrier to Love to heal. Those who trigger your anger are to be treated with gratitude rather than having anger thrown back at them.

  Like anger, every emotion that arises inside you is an indicator that you have an unhealed barrier to Love.

- *Fear* – Fear is another of your greatest allies on the healing journey. If you feel fear arising in your body then you are being shown that an unresolved barrier to Love has been triggered.

- *Non-Loving Motivation* – The final signpost is to have a non-Loving motivation behind your words, thoughts, or deeds. You can respond to life either from Love or from the ego. You cannot do both. If you have an ego based motivation then you are being non-Loving.

  By bringing honesty and integrity to the true motivation for anything you think, say, and do, you can use mindful awareness to observe when you are being non-Loving. You will have then found another signpost indicating that an unhealed barrier to Love inside you has been triggered.

That is step one, looking in the mirror. It enables you to observe the signposts indicating that healing is required.

You then have the opportunity to heal yourself by first finding the barrier to Love underlying that signpost (step 2) and then removing that barrier to Love (step 3). Removing the barrier to Love initiates the healing process because doing so releases its associated energetic disturbance. If that disturbance had already led to a pain or illness then the body will begin to heal itself. If the disturbance had not yet resulted in a pain or illness then removing the barrier to Love will have the effect of performing preventative maintenance on your body and mind.

Step Two: Find the Barrier to Love

Once you have observed that one of the four signposts has arisen inside you then the next step is to find the underlying barrier to Love. This is done through a combination of Self-Love, Insight Meditation, and Trust.

- *Self-Love* – Love is acceptance. Self-Love involves accepting the way you feel without judgment or reservation. It is only when you truly accept the way you feel that you can then begin to heal yourself.

  For example, if you deny that you are angry, perhaps because you think that you shouldn't be angry, then you will not be able to heal the root cause, inside you, of that anger. The root cause is a barrier to Love and it will remain inside you like a poison that will eventually manifest as a physical or psychological ailment.

  Loving yourself is to accept yourself the way you currently are; warts and all. It does not mean that you have to remain that way forever. It simply means that you feel that way now. By bringing honesty, integrity, and acceptance to the way you feel, you can then delve inside to find and heal the barriers to Love underlying any signposts that arise.

- *Insight meditation* – This is a form of meditation that enables you to glean insights into a particular issue from your own inner guide. The insights that you will be receiving are not coming from your rational mind and they are not coming from an external being. They are coming from you.

  Insight meditation is used in the self-healing process to find the barrier to Love underlying a signpost. Basically, you allow yourself to feel the signpost and then ask your inner guide to show you the root cause, inside you, of that signpost.

- **Trust** – Cultivating trust is a necessary part of becoming a self-healer. You will be learning to trust your own inner guide.

  You will not be putting your trust in your own mind or in the mind of anyone else. Your mind is not trustworthy. It is full of barriers to Love that can be triggered at any time. Similarly, the minds of others are full of their own barriers to Love and their minds cannot be trusted either.

  You will also not be putting your trust in anything outside of yourself: no being; no belief system; and, no ideas of an external God. If you did that then you would only be taking on their beliefs and fears. You would effectively be adding to your barriers to Love rather than dissolving them.

  Becoming a self-healer requires you to cultivate trust in your own inner guide. It is only your inner guide that can show you the barriers to Love underlying your signposts.

Self-Love forms the foundation for finding your barriers to Love as it enables you to truly accept whatever is going on inside you. It does not allow you to deny the way you feel as you dive deeper inside yourself. Insight Meditation and Trust then allow you to actually delve inside and find the barrier to Love.

If the signpost was a fear, pain, or emotional reaction then you allow yourself to feel the signpost and then use insight meditation to ask to be shown the barrier to Love that lies at its root. You then sit silently, in mindful awareness, and wait to either 'hear' or 'see' the answer. All you then do is trust that your inner guide will show the barrier to Love and you patiently wait for it to do so.

Similarly, if the signpost was a non-Loving motivation then you recall the scenario in which you were being non-Loving and then use insight meditation to ask to be shown the barrier to Love that triggered you into being that way.

Your inner guide will show you the root cause of the signpost that has arisen. In the vast majority of cases, that root cause will be one of the four barriers to Love (a fear, belief, desire, or emotional trauma). You can then complete the healing journey by removing that barrier to Love.

There is one exception to the rule that there is always a barrier to Love underlying a signpost. That exception is the case of your having a misalignment between the life you are living and the life you incarnated to live. We will deal with that exception shortly.

Awareness often removes a barrier to Love

For the most part, your insight meditation will reveal one of the following four types of barriers to Love as the root cause of your signpost:

- *Fear* – a particular fear is considered a barrier to Love because it causes you to make fear-based choices rather than Loving choices. You cannot function from both fear and Love. If you are functioning from fear then you are lost in your ego and there is no Love in your thoughts, words, or deeds.

- *Belief* – a belief is a barrier to Love because you are functioning from the ego whenever you are espousing or defending a belief. Again, there will be no Love in your thoughts, words, and deeds.

- *Desire* – seeking to fulfill a desire of any kind disconnects you from Love and throws you into your ego. You will then be seeking either to get something you want or to avoid something you don't want. Your words, actions, and deeds will be non-Loving.

- *Emotional Trauma* - an unresolved emotional trauma is also a barrier to Love. It causes you to function from the emotions and false beliefs that were taken on at the time of the trauma. You will not be functioning from Love.

The good news is that simply becoming aware of a barrier to Love will heal the vast majority of them. Awareness of a barrier, and how it affects your interactions with yourself and others, is often all the incentive you need to let it go. The energetic disturbance that it created will then be released and the body will heal itself. Your self-healing journey for that particular signpost will be over.

I was once told that upwards of 90% of all healing occurs simply by becoming aware of the barrier to Love underlying a signpost. I chuckled when I heard that number. How could anything be that precise? However, I then found, through my own self-healing journey, that it did seem to reflect my experience. Awareness did heal most of my barriers to Love. When that occurs, the self-healing process is complete. The barrier to Love will be gone, the signpost will have fallen away, and the body will heal itself.

However, simply becoming aware of my barriers to Love did not remove all of them. There were a number of barriers to Love inside me that I was holding onto so strongly that I could not release them solely by becoming aware of them. For example, I had a deep-rooted anger towards my mother. Simply becoming aware of the source, inside me, of that anger was not enough for me to let it go. I had to use a combination of Love, learning my lessons, and forgiveness to remove the barriers to Love underlying that anger.

Thus, I created an additional step in the self-healing process. It is step 3 and it is for removing the barriers to Love that awareness does not heal. We will review that step after first dealing with the exception to the rule that there is always a barrier to Love underlying a signpost.

A Misalignment in your life may underlie a signpost

When you use insight meditation and trust to follow a signpost down inside yourself, you may find that you have a misalignment between the life that you are choosing to live and the life that you incarnated to live.

A misalignment occurs when you use your free will to pursue your ego-based desires rather than listening to your inner guide. Your inner guide will constantly be bringing situations into your life in order to show you both the lessons that you are to learn and the direction that you are to take with your life. You may be consciously or unconsciously choosing to ignore your inner guide.

If you are identified with your ego then you may not be able to hear your inner guide at all. Furthermore, even if you can hear your inner guide, you may be choosing to ignore its guidance because of fear, resistance, or desire. By choosing to follow the whims of your ego, it is possible for your life to become misaligned with the life you incarnated to live.

Thus, when you follow a signpost down inside yourself, you may find a misalignment as its root. You will then need to resolve that misalignment in order to heal yourself. You can do that in one of two ways.

You can simply choose to follow the guidance of your inner guide and thereby bring your life back into alignment with your soul. You will have healed yourself and the signpost will disappear.

However, healing yourself of a misalignment is not always that easy. There is often a feeling of fear or resistance that is preventing you from either hearing or heeding the guidance that you are receiving. If that is the case for you then the second way to heal yourself is to first delve inside to find and remove the barriers to Love underlying the fear or resistance.

You can find those barriers to Love using self-Love, insight meditation, and trust. You then either watch the barrier to Love dissolve away through awareness or you follow step 3 to remove it. Once removed, the fear or resistance will dissolve away and you can then follow the guidance of your inner guide to bring your life into alignment.

The full process for resolving a misalignment between your chosen life and the life you incarnated to live is described in exercise '*5. Bringing your Life into Alignment with your Soul*'.

Step Three: Remove the Barrier to Love

The process for removing the barriers to Love that awareness does not heal is summarized in Diagram 3.

BECOMING A SELF-HEALER (PART TWO)

3. REMOVE THE **BARRIER TO LOVE:**

FEAR: Every FEAR is based on a LIE. Face the FEAR or find the LIE.
> **USE:** FEEL, INSIGHT MEDITATION and TRUST to see the LIE. LET IT GO.

BELIEF: Every BELIEF is based on a LIE. Find the LIE.
> **USE:** FEEL, INSIGHT MEDITATION and TRUST to see the LIE. LET IT GO.

EMOTIONAL TRAUMA: Can be HEALED ON YOUR OWN or with SUPPORT

- ALLOW YOUR HIGHER SELF TO GUIDE YOU THROUGH HEALING ON YOUR OWN OR TO A HEALING TECHNIQUE AND THERAPIST TO SUPPORT YOU IN HEALING YOURSELF.
- YOU MAY USE DIFFERENT HEALING TECHNIQUES FOR DIFFERENT TRAUMAS.
- THIS IS A SELF-HEALING JOURNEY. YOU HAVE TO "FEEL IT TO HEAL IT". ALLOW YOURSELF TO ENTER A BREAKDOWN CONSCIOUSLY TO FIND THE ROOT EVENT.

> **USE:** CATHARSIS TO GO DEEP INTO YOUR EMOTIONS AND THEN USE FEEL, INSIGHT MEDITATION AND TRUST TO SEE THE ROOT EVENT. ACCEPT IT HAPPENED AND HEAL IT:
>
>> IF OTHERS ARE INVOLVED THEN FORGIVE THEM AND SEND THEM LOVE.
>>
>> USE SELF-LOVE AND FORGIVENESS TO HEAL THE WOUNDED PART OF YOU.
>>
>>> IF YOU FEEL GUILT OR SHAME THEN **APOLOGIZE**, LEARN YOUR **SOUL LESSON**, **FORGIVE YOURSELF**, AND **LOVE YOURSELF** (ACCEPTANCE).
>
> **NOTE:** THERE MAY BE MANY LAYERS TO AN EMOTIONAL TRAUMA. YOU MAY NEED TO REPEAT THIS PROCESS FOR EACH LAYER UNTIL YOU REACH THE ORIGINAL ONE.

DESIRE: Make the Choice to either Be LOVE or Pursue DESIRES and suffer.
> **USE:** FEEL, INSIGHT MEDITATION and TRUST to see the EGO-BASED NEED underlying the DESIRE. Either LET IT GO or PROVIDE IT FOR YOURSELF (*)
>
> * IF YOU ARE UNABLE TO DO EITHER OF THESE THEN USE FEEL, INSIGHT MEDITATION AND TRUST TO FIND THE FEAR, BELIEF, OR EMOTIONAL TRAUMA UNDERLYING THE NEED. USE THE APPROACHES ABOVE FOR REMOVING THAT **BARRIER TO LOVE** AND THEN LET GO OF THE NEED.

Diagram 3 – Becoming a Self-Healer (Part Two)

There is a different healing process for removing each of the four types of barriers to Love. We will discuss each of them in turn.

Removing the first Barrier to Love: A Specific Fear.

Every fear is based on a lie. If you can find the lie and stop believing it then the fear will be released. There are two approaches to releasing a particular fear that I found to be effective.

The first approach was to face a fear directly. I would simply do whatever it was that I was afraid to do and, more often than not, the fear would not be realized. I would then see that there had been nothing to fear in the first place and the fear would dissolve away.

This first approach didn't always work. With some of my fears, I believed the lie underlying the fear so strongly that I would draw situations into my life that seemed to confirm it. I needed a second approach for healing the fears that were not released by my facing them.

I also couldn't use this direct approach for facing a fear if facing it would result in harm to my body. For example, I would not face my fear of heights by jumping off a cliff. I needed a second approach for healing the fears that I couldn't face directly.

That second approach was a meditative one. I would find a quiet space where I could sit on my own and allow myself to feel the fear as strongly as I was able. I did that by visualizing whatever scenario created the fear and then letting myself feel afraid. I would then use insight meditation to ask my inner guide to show me the lie underlying the fear. It was then simply a matter of trusting that my inner guide would show it to me and patiently waiting for it to do so. Once I saw the lie, I would stop believing it and the fear would be released. I would have healed one more barrier to Love.

The process for healing a specific fear is outlined in exercise '*6. Letting Go of a Particular Fear*'.

Removing the second Barrier to Love: A Belief.

Every belief is based on a lie; every single one. Even believing that the sky is blue is a lie. It only appears to be blue when viewed through the limited perspective of the physical eyes. It is not blue. You can find out for yourself what is really in the sky if you open up to the possibility that everything is not necessarily the way your eyes perceives it to be. I invite you to remain open to the possibility that every belief is based on a lie. You will then be able to explore your beliefs for yourself.

The approach that I adopted for removing my beliefs was a meditative one. I would find a quiet space where I could sit on my own and silently state the belief to myself. I would then use insight meditation to ask to be shown the lie underlying that belief. It was then simply a matter of trusting that my inner guide would eventually show it to me and patiently waiting to see it. Once I saw the lie underlying the belief, and stopped believing the lie, the belief would be released. I would then have healed one more barrier to Love.

This process for letting go of a belief is outlined in exercise '7. *Removing a Belief*'.

Removing the third Barrier to Love: An Emotional Trauma.

How is an emotional trauma created?

An emotional trauma is created inside you when the original event is too painful for you to handle at the time. Your ego then creates the false beliefs that 'you' had been threatened and that 'you' have to protect yourself from that ever happening again. Those false beliefs then become part of your ego. The memory of the event, along with the emotions that arose at the time of the event, are then typically buried away and forgotten.

There are two ramifications to the rest of your life from having this happen. The first is that the false beliefs will have created disturbances in your life force energy and, unless they are released, they will eventually manifest as a pain or illness. The second is that the false beliefs will be affecting your interactions with others. They will have you unconsciously trying to 'protect' yourself from having the trauma recur. You will end up reacting to external events that feel threatening to your subconscious with either fear or with an emotion such as anger or sadness. You will basically be reacting to present time events from past time emotions.

However, there is a silver lining in all of this. An external event that triggers the emotions of fear, anger, or sadness is actually giving you a gift. Those emotions are your signposts. Instead of reacting in the world from them, you can use them to turn inwards and recall the underlying emotional trauma. That will then give you the opportunity to heal that trauma.

How do you heal an emotional trauma?

In order to heal an emotional trauma, you will need to let go of both the false beliefs and the emotions that were stored with the memory of the original traumatic event. Once you have healed a trauma, you will retain the memory of the event but the associated emotions and the false beliefs will be gone. You will know that you have healed a trauma when you can recall the original event without becoming either emotional or afraid.

You have to feel it to heal it

You have to feel it to heal it. Your rational mind cannot heal you. Simply becoming mentally aware of an emotional trauma opens the door to healing but does not heal you. Mentally forgiving someone does not accomplish any healing.

I found this out the hard way. I 'thought' that I had forgiven my mother yet I remained angry with her. This went on for years and I couldn't understand why. I had forgiven her! Why was I still so angry? I was still angry because the wounded part of me had not forgiven her; only my mind had. It was the traumatized part of me that had to forgive her. I had to feel it to heal it.

Healing an Emotional Trauma

The process of healing an emotional trauma begins by bringing your awareness back to the signpost (the anger, fear, or pain) that had first shown you that you had an underlying emotional trauma. You then allow the feelings of anger, fear, or pain to grow stronger and ask your inner guide to again show you the underlying trauma. As you recall the event, you then allow yourself to feel the associated emotions.

Feeling those emotions can be a deeply painful process. I often found it useful to use some form of catharsis to fully access the emotions associated with my traumas. I also found that those emotions were sometimes too much for me to handle initially. I would then allow myself to scream and yell out the emotions in a healing setting (not in front of anyone involved in the traumatic event). That kind of cathartic yelling did not actually heal anything for me. However, it did allow me to access the way I had really felt at the time of the trauma and enabled me to gradually accept those emotions.

Eventually I would be able to feel the emotions without getting lost in them. I would be ready to do the deep healing work. I would then release the emotions using a combination of Love, forgiveness of others, learning my lessons, and forgiveness of self. Releasing those emotions would accomplish the core of the healing journey for the trauma.

However, healing of the trauma would not yet be complete. The false beliefs would still need to be released and there may be additional layers of emotional pain to be healed.

An emotional trauma may have multiple layers of emotional pain associated with it. Each of those layers will need to be healed. For example, an abused child may have healed the anger that they feel towards their abuser and yet still feel angry. They may have another layer of anger towards a parent or guardian for not having protected them.

You will know whether or not there are additional layers of emotions to be healed because you will have already felt them. You will have passed through them on the journey of feeling the original signpost and then following the signpost down inside yourself to find the traumatic event. If you passed through multiple emotional layers on that journey then you will need to return to each of them.

You do that by returning to the signpost to see if it is gone. If you can no longer feel the fear, anger, pain, then the healing of all of the emotional layers is complete. If you can still feel the signpost then you can go back down through the emotional layers and do whatever healing is required for the layers that are still present.

The last step in healing an emotional trauma is to let go of the false beliefs that were taken on at the time of the traumatic event. If that is not done then the energetic disturbances will remain in place and they will eventually manifest as a pain or illness. It is the traumatized part of you that took on those false beliefs and it is only that part of you that can let them go. This is where inner child work becomes so important in the healing of an emotional trauma.

Removing false beliefs involves visualizing yourself as the person you were when the original trauma occurred. You then visualize the person you are today telling that younger part of you that you will look after it now and that it no longer has to be afraid. You then watch to see how the inner child reacts. If it is receptive to you then you can invite it to accept a hug. If it allows you to hug it, and then allows itself to merge back into you, then the healing journey is over. The false beliefs related to that traumatized part of you feeling the need to protect itself will have been released.

On my healing journey, that final step in the healing process often required me to visit with my traumatized inner child a number of times. That traumatized part of me was often reluctant to let go of its anger and its pain. It would not let me hug it and would not merge back into me. In those cases, I had to repeat the visualization process until it trusted me enough to allow itself to merge back into me.

Once the inner child work is complete, the emotional trauma will be healed. You will still have the memory of the original traumatic event. However, the false beliefs and the associated emotions will both be gone. In addition, the signpost that had pointed you towards the emotional trauma will also be gone. You will have healed one more barrier to Love.

This process for healing an emotional trauma is outlined in exercise '*8. Healing an Emotional Trauma*'.

Healing a trauma on your own or with Support

This process for healing your emotional traumas can be done either on your own or with the support of a therapist.

I was able to heal many of my emotional traumas on my own using this process. However, a few of my most deeply held traumas were extremely painful for me to face. I sometimes found it difficult to avoid getting lost in the overwhelming flood of emotions that would be arising from those traumas. When that happened, I found it invaluable to have a therapist there for support.

The therapist was not there to heal me. I had to do that myself. They were there simply to guide me through the healing process when the emotional pain was too strong for me to be able to heal a trauma on my own.

I would look to my inner guide for guidance on whether I was to heal an emotional trauma on my own or with the support of a therapist. When I was first recalling a traumatic event, I would ask my inner guide if I needed therapeutic support. If I felt drawn to have support then I would also trust that my inner guide would direct me towards the appropriate therapy technique and therapist to support me.

I found that a therapist could play an invaluable role in supporting me with:

- accepting that the traumatic event had occurred;

- allowing myself to feel the way I had at the time of the trauma; and,

- applying whatever forgiveness and learning of lessons was necessary in order for me to heal myself.

The therapists that used their technique solely to guide me through the self-healing process outlined above were the ones I resonated with. They didn't try to heal me. They simply created space for me to heal myself, and provided me with tools for doing so.

I did not resonate with therapists who thought they could heal me. I knew that the only one who can heal me is me. If someone believed that they could heal me then I knew that their technique was not for me.

I also did not resonate with therapists that either advocated pharmaceuticals to numb pain (emotional or physical) rather than heal the source of that pain or operated solely in the world of the rational mind. I feel that healing involves following my feelings down inside myself in order to dissolve the illusions of my ego. Therefore, I feel that either numbing myself or reprogramming my ego does not provide any healing benefit.

Removing the fourth Barrier to Love: A Desire

My biggest challenge in removing my desires came in first accepting that I actually wanted to. What was wrong with pursuing a desire? Isn't that a big part of the human experience? Do I really want to let them go?

It was only after I began to see what desire did to 'me' that I started to feel drawn to rid myself of desire. Through bringing mindful awareness to my motivation for everything that I said, thought or did, I soon realized that the pursuit of desire was a major cause of my becoming non-Loving. For example, if I wanted my hockey team to win then I found that I would get upset or even angry if they lost. Once upset or angry, my interactions with others were non-Loving. I realized that my either wanting something to happen or wanting to prevent something from happening sent me into my ego.

It became clear to me that my pursuit of a desire only led to suffering for myself and those around me. I had a choice to make. Do I want to become Love or do I want to continue pursuing my desires?

My answer to that question was easy for most of my desires; of course I wanted to become Love!

However, there were certain desires that I held onto rather strongly. I may have been trying to convince myself that I wanted to become Love but my 'desire' to become Love was occasionally weaker than my other desires. I would then pursue those deeply held desires and fall from grace (act in a non-Loving way towards myself and others). It was abhorrent for me to act in a non-Loving way and I eventually came to accept that I was going to have to remove all of my desires.

Note: the desire to become Love is known as the highest desire. It is to be held onto until all other desires have been dropped. We will explore the highest desires in more detail in chapter '*9 Distractions*'.

How do I remove a desire?

Every desire is based on an ego-based need. The essence of who I truly am does not desire anything from this world of form. It is only the ego that creates a desire and it does so because it believes that it needs something. The approach that I used for removing a desire from my being was to find and remove the underlying ego-based need.

I did this by first finding a quiet space where I could be on my own. I would then visualize whatever it was that I desired and allow the feeling of desire to arise within me. I would then use an insight meditation to ask my inner guide to show me the ego-based need underlying the desire.

Once I was shown the ego-based need then I could remove it. I would start by exploring the possibility of either providing that need for myself or simply letting it go. That worked sometimes, but not always. Often, I was holding onto the need too strongly to simply let it go and I was doing that because of an underlying barrier to Love. Perhaps I was afraid that I would feel worthless if I did not satisfy that need or perhaps I had been traumatized in the past and was desperately trying to prevent a similar situation from recurring. In order to let go of my more deeply held ego-based needs, I found that I would first have to find and remove the underlying barriers to Love.

I would do that by continuing to sit in meditation and allowing myself to feel the need strongly. I would then use insight meditation to ask my inner guide to show me the barrier to Love underlying the need. I would then trust and be patient. The barrier to Love that my inner guide would show me was invariably a fear, belief, or emotional trauma. I would remove that barrier to Love as outlined above. Once that barrier was removed then I would be able to let go of the ego-based need and the desire would be gone. I would have healed one more barrier to Love.

This process for letting go of a desire is outlined in exercise '9. *Letting Go of a Desire'*.

****

Summary of the Self-Healing Process

In summary, the process that we have explored for becoming a self-healer involves using:

- *Mindful awareness* to find the signposts indicating that healing is needed;

- *Self-Love, insight meditation,* and *trust* to find either the misalignment in your life or the barriers to Love underlying a signpost; and,

- *Self-Love, insight meditation, trust, forgiveness, and learning your lessons* to remove the barriers to Love underlying a misalignment or signpost.

The detailed steps for healing the barriers to Love underlying each of the four signposts are provided in exercises: '1. *Healing the Source of a Pain or Illness';* 2. *Healing the Source of an Emotional Reaction (such as Anger)';* '3. *Healing the Source of Fear';* and, '4. *Healing the Source of a Non-Loving Motivation'*.

That completes this overview of the self-healing process. Again, please don't believe any of it. Instead, I invite you to explore it for yourself. Apply it to your own life and then decide whether or not it has any merit for you.

****

The Three Pillars of Becoming a Self-Healer

Mindful awareness, self-Love, and *trust* form the core of the self-healing process. They are referred to as '**The Three Pillars**'. It is only by becoming proficient with all three of them that you can master self-healing.

However, a rudimentary proficiency is all you need to begin healing yourself. You will be able to use them to find and remove some of your barriers to Love. As you do so, you will begin to master them and will be able to use them to remove more and more of your barriers to Love. In this case, the expression 'practice makes perfect' does apply. We will discuss these three pillars in more detail in the next chapter.

****

The Role of Western Medicine in Healing

Western Medicine can play an invaluable role in this alternative approach to healing.

I made the mistake of dismissing Western Medicine entirely when I first discovered this alternative view of healing. I dismissed it because I was blinded by anger. I was angry at the medical system for not including the possibility that pains and illnesses were messengers of unresolved energetic disturbances. I felt that the western approach was too focused on the body and was not actually healing the root cause of disease.

I also felt that the western health care system was doing a disservice to practitioners and patients alike. Many corporations that are involved in the system are at least partially motivated to generate a financial profit. I felt that this opened the door to health care providers being influenced by the need to generate a monetary return rather than focusing solely on providing healing services. That influence could result in:

- the turning away of patients who cannot pay for services;

- a hospital providing unnecessary services in order to generate a financial return on investment;

- pharmaceutical companies benefitting financially from people being sick rather than from their being healed; and,

- a health practitioner performing unnecessary services in order to pay their bills.

All of this made me angry and I owned that anger. I knew that the anger was sourced from inside me. The western medical system was simply showing me that I had unresolved barriers to Love that needed to be healed. Rather than lash out at that system, I used the anger as an opportunity to delve inside and heal myself.

I began by accepting that there were beautiful and well-meaning people in the health care industry. I had spent a year consulting at a pharmaceutical company and another year consulting at a provincial health care provider. During that time, I had met many dedicated and caring people. I had even come to feel that the vast majority of health care practitioners were indeed well-meaning and were doing the best they could under the circumstances. That helped me to forgive the western medical system and its practitioners for being too, in my mind, body-centric and for ignoring this alternative perspective on healing.

Unfortunately, that didn't heal all of my anger. I had a deeper layer of anger. It turned out that I was angry at myself for a choice that I had made many years earlier. In my early twenties, I had been accepted into medical school and had chosen not to go. Something about western medicine had not resonated with me even then. I had felt drawn to the world of healing but could not see myself becoming a medical doctor. Instead, I had gone in a completely different direction. I had completed an engineering degree, obtained an MBA, and pursued the 'Canadian dream' of material success.

That decision to go another way was the source of the deeper layer of anger. I was angry at myself for having given up on my calling towards healing in order to become a materially successful corporate guy. That decision had 'cost' me twenty years of my life. I struggled to forgive myself for that.

The first step in forgiving myself was to accept that becoming a medical doctor was not my path in this life. I had made the choice not to go to medical school because it simply wasn't for me. It was easy to forgive myself for that choice because I didn't really feel that there was anything to forgive.

However, forgiving myself for pursuing material success was much harder. That choice essentially meant that I had turned my back on me. I had chosen to succumb to the pressures of my society rather than to follow my own inner calling to explore healing. I struggled to forgive myself.

In order to do so, I had to first learn the soul lesson that this scenario from my life was teaching me. That lesson was to always follow the guidance of my inner guide no matter what. It did not matter what anyone else thought of me and it didn't matter what I thought I had to give up. In order to live my life, I had to follow my inner guide rather than follow the whims of my, or anyone else's, rational mind. I embraced that lesson to the depths of my being. I was then able to forgive myself for turning my back on me. The anger was then gone. I wasn't angry at myself or the western medical system any more.

I was then able to see the gifts that western medicine does offer. It may not accomplish any actual healing but it can keep the body alive long enough for healing to occur. For example, if I slice my leg open, or contract flesh eating disease (which did happen to me), then I want to be taken straight to emergency. I want my body to be taken care of before I delve inside and heal myself. The western medical system can do that.

I feel that treating the physical symptoms of a disease is an important part of the healing journey. If an energetic disturbance has been left in place long enough to result in a physical ailment then western medicine can be used to treat the body. Once the body is stable, the patient can then focus on healing themselves. Similarly, if an energetic disturbance has resulted in a psychological ailment then psychotherapy may be needed in order to help a person to move into a mental state that enables them to be guided through their own self-healing process.

I do feel that the western approach to healing could be brought into alignment with the energetic disturbance perspective on healing. They could work together seamlessly. However, that is not the focus of this book. The intention for this book is solely to provide you, the reader, with a process for becoming a self-healer. Any work on bringing the two alternative perspectives on healing into alignment is left for others.

****

Providing Guidance for your Self-Healing Journey

I could have ended the book at this point. You have all the tools that you need to become your own self-healer.

However, there were many insights that I gained through my own self-healing journey. For example, I learned far more than how to heal my body of a given pain or illness. I also learned how to heal things such as sexual insecurity, depression, and guilt.

I feel drawn to pass on those insights as they may smooth your path of self-healing. I mostly felt like I was flying blind on mine. A few people did appear in my life to pass on their insights but, for the most part, I was left to my own devices. I often wished that someone could have been there to give me guidance on how to cultivate things like trust, patience, and self-Love, and on how to deal with sexual issues, deep emotional traumas, loneliness, guilt, fear, depression, and so much more.

In order to perhaps streamline your self-healing journey, I have included all that I have learned about this self-healing process in the remainder of the book. In the coming chapters, we will:

- delve deeper into how you can use the three pillars (mindful awareness, self-Love, and trust) to heal yourself;

- clarify how the fours signposts can be used to find your Barriers to Love;

- explore the form of Love that you can become;

- discuss a few things that can cause you to have a non-Loving motivation for your thoughts, words, and deeds;

- provide insights into healing issues such as guilt, depression, and loneliness in order to accelerate your healing journey; and,

- highlight a few distractions that could slow down, or even derail, you on your self-healing journey.

Welcome to the journey of becoming a self-healer. Enjoy the ride.

Before time, there was one. You are that one.

5. The Three Pillars

The three pillars that form the foundation of becoming a self-healer are Self-Love, Mindful Awareness, and Trust. You will need all three in order to find and remove the barriers to Love that underlie all of your physical and psychological ailments.

In this chapter, I will describe each of them in more detail and provide suggestions on how to cultivate them.

****

The First Pillar: Self-Love

What is self-Love?

The word 'love' was a challenging one for me when I first set out on my own voyage of self-discovery. I had grown up with a form of love that was conditional and I had not resonated with it. I had also felt confused as to how love could be used interchangeably in reference to chocolate, sports, friends, ice cream, family, and lovers. How could all of that be love? I felt like I was definitely missing something.

I gave up on my society's perspective on love very early in my life. I stopped telling anyone, even my long-term partners, that I loved them. I dated a woman for seven years and not once did I tell her that I loved her. I couldn't say it because it would have been a lie. I didn't know what love was.

I had then set out on a quest to find both happiness and a form of love that did resonate with me. That quest turned into an inner journey of self-discovery. I then found the Love that I had been looking for. I call it 'Divine Love' and it appeared from inside me when I fell silent inside. I became it.

I realized that the only thing that was stopping me from becoming this kind of Love was my choosing to function in the world from my ego. If I could remove the barriers to Love, the things inside me that triggered me into my ego, then I could remain in my natural state of Love. This was an exciting discovery for me. I had found a form of Love that I resonated with, and a way to become it.

The journey of becoming Love is the self-healing journey. I dove head first into that journey. I wanted to become Love more than anything else in the world, and was willing to do whatever it took to return there.

I explored the use of the word 'love' extensively during my self-healing journey. I found that I could love a thing, love a person, use Love for healing, practice self-Love, and become Love.

As mentioned earlier in this book, I eventually came to feel that there are three ways in which people are using the word love in today's world.

- *Mind-Based love* – this is the love that a person is using when they say things like: I love Chocolate; I love movies; and, I love you because you make me happy. This form of love is based on what a person gets in return for what they love. It is a game of the ego. It is given and received. There is no healing power in this form of love.

- *Heart-based love* – this is the love that a person is using when they want what they think is best for someone else. This form of love is focused on the other rather than the self. It is generally a nicer form of love than mind-based love but it is still a game of the ego. What you think is best for another is your ego talking. Again, this form of love is given and received. There is no healing power in heart-based love.

- *Divine Love* – this is the energy of both Source and your Higher Self. Source is a field of pure awareness that flows through everything in this world of form. The energy of Source is Divine Love. You are literally swimming in an ocean of Divine Love. It accepts everyone exactly as they are and wants nothing from anyone. It is something you become when you drop your identification with the false self (the ego and body). This form of Love has tremendous healing power.

Divine Love will support you on your healing journey. Its primary quality is acceptance. It is aware of everything and accepts everything exactly as it is. It does not interfere and it does not try to change. It simply accepts.

The journey of becoming Divine Love begins with cultivating self-Love. Love is acceptance. Self-Love involves simply accepting yourself; nothing more and nothing less. That means accepting yourself exactly as you are without judgment, without blame, and without wanting to change anything. You simply accept:

- the way you feel about yourself and others;

- what is truly motivating everything that you think, say, and do;

- your inner emotions and inner demons;

- your ailments, and,

- your body.

For example, if you bring your awareness to how you are feeling in any given moment, and simply accept that the way you feel is the way you feel, then you are Loving yourself.

Loving yourself does not mean that you will have to feel that same way for the rest of your life. It simply means that you are accepting that you feel that way right now. That is self-Love. It opens the door to your being able to find and remove the barriers to Love that have led to your feeling that way.

No healing can happen until you Love yourself. If you either deny the way you feel, tell yourself that you shouldn't feel the way you do, or blame someone else for the way you feel then you will remain trapped in the world of the ego. You will continue to ride the roller coaster of emotions that is the ego-based existence. You will remain disconnected from Love and you will not become a self-healer.

Accepting yourself applies to your body as well as to your feelings. You are Loving your body by bringing your awareness to it and accepting it exactly as it is. For example, if you focus all of your attention on your right foot then you are Loving that foot.

How do you cultivate self-Love?

You cultivate self-Love by practicing awareness and acceptance in your daily life. You are Loving yourself whenever you are:

- giving yourself permission to feel the way you do;

- expressing the way you feel with honesty and integrity;

- owning your emotions as being sourced from inside you and not blaming anyone else for the way you feel;

- being honest with yourself about the true motivation for everything you think, say, and do;

- accepting your body exactly as it is;

- dropping all judgments of your feelings, motivations, and your body; and,

- bringing mindful awareness to your inner reactions to external events.

You can also cultivate self-Love by using the following exercises.

1. **Learning to feel again** – many of us, myself included, were raised to repress the way we felt. For example, I was told that "big boys don't cry" and that I shouldn't get angry. As a result, I became very good at suppressing my emotions. My answer to "How are you?" was always either "Good" or "Fine". In fact, I was so good at suppressing my emotions that I couldn't have told someone how I felt even if I had wanted to. I no longer knew.

   This exercise was designed for people like me. It gives us a way to learn how to feel again. You begin by recalling a situation in your life that made you angry. You then bring your awareness to how the emotion of anger feels in the body. You then pick another emotion, such as sad, happy, ashamed, frustrated, jealous, or guilty, and repeat the exercise. You do this for all of the emotions. With practice, you can learn to feel the difference between each emotion as it flows through the body. This process is described in exercise '*10. Learning to Feel Again*'.

2. **Expressing the way you feel out Loud**– This exercise is done in a group setting. Pick a question such as 'How do you feel about the opposite sex?' or 'How do you feel about your body?'. Take it in

turns to stand up and express your honest answer to that question. When you are speaking, have everyone else stay sitting until they feel that you are expressing the way you truly feel. At that point, they are to stand up. Keep talking until everyone else stands up.

This exercise gives you an opportunity both to practice expressing your feelings openly and honestly, and to listen to how other people sound when they are expressing the way they feel. You are Loving yourself when you are able to express the way you feel without any reservation or self-judgment. This process is described in exercise *'11. Expressing the Way you Feel'*.

3. **Do a dyad** – a dyad is an exercise in which two people sit opposite each other and take it in turns talking. The two of you agree on a statement that you are going to talk about such as 'tell me how you feel right now'. You then pick one person to talk and the other is to listen. The one who is going to listen then says 'tell me how you feel right now'. The speaker then spends the next five minutes expressing how they feel. The listener does not comment and does not react in any way. They simply listen in silence. After five minutes, you switch roles. The speaker becomes the listener and the listener becomes the speaker. You repeat this process until each person has had four chances to speak. The exercise takes a total of 40 minutes. This process is described in exercise *'12. Dyading'*.

    This exercise enables you to express the way you feel at deeper and deeper levels. That is Loving yourself. It also gives you an opportunity to practice the art of listening; listening from a silent inner space without feeling the need to reply, comment, or judge the speaker in any way.

4. **Take yourself on a date** – pick something that you have always felt drawn to do, and give yourself permission to do it. Take an art course, have a massage, lie at the end of a runway and watch planes land, or take a stroll through a neighborhood you have always wanted to explore. Do anything that feels like a gift to yourself.

I would recommend that you find little ways to cultivate self-Love every day. Be imaginative and have fun with it.

Self-Love is a Flame of Transformation

It would be remiss of me to discuss self-Love without providing a warning. Self-Love is referred to as a flame of transformation or sacred fire.

Why? What does that mean?

The answer lies in what self-Love will do for you, or should I say 'to you'. Self-Love will burn away all of the illusions that you hold about yourself. Love is acceptance and self-Love means to accept yourself exactly as you are. You are literally shining the light of awareness on yourself. That awareness will illuminate the barriers to Love that make up your personality and they will begin to fall away. In essence, the false self that you thought you were will be burned away by self-Love.

That is why self-Love is called a sacred fire or flame of transformation. It will transform you from a lost person who is functioning in the world through their ego to a being of Love.

Another way of saying this is to state that Self-Love will destroy your personality. Your personality is essentially a set of false beliefs that you have taken on from your society.

Freud referred to the personality as having three components, the id, the ego, and the super-ego. The id is instinctive, the ego adopts societal rules, etiquette, and norms, and the super-ego incorporates all of the learned values and morals of society. For simplicity, we have rolled the ego and super-ego into one construct and simply call it the ego. The personality, with the exception of the id, will be dissolved by self-Love.

Hence the warning. The personality that you think is you is not you. The personality is simply a set of false beliefs. Self-Love will expose that truth. It will also dissolve away your personality leaving only who you really are. In essence self-Love burns away the false self leaving only Love. That process is the underlying truth of what the self-healing process is all about.

My ego struggled to accept this possibility when I was first exposed to it. 'I' really didn't like the idea that 'I' was false. 'I' tried to resist it but, when I allowed myself to open up to the possibility that it might be true, I knew in my heart that it was.

Accepting that truth was one of the biggest 'ah shit' moments on my journey. I wrote the following statement in my journal.

"I am a set of false beliefs. Ah shit."

I felt like I had wasted my whole life trying to be something, a personality, that was just a bunch of lies. 'I' had even believed that I was a normal and highly successful human being. I wasn't. I was living a lie. This realization resulted in a few moments of self-recrimination. I indulged myself in a brief rant that I captured in my journal.

> *"What an idiot! I had actually believed that a bunch of lies was 'me'. What is more insane than that? Bugger, bugger, bugger. That just plain sucks".*

I was angry at myself for having been such an idiot. I had actually thought that I was doing very well at living this thing called life when all the while I had been completely and utterly insane. What could be more insane than believing that I was a set of lies? I felt like I had wasted the first forty years of my life and that sucked.

That anger only lasted for a few moments. I was soon feeling resigned to the 'fact' that I had indeed been lost in believing that 'I' was my personality. I accepted that my personality was a set of lies. That was a huge leap forward in Loving myself. It opened the door to my dropping the false and returning 'home' to Love.

It also led to my understanding why the false beliefs that made up my personality were known as the barriers to Love. Whenever I became triggered into functioning from one of those barriers, I would be operating from my ego and would be disconnected from Love. Removing the barriers to Love would destroy the only thing that was preventing me from knowing that I was, and always had been, Love. That one thing was my own ego or personality.

After accepting that my personality was a set of lies, I was left with a very strange feeling inside. Deep down, I was excited that removing my barriers to Love would enable me to return 'home' to Love. However, the ego-based 'I' was sad because 'he' was going to have to disappear in order to make that happen. Basically, 'I' was asking my ego-based mind to accept its impending doom. That was not an easy thing for my ego to do.

Fortunately, 'I' was ready to do that. I had played out the ego game. I had become a roaring 'success' in the ego-based world and had discovered that 'success' did not work for me. I had become successful and had been miserable. The so-called 'successful' life had felt absolutely soul destroying to me. There was no way I could return to that kind of life. I had to find an alternative. If the alternative was to dissolve the 'I' that was just a bunch of lies then so be it. 'I' was okay with that.

I soon began to relax. It still felt weird for 'me' to accept that I was on a 'self' destructive journey but I was determined to do it anyway.

That is why self-Love is called the sacred fire. It will destroy everything that you think you are and leave behind only what you truly are.

There is a tremendous beauty that will result from stepping into the sacred fire of self-Love. It will transform you from living a conditioned existence that is a lie to living life as the eternal being of Divine Love that you are.

Nisargadatta Maharaj described the result of embracing self-Love in the book 'I am That'.

"The search for reality is the most dangerous of all undertakings,
for it will destroy the world in which you live. But if your motive is
love of truth and life, you need not be afraid." (2)

This is where the symbolism of the phoenix rising from the ashes applies. Removing your barriers to Love will destroy the illusory self that you have believed yourself to be. It will destroy the very world that you have thought you were living in. In return, you will be gifted with becoming truth and Divine Love. As Nisargadatta says in the above quote, *"you need not be afraid"*.

I invite you to step into the garden of self-Love. However, before you do, I suggest you ponder the words of Rumi.

"If you can't smell the fragrance don't come into the garden of
Love. If you're unwilling to undress don't enter the stream of
Truth. Stay where you are. Don't come our way."

Unless you are willing to undress completely (to expose the way you truly feel inside and to let go of all of the illusions that you hold about yourself) then self-healing is not for you. On the other hand, if you are open to the possibility that your personality is simply a set of false beliefs, and you are ready to let go of those false beliefs, then welcome. Welcome to the journey of becoming a self-healer. Welcome to the journey home to Love.

The reward for undertaking this journey is arguably the greatest gift that you can give yourself: you.

****

The Second Pillar: Mindful Awareness

What is mindful awareness?

The term mindful awareness can be described by breaking it down into its two component parts; mindful and awareness.

The first part is mindful. To be mindful is to bring your full attention to what is going on, both inside and outside you, in the present moment. One simple way to know if you were mindful in the past is to look at your memory of a past event. If you have a clear memory of everything that was taking place during that event then you were fully mindful. If the memory is hazy, or you have trouble remembering it at all, then you were not fully mindful. Your attention was at least partially elsewhere. Perhaps you were daydreaming about the past or future.

The second part is awareness. In this context, awareness means to be aware of everything going on both inside you and outside of you without getting caught up in reacting to any of it. For example, you are aware of any thoughts, emotions, pains, or sensations that arise in the body and mind but you do not react from any of them. You are simply aware of them. You are also aware of everything going on outside of you without judging it or wanting it to change in any way. You are simply aware of it.

Thus, mindful awareness enables you to be aware of everything that is going on, both inside and outside of you, in the present moment without reacting to it. It gives you the ability to treat life as a mirror. You are able to observe the signposts (fear, pain, an emotion such as anger, and a non-loving motivation) arising inside you without becoming identified with them. You can then follow those signposts down inside yourself to find and remove the underlying barriers to Love. You are able to heal yourself.

The key to practicing mindful awareness is not to 'become' the emotions, thoughts, or sensation that you observe arising in the body and mind. You 'become' something by identifying with it. For example, if anger arises in the body and you say 'I am angry' then you have 'become' angry. You have identified with being angry. You may then act out in the world from that anger.

With mindful awareness, you accept that the essence of who you really are is not angry. The emotion of anger has arisen inside the mind and body because a part of your ego, a barrier to Love, has been triggered. You are not angry. It is only your false self that is angry.

If you can use mindful awareness to be aware of an emotion arising without 'becoming' lost in that emotion then you have created a healing opportunity. Instead of becoming the emotion and reacting from it, you can use it as a signpost indicating that healing is required. You can then delve inside to find and remove the barrier to Love underlying that emotion.

Similarly, if a feeling of fear arises inside you and you say "*I am afraid*" then you have become lost in fear. Instead of becoming a fear, you can use mindful awareness to observe fear arise in the mind and body and then treat it as another signpost.

Lastly, a pain or illness can arise in the body without your having to identify with it. There is illness in the body but the essence of who you really are is not ill. The illness is simply a messenger indicating that you have a barrier to Love that needs to be healed.

There are Multiple Levels of Awareness

There are many levels of awareness. For example, if you read something in a book then you have become 'mentally aware' of the concepts outlined in that book. Mental awareness is one level of awareness. However, there is no healing power in mental awareness. Mental awareness opens the door to what is possible but does not take you through that door.

The level of awareness that is required for practicing 'mindful awareness' is achieved by going beyond the mind. You will need to connect to your Higher Self or witnessing consciousness. You will then be beyond the ego and can observe the functioning of the ego rather than becoming lost in it.

There are more levels of awareness beyond that of the Higher Self or witnessing consciousness. You can explore those deeper levels through meditation. However, moving your awareness to the level of the witnessing consciousness is enough for you to be able to practice mindful awareness. Awareness at that level has tremendous healing power.

How can you bring your awareness to the level of the higher self or witnessing consciousness?

Meditation is the tool for shifting your level of awareness. Meditation is an art, not a science. It has been described in many different ways. It has been referred to as residing as the witnessing consciousness, being mindfully aware, abiding in a silent inner space, creating separation from one's thoughts and emotions, a state of being, and more.

In the book 'I am That', Nisargadatta Maharaj summarized meditation as follows.

"The art of meditation is the art of shifting the focus of one's attention to ever subtler levels, without losing one's grip on the levels left behind." (3)

In order to fully understand that statement, we first need to clarify what is meant by the focus of one's attention. The focus of one's attention is also called the focus of one's awareness. Meditation is used to shift the focus of your awareness to ever subtler levels of consciousness. Shifting the focus of your awareness out of your ego and into your higher self enables you to practice mindful awareness.

How do you shift the focus of your awareness?

You can begin by playing with shifting the focus of your awareness around within the body. For example, while you are identified with your thoughts (you do that by starting a sentence with the words 'I think'), the focus of your awareness is inside your head just behind your forehead. Holding the focus of your awareness there keeps you lost in identifying with your monkey mind.

You can shift the focus of your awareness out of your thoughts and into the center of your chest by either focusing on any sensations that you feel in your chest or simply intending to do so. The focus of your awareness will then be in your heart chakra. You will be heart-centered. You will have shifted the focus of your awareness!

You can also move the focus of your awareness to the center point of your head (between your temples and in the middle of your head) by simply intending to do so. You will then be centered. You will not be identified with your thoughts nor with the emotions that are stored within your heart chakra. Having the focus of your awareness centered in this way allows you to respond to external events from a calm inner space. You do not get lost in any thoughts, emotions, or pains that arise in the body.

This process for centering the focus of your awareness is described in exercise '*14. Center yourself*'.

Practicing meditation allows you to shift the focus of your awareness out of the false self (the ego and body) entirely. You are able to shift it into your higher self or into one of the other subtler levels of consciousness. You can even shift it all the way to Source.

For our purposes, the art of meditation is used to shift the focus of your awareness to your higher self while retaining a grip on your ego and body. You are then able to observe the functioning of the false self without becoming it.

The ability to shift the focus of your awareness in this way is what makes mindful awareness one of the three pillars of becoming a self-healer. By using mindful awareness, you can observe the signposts arising inside you without becoming identified with them. You can look in the mirror.

How do you Cultivate Mindful Awareness?

There are a wide variety of meditation techniques available to support you in learning the art of meditation: Vipassana, Guided, Walking, Active, Dynamic, Insight, Concentration, Aum, Kundalini, and so on. Each technique provides you with an opportunity to practice shifting the focus of your awareness to subtler and subtler levels.

The meditation techniques that work for you will likely be different from the ones that work for others. I suggest that you try a variety of techniques and then focus on practicing the ones that resonate with you.

I also recommend that you focus on meditation techniques that are designed specifically to cultivate mindful awareness. For example, Vipassana meditation is known as Gautama Buddha's gift to the world and it specifically teaches mindful awareness. I highly recommend that you begin your exploration of meditation by attending a Vipassana retreat. It will provide you with an introduction to mindful awareness and you can then cultivate mindful awareness by bringing it to every moment of your daily life.

Insight Meditation includes Mindful Awareness

The ability to perform an insight meditation is another key tool in becoming a self-healer. Insight meditation is a way to glean answers, from your inner guide, to any question about yourself that you choose to ask. It is used in the self-healing process to find the barrier to Love underlying a signpost.

It is only your inner guide that can assist you in finding your barriers to Love. Your rational mind cannot help you in this process. You need to be able to tune in to your inner guide and ask it to show you the barrier that has been triggered. Insight meditation enables you to do that. Thus, the ability to do an insight mediation is a prerequisite to becoming a self-healer.

The process for performing an insight meditation involves sitting in silence and focusing your attention on whatever question you would like to ask your inner guide. You then enter into a meditative state and practice mindful awareness while you patiently wait for your inner guide to show you the answer. This process is described in exercise '15. *Performing an Insight Meditation*'.

****

The Third Pillar: Trust

Trust is a vital part of becoming a self-healer. You need to trust that you will be able to find a barrier to Love, that you are ready to face whatever it is surfacing from inside you, and that your inner guide is bringing events into your life that will enable you to learn your soul lessons and heal yourself.

However, who or what do you trust?

I explored the word trust a great deal on my journey and was told countless times that the only one I could trust was myself. I didn't!

At the beginning of my journey, I was attached to the false self (ego and body) and I certainly didn't trust it. In the morning, my ego would be triggering me into sadness or frustration and, in the afternoon, it would be triggering me into excitement. It was basically sending me on a roller coaster ride of emotions and associated thoughts based on whatever external event appeared in my life. I came to refer to my ego as my 'monkey mind' and I felt like I was a prisoner of its whims. There was no way I was going to trust my monkey mind.

I couldn't trust myself but could I trust other people?

Initially, whenever I thought about trusting others, I would automatically picture a used car salesman in Vancouver who had misled me when I was a naive young man buying his first car. He had 'tricked' me into paying far more for a car than it was worth. At the time, his actions had left a very sour taste in my mouth. However, I eventually came to feel that he had given me a tremendous gift. He had shown me that I could not trust people who were caught up in satisfying their own ego-based desires.

Unfortunately, that included pretty much everyone I knew. I was left feeling that people were basically untrustworthy.

It wasn't until I met His Holiness - an enlightened master who taught me the nature of mind – that I found someone who I felt I could trust. He was completely selfless. I felt that he didn't want anything from me and was there simply to guide me. Him I trusted.

This was good news. It seems that I could actually trust a person. However, I could only trust them if they were functioning from beyond their ego. I didn't come across too many of those people during my travels. It was very rare for me to find a person who was functioning from their higher selves and was therefore trustworthy. I gradually came to accept that, for the most part, I could not trust other people.

Where did that leave me? I couldn't trust my monkey mind and I couldn't trust yours. What was left for me to trust?

I had been raised as a Christian and I briefly considered putting my trust in its version of 'God'. My grandmother was devoutly catholic and she had been one of the kindest and most gentle women I had known. If she was a product of Christianity then I felt that it had to be doing something right.

However, as a young boy, I had been given parts of the Bible to read by a minister. I had read them and they left me with a bunch of questions which I then posed to the minister. He didn't seem to like my attitude and wouldn't answer my questions. To this day, I don't really know why. Maybe it was the resistance that I was feeling to him and his ways. Regardless, I came away from that interaction feeling like I wasn't allowed to question him or the Bible. The Bible was supposedly 'gospel' and I was supposed to just blindly believe it and his interpretation of it. That had left a very sour taste in my mouth. I wasn't a fan of blind belief even at an early age. I had then turned away from my parent's religion.

Upon making the choice to leave the material world behind, I reconsidered the role of religion in my life. I briefly considered embracing Christianity but just couldn't do it. I didn't resonate with it because I felt that it was asking me to believe stuff without having the opportunity to verify it for myself.

I also found myself feeling turned off by the idea that there was a judgmental God who could send me to eternal damnation. Where was the Love in that? Wasn't Christ a forgiving being of Love? Was he really the son of a non-Loving God who used fear to control his or her people rather than used Love to inspire them?

Something about the Bible and the Christian religion simply didn't resonate with me. Nope, I wasn't going to trust that kind of God.

I then explored other religions and belief systems. I briefly explored Hinduism, Jainism, Islam, Buddhism, and Shamanism. I found that there were beautiful parts to all of them but none of them completely resonated with me. I did explore Buddhism rather deeply. I had been told that it was an experiential religion. If you completed the Buddhist path then you were no longer a Buddhist, you were a Buddha. I resonated with that idea. I love a great deal about the Buddhist philosophy that I explored. However, my exposure to life in two Buddhist monasteries left me feeling that its path simply wasn't for me.

The other belief system that I explored deeply was Shamanism. It was another experiential system that invited me to explore the capabilities of the human being for myself. Again, I resonated with a great deal of what I learned but came away feeling that becoming a shaman was not my path; at least not in this lifetime.

That exploration of various belief systems gave me some wonderful insights into the human experience and the underlying commonalities between those systems. However, I came away from it feeling that I could not put my trust in any religion or belief system that asked me to blindly believe anything. That pretty much eliminated them all.

Even Buddhism had me doing some rather strange, at least to me, stuff related to where I pointed the soles of my feet and where I was allowed to put the teachings. I also struggled with the Buddhist code of ethics that I was meant to follow. It struck me that Buddhism did have its own set of beliefs and I felt completely finished with any form of blind belief.

In the end, I was left with nothing to trust.

I didn't know which way to turn. I did look back over my shoulder at the society that I had left behind. Was there anything or anyone in my society that I could trust?

I was skeptical about that possibility because my society's definition of how to become successful and happy had not worked for me. I no longer felt aligned with my society's chosen way of life. However, I didn't know where else to turn. My mind, your mind, and religion couldn't be trusted.

I thought about going back into my old life but I simply couldn't see myself returning to the corporate world. I felt that the capitalist economic system had been implemented in a way that resulted in corporations that were driven primarily by greed rather than Love and harmony. I also felt that the prevailing form of democracy in the west was biased towards putting the interests of lobbyists ahead of providing Loving and selfless service to the people. I really couldn't see any social structures in my society that were designed to have its leaders be Loving and selfless; no religion, no business model, and no political institution met that basic requirement.

Basically, I felt like I couldn't trust anyone or anything. I could not trust myself, you, my religion, or my society. I felt totally lost and alone in the world.

Fortunately, my global meanderings did eventually lead me to discover something that I could trust; my own inner guide. It began with an 'inner knowingness' that would arise from inside me whenever I allowed my conditioned mind to fall silent. That knowingness grew stronger through the efforts I put in to interpreting my dreams, meditating, activating my sense of clairvoyance, and doing automatic writing. I found that thoughts would literally pop into my head or words appear on the page that my rational mind did not know.

For example, 'I' am not a poet yet poetry would occasionally flow through me. I was in Bali at a time on my journey when I did not have a clue about where I was going or what life was all about. I was spending hours every day simply sitting by the ocean and writing. The answers to my questions began to come from inside me, through poetry. These are a few of the poems that emerged:

LOVE

    Love is not a word.
    Love is an act.
    It is not physical.
    It is not mental.
    Love is a way of being.
    Love is the answer

we are all seeking.
There is nothing out there.
It is only in you.
Give yourself away,
You give peace,
You create a new world.
Love is the Path
humanity has lost.
It's right inside you
waiting to be released.
Stop the seeking
and be yourself.
Be Love.

This was my first real introduction to the idea of becoming Love, and it had come from inside me! I had no idea that I could become Love and yet something inside me was letting me know. It certainly wasn't my rational mind doing that.

THE PATH REVEALED

A feeling of contentment descends.
A sense of spiritual awakening arises.
The veils of darkness are lifting.
The connection to Source is revealed.
The purpose of life laid bare.
There is but one destination.
All paths lead to it.
In Bali, you breathe it.
Breath is Life, life is Love.
That is the destination.

So simple yet so complex.
How to attain it?
We all know but have forgotten.
Life is a mirror showing the way back to it.
Trust the mirror and your path is found.
The journey becomes easy with trust,
Life is a struggle without.

In this poem, I was introduced to the ideas of looking in the mirror to find my path and trusting what I saw. The poem also reinforced the idea that life is Love.

I did not understand this poem when it came out of me. I was newly embarking upon the inner journey and did not know anything about 'the mirror' or how life could be Love. It would be years before I began to understand what this poem meant yet it had come out of me. Something inside me clearly seemed to know more than 'I' did.

CIRCLE OF LIFE

The light has gone out
In the eyes of so many around me.
The struggle has been lost.
Temptation has won.
The path to Nirvana has been abandoned.
A life to be relived.
No lessons learnt.
It will all begin again,
Stuck in the circle of life.

This last poem reflected the way I felt about myself and those I saw around me. I didn't understand what it meant to say that the light had gone out and I hadn't yet learned about soul lessons. This poem was pointing me towards things that I had not yet discovered.

These poems, and many others like them, simply flowed out of me. They were answering my questions in a way that didn't appease my turbulent rational mind. For the most part, my mind didn't understand what they were saying. However, the words were touching a deep place inside me. I was being shown what the journey through life was all about in a way that was not allowing my ego to latch onto anything. Something beyond my mind was pointing me to go beyond my mind.

I called this something my 'inner knowingness'. I began to pay attention to it in whatever form it appeared. Much to my delight, I discovered that it both knew things that my mind did not know and seemed to have my best interests at heart. I eventually came to realize that this 'knowingness' was coming from my own inner guide.

I began to trust its guidance. I would go wherever my inner guide asked me to go and do whatever it asked me to do. I would also trust that it was bringing experiences into my life that were enabling me to both learn my lessons and remove my barriers to Love. With that trust, I stopped perceiving difficult situations in my life as challenges but rather as opportunities.

Life even started to become a joyful ride. A statement eventually arose from inside me: *Life is not a struggle to be endured, life is a journey to be enjoyed.*

Upon reflection, I started to feel that my inner guide had always been there for me. For example, it had tried to reach out to me when I was in my early twenties to invite me to explore the world of healing. I had gotten as far as to be accepted into medical school but had then turned and gone another way. I had ignored my inner guide on that occasion, and on many other occasions, because of my attachment to my own ego.

I also felt like there had been times in my life when my inner guide had been able to penetrate my ego and guide me. That seemed to have happened when I was faced with situations that my rational mind did not know how to handle.

Two scenarios in particular stood out for me as examples of when my inner guide had taken over. In both cases, I had felt that female friends of mine were under threat from other men and that I had to do something about it.

The first had occurred when I had been in Jamaica with my then girlfriend and two other couples. The six of us had rented three scooters and gone for a tour of the island. The scooter that I had been driving had broken down in a poor area of a town. The two other guys that I had been with had then taken one of the two remaining scooters and gone to get a replacement for mine. That left me standing in the equivalent of a slum with three beautiful, and scantily clad, young women.

We were standing in the driveway of a house and a friendly woman came out of the house to ask if we were okay. I explained the situation, thanked her for her concern, and said that we were fine. Two men then appeared at the far end of the street. They talked together for a few minutes before one of them began to approach us. As he got closer, I started to feel like we were in trouble.

I had then gone completely calm inside and had walked away from my female friends to meet him on the sidewalk. We stood face to face for a few moments and looked at each other. We didn't say a word and I felt like he was sizing me up. He then turned and walked away. I had remained calm throughout our silent interaction and only began to shake a little bit as I walked back to the three women.

The second incident had occurred on the south side of Chicago. I was on an elevated train when a man had walked up to a female friend of mine and began to yell at her from a few inches away. He was yelling about how he had not raped his daughters and had not deserved to go to jail. Again, I felt like I had to do something. I had then gone completely calm and stepped in between them. I remained silent as he yelled at me for a few minutes before he also turned and walked away.

In both of those situations, my first instinct had been that these men were a threat and that I needed to do something. An amazing feeling of calm had then come over me and I had simply acted from what felt like a kind of autopilot. Throughout the subsequent interactions, I had remained completely calm inside. It was only after the incidents were over that any fear had arisen. At the time, I didn't know what had come over me. I just knew that I had somehow managed to defuse both situations.

It was only much later that I discovered what may have happened to me. The feeling of deep inner calm that I had experienced in both situations was very similar to the inner calm that arises from inside me when I allow my monkey mind to fall silent and my inner guide to take over. I am then able to act on whatever I feel inspired to do without having to think about what to do. It simply happens. I flow with life.

I have a feeling that this is exactly what had happened to me in both Jamaica and Chicago. My monkey mind had simply gotten out of the way and allowed my inner guide to take over. I had then been able to do whatever it inspired me to do while remaining completely calm.

Upon reflection, I felt that my inner guide had been guiding me through life, without my even knowing it. Now I knew.

I had finally found something that I could trust: my own inner guide. I began to cultivate that trust.

I now feel that life really is a mirror and that my inner guide is the one that is placing things in that mirror. All I have to do is trust that my inner guide is bringing me the life situations that I need in order to learn my soul lessons. I also trust that it, together with insight meditation, awareness, self-Love, and forgiveness, will enable me to remove all of the obscurations that appear in that mirror.

My self-healing journey began to accelerate exponentially after I learned to trust my inner guide.

Cultivating Trust in Your Own Inner Guide

There are many ways to cultivate trust in your own inner guide.

I recommend that you start with a spiritual practice of at least 20 minutes per day. A spiritual practice involves doing something on your own that does not include anything that could stimulate your intellectual mind. It could be a walk in nature, sitting in meditation, chopping vegetables, surfing, wood carving, or any number of activities. It is anything that allows you to take a break from functioning in the world through your rational mind.

You can choose any activity that supports you in falling silent inside. The only requirements are that you do not talk to anyone and that you avoid all forms of mental stimulations such as such as reading, talking, watching TV, watching a move, listening to recordings, and even listening to music. You can do those activities during the rest of your day but not during your spiritual practice.

Over time, you will find that your mind will eventually begin to fall silent during these periods. You will have then accessed the inner environment that allows you to hear your inner guide.

There are also a number of exercises that you can use to connect with your inner guide. I have listed a few of these exercises below.

- **Automatic Writing** – write in a journal every day for a minimum of three weeks. Write the equivalent of at least three full sized (8.5 inch by 11 inch) pages, single spaced. Begin by writing whatever is on your mind and then just keep going. Keep writing until you are writing things without knowing why you are writing them, and without even knowing how the current sentence is going to end. At that point, you will be doing automatic writing and messages from your inner guide will often appear on the page.

- **Dream Interpretation** – acquire a dream journal and leave it beside your bed with a pen. Set the intention to remember your dreams and then write them down as soon as you wake up; even if you wake up in the middle of the night. Don't go back to sleep until you have written down your dreams as you will invariably forget them if you wait until morning.

    Everyone dreams and everyone can recall their dreams. Have someone teach you how to interpret your dreams or buy a book on dream interpretation. Begin interpreting your dreams and pay attention to the messages that they contain. Those messages are coming from your inner guide.

It does not matter what dream interpretation method you use. Your inner guide will send you messages through your dreams that fit with whatever method you have chosen.

- **Go on a Date with Yourself** – give yourself permission to do something that you have always felt drawn to do. Pick an activity that does not harm you or any other being in any way. Do that activity on your own. This practice is about tuning into see what, deep inside you, you have always felt inspired to do, and then actually giving yourself permission to do it. This exercise will prepare you for acting on the guidance that you receive from your inner guide, once you are able to hear it more clearly.

- **Practice Flowing with Life** – start doing things in your daily life without thinking about why you are doing them. For example, allow yourself to simply walk or drive a different route than you normally do. Pay attention to everything that is happening around you as you do so.

  You can also allow yourself to be drawn to something, such as a movie or a bookstore, rather than thinking about which one to choose or go to. Another thing you can do is to tune into your body whenever you go to a restaurant and see if you can allow your body to choose what it would like to eat rather than ordering your usual item. Another possibility is to go for a walk in nature, without any time limit or goal in mind, and simply be aware of everything you encounter on your walk.

  Be imaginative in finding your own ways to flow. The key with all of these activities is to let go of the need to know why you are doing any of them. Instead, open yourself up to embracing whatever comes your way. In that way, you are opening yourself up to having your inner guide driving your life rather than having your rational mind in charge.

  You will likely find that you begin to feel a deep sense of inner peace during these activities, and that amazing synchronicities begin to happen.

  This exercise is preparing you for the day when you have removed enough of your barriers to Love that your ego begins to fall silent. At that point, you will automatically fall into functioning with your inner guide in charge of your life.

- **Insight Meditation** – Play with performing an insight meditation on any of the questions that you have about yourself and your life. For example, pick a simple pain that you have in your body and ask your inner guide to show you the barrier to Love that lies at its source. Another example would be to use an insight meditation to glean an answer as to where to go on your next vacation or long weekend. The instructions for performing an insight meditation can be found in exercise '*15. Performing an Insight Meditation*'.

  At first, you may find this exercise difficult but, with practice, you will find that your inner guide will answer your questions.

- **Guided Meditation** – guided meditations can be used to help you to: fall into a silent space inside yourself; to retrieve messages from your higher self; and, to do more esoteric activities such as finding your power animal or soul purpose. Select a guided meditation online, or attend a course that you feel drawn to, and try doing a guided meditation.

  This exercise will enable you to cultivate trust in your own ability to enter into a meditative state and to receive messages from your inner guide. You may initially find it difficult to follow the meditation because of interference from your mind. Be patient. Practice trusting that you are able to do it and eventually your mind will fall silent enough for you to be able to follow the meditation.

- **Shamanic Drumming Circle** – shamanic drumming can support you in shifting your awareness out of your rational mind and into your witnessing consciousness. That will then enable you to hear your inner guide. This exercise is a way for you to cultivate trust in your ability to shift your awareness and to receive guidance.

These are just a few examples of how you can cultivate trust in your inner guide. Please do whichever ones resonate with you and also allow yourself to be drawn to other techniques. With practice, you will discover that there is something inside you that you can trust; your own inner guide.

One of the main obstacles that people face in hearing their inner guide is to be attached to how they are 'supposed' to receive that guidance. Your guidance may appear:

- in the form of inspiration that comes to you during your spiritual practice;

- through the people that are drawn into your life;

- during a movie that you feel drawn to watch;

- while reading a book;

- in your dreams; or,

- even in a sign on the side of a bus.

Allow yourself to be open to your guidance appearing in any way imaginable.

Another obstacle that commonly arises for people is to start thinking that everything that you see in your life is guidance from your inner guide. You may then waste your time doing what your mind thinks you 'should' do rather than following your inner guide. Over time, you will learn to feel the difference between something being guidance from your inner guide and something just being your mind playing its games. Until then, one rule of thumb to use is, if a message comes into your life three times, in three different ways, then it is time to pay attention.

Cultivating trust in your inner guide will enable you to trust that:

- every situation in your life that triggers a signpost is an opportunity for you to heal yourself;

- you can cultivate mindful awareness;

- you can use an insight meditation to receive answers from your inner guide;

- a particular fear will only be placed in front of you when you are ready to face it;

- an emotional trauma will only surface when you are ready to heal it;

- you are Loveable no matter what surfaces from inside you;

- your inner guide will show you everything that you need to do in order to heal a particular barrier to Love;

- your inner guide knows your unique way 'home' to Love; and,

- you are best served by following the guidance of your inner guide rather than the desires and whims of your ego.

****

The Three Pillars and Self-Healing

The combination of trust, self-love, and mindful awareness will enable you to become a self-healer.

- Trust will enable you to accept that your inner guide is bringing experiences into your life that you need in order to learn your soul lessons, heal yourself, and return 'home' to Love.

- Mindful awareness will enable you to use life as a mirror and to thereby become aware of the signposts indicating that self-healing is needed.

- Trust and insight meditation will then allow you to follow those signposts down inside yourself to find the barriers to Love that triggered them.

- The combination of awareness, self-Love, insight meditation, trust, forgiveness, and learning your lessons allows you to remove those barriers.

  Removing your barriers has the effect of removing any energetic disturbances that may have led to a pain or illness. The body will then heal itself.

That is the self-healing journey. Self-Love, mindful awareness, and trust form the foundation of that journey. They are the 'The Three Pillars'.

Life is a journey to be enjoyed not a struggle to be endured.

6. The Four Signposts

There are four signposts that you can follow on your self-healing journey. They are anger (or any other emotional reaction), fear, pain, and a non-Loving motivation.

They are called signposts because they are triggered by either your barriers to Love or by a misalignment in your life. The key to becoming a self-healer is to find and remove both your barriers to Love and your misalignments. The signposts show you the way.

In this chapter, we will be discussing in more detail how to use each of the four different types of signposts as your starting point for self-healing.

****

The First Signpost: Anger (or any other emotion)

Anger can be a powerful ally for you on your healing journey. If you are able to accept the possibility that every feeling of anger is sourced from inside you then anger becomes a signpost. You can then use anger as a healing energy. Anger arising in you represents an opportunity to heal yourself.

Unfortunately, many people do not have this kind of healing relationship with anger. I know I didn't. I used to think that others were responsible for making me angry. I would blame others for my anger and then lash out at them from my anger. Basically, I was getting lost in the energy of anger and becoming disconnected from the inner space of Love. Everything that I then said or did would carry the energy of violence not Love. I would be acting in a destructive way towards myself and everyone around me.

This destructive relationship with anger represented my modus operandi for most of my life. I was raised to believe that anger was 'bad' and that 'nice guys' don't get angry. I wanted to be 'nice' and so I did my best to suppress any anger that I felt. Unfortunately, suppressing my anger didn't make it go away. It just simmered away inside me and would occasionally burst out.

The worst part of suppressing my anger was that I didn't even realize that I had a ton of anger inside me. I actually thought that I really was a 'nice' guy. I was very much in denial. My ex-partner of seven years later told me that she had been scared of me the whole time we dated! It seems that the only one had been fooled by my suppressing my anger was me.

It was rather shocking for me to discover that I was an angry, rather than 'nice', person. However, once I did, I became determined to free myself of that anger. In the beginning, I didn't know about the relationship between anger, barriers to Love, and self-healing. All I knew was that anger was toxic and that I wanted to get rid of it. Thus, my initial forays into healing anger were full of trial and error. I was blindly going where only I could go. I did have some beautiful people supporting me through this process but I really didn't have a clue as to what I was doing.

My relationship with anger began to change after I was exposed to the possibility that anger was sourced from inside me. I was told that anger could only arise inside me if one of my barriers to Love had been triggered. Basically, I would only feel anger when my ego was trying to protect a part of itself. No external person or event could make me angry. Only my ego could do that.

This explained a lot for me. Throughout my life, I had occasionally become vehemently angry over seemingly trivial things. It had always surprised me as to how I could get so angry over something so small. I now had an explanation. It wasn't the trivial event that was causing me to become angry. It was the belief that a part of me was being threatened that was triggering the anger.

This was a profound realization for me. I felt like so much of the conflict that had arisen in my life was because of this effort by my ego to protect itself. It was time for me to stop fighting the world and at least explore the possibility that anger was sourced from inside me.

I was then able to confirm for myself that anger was indeed coming from my barriers to Love. I used anger as a signpost and, invariably, I found that I was indeed protecting a part of my false self whenever I got angry. For example, I felt deep anger towards my mother and I allowed myself to delve into that anger. It turned out that I was furious at her because I felt that she had made me give up on being me in order to become what she thought I 'should' be (materially successful and emotionally cold).

I then began the process of forgiving her for conditioning me into becoming something that I was not. I discovered that I had created a false belief that she would only love me if I became what she wanted me to be. That false belief was triggering my anger. Every time she did anything for me I would subconsciously think that she was trying to manipulate me into being something I was not, and I would get angry. The false belief was creating the anger and it simply wasn't true. She did love me and was only doing what she thought was best for me. I let go of that belief. I also forgave her for getting lost in her own ego-based ideas of what was best for me and for trying to turn me into something I was not.

It turned out that forgiving her did heal the anger that I felt towards her, but I was still angry. Bummer. I delved further into the anger and discovered that, underneath my anger towards my mother, was anger at myself. I was angry at myself for having succumbed to her conditioning and giving up on myself. I had chosen to become what she wanted me to be. She may have pushed me towards becoming emotionally cold and materially successful but I had chosen to go there. I had given up on me! It was not my mother's fault at all. It was mine.

I then went through the process of forgiving myself. That was much harder than forgiving her. How do you forgive yourself for doing something that costs you twenty-seven years of your life?

Fortunately, I knew that every experience that came into my life was an opportunity for me to learn my soul lessons. I knew in my heart that my giving up on me was how my journey was meant to unfold. However, simply knowing that didn't release the anger I felt. I would have to learn the soul lesson before I could forgive myself.

The lesson was to always be true to myself no matter what anyone else asked of me. I embraced that lesson to the very core of my being. I was absolutely determined not to give up on me again no matter what. I told myself that I would rather leave this body than make that mistake again, and I meant it.

At that point, I felt like I knew what Shakespeare had meant when he had written (in Hamlet):

"This above all: to thine own self be true".

I was going to be true to myself no matter what came my way.

After learning that lesson, I began the process of forgiving myself. I initially found it difficult to forgive myself because of how many years I had 'lost' through making that choice. How could I forgive myself for that? I was too mad at me to forgive myself.

This is where self-Love came into play. Self-Love includes accepting both the truth that I had given up on me and the feeling that doing so had cost me twenty-seven years of my life. I embraced the feeling of losing so many years. I let that feeling sink in, and it hurt. I let myself feel the pain. I didn't deny it. I was practicing self-Love.

While sitting with the pain, I began to wonder if it had been necessary for me to go through those years of descending into the darkness of an ego-based materialistic existence. I had learned a great deal about what it was like to live that kind of life during those 'lost' years. That had given me the ability to relate with others who had made similar choices with their lives. I had also subsequently learned how to break free of that conditioned existence.

Were those 'lost years' actually a necessary part of my journey through life? Could I have lived that kind of life so that one day I would be able to guide others in breaking free of their conditioned minds?

I didn't know. However, the possibility that those years may not have been a complete loss opened the door to my being able to forgive myself. I did that, and the anger was gone.

This example of using anger as a healing energy showed me the futility of blaming others for the way I felt. I had spent most of my life blaming my mother for pushing me into becoming just one more member of the corporate treadmill. That anger had been toxic for me, and for everyone around me. Blaming her also meant that I was not owning the anger as being sourced from inside me. That lack of ownership had been preventing me from learning one of the main lessons that I had incarnated to learn. It was definitely time for me to stop playing the blame game and to own my emotions.

Where does that leave us on this discussion of anger as a signpost?

Basically, other people do not make you angry. The false beliefs that you hold inside yourself create all of the anger that arises inside you. A person who triggers you into feeling anger is actually giving you a gift of showing you that you have some healing to do. Own your emotions and you can become a self-healer. Blame others for the way you feel and you will not heal yourself.

I highly recommend that you confirm this for yourself. I did.

A Process for using Anger as a Signpost

For me, anger is a healing force. It is not something to be either thrown at others or repressed. It is something to be embraced through self-Love. It represents a healing opportunity. It is a signpost.

Whenever anger arises inside me, I know that it is pointing at either a barrier to Love inside me or a misalignment in my life. If I don't remove that barrier, or rectify the misalignment, then the energetic disturbance that has been created inside me will eventually manifest as a pain or illness.

I use the following process to find the barrier to Love or misalignment underlying any anger that arises inside me. I begin by finding a quiet space where I can be on my own. I then picture the event that triggered me to feel angry and allow myself to feel that anger as strongly as I am able. I then go into an insight meditation and ask my inner guide to show me either the barrier to Love or misalignment that is triggering the anger.

This process is outlined in exercise *'2 – Healing the Source of an Emotional Reaction (such as Anger)'*.

Once I see the source of the anger, I heal myself by removing either the misalignment or barrier to Love that I have discovered.

If the source of the anger is a misalignment in my life then I will resolve that misalignment using the process described in exercise *'5. Bringing your Life into Alignment with your Soul'*.

If the source of the anger is a barrier to Love then I heal it using one of the following four exercises: *'6. Letting go of a Particular Fear'; '7. Removing a Belief'; '8. Healing an Emotional Trauma';* or, *'9. Letting go of a Desire'*.

I have been able to heal many of my barriers to Love in this way. Anger continues to be one of my greatest allies in healing myself. I now find myself feeling tremendously grateful to anyone who is able to trigger anger in me. They are giving me the gift of showing me that I have something inside me that needs to be healed.

Every Emotional Reaction is a Signpost

Every emotional reaction, not just anger, is triggered by a false belief. In other words, every emotion that arises in your body is sourced from either a barrier to Love or a misalignment.

I have spent many years using all of my emotions as signposts. During that time, I have been able to verify for myself that every one of them is indeed sourced from a barrier to Love or misalignment; every single one.

At first, I worked with the 'negative' emotions such as jealousy, lust, frustration, sadness, shame, and guilt. All of those emotions felt poisonous to me and I was happy to do anything I could to free myself from them. Sure enough, removing the barriers to Love and misalignments that they were pointing at did heal them.

It was with the so-called 'positive' emotions that I initially struggled. Were emotions such as happiness and excitement also created by my false beliefs? Did my becoming happy or excited disconnect me from Love? If so then did I even want to remove those barriers to Love? I liked feeling happy. What was wrong with happiness?

I began to observe what happened to me when I became either happy or excited and discovered that, sure enough, I would get lost in my ego. I would then say or do things that came from a non-Loving space. For example, when I got excited, I would talk loudly, play music loudly, or even yell. I would often be disturbing the peace and serenity of everyone around me without caring about my impact on them.

Initially, I tried to justify my actions by telling myself that I was just having fun and that the others should either join me or leave if they didn't like it. However, I was being non-Loving and I knew it. Basically, my becoming excited was disconnecting me from Love and was having me function in the world from the false self.

This is where I struggled. I liked being excited and was reluctant to give it up.

I also explored what happened to me because of my desire to be happy. I discovered that this desire also disconnected me from Love. For example, I would become happy if my hockey team won a game. Therefore, I wanted them to win. I soon noticed that I would become irritable during a game if they were losing and morose afterwards if they lost. The desire to be happy was throwing me into the false self and disconnecting me from Love.

Bugger. I liked being happy or excited and felt reluctant to do anything about the barriers to Love that were triggering them.

Initially, I decided to focus on the 'negative' emotions and leave the 'positive' ones for another day. The turning point in my relationship with the 'positive' emotions came when I was attending a U2 concert in Vancouver. I loved U2 and was having a great time at the concert. I could feel excitement coursing through me. And then it happened. Bono took a couple of minutes between two songs to talk about his feelings on George Bush's foreign policies. It was clear to me that he was not a fan. He then had Bush's phone number displayed on a large screen, and invited all of us to text Bush and tell him what we thought of his policies.

I was shocked. My enjoyment of the concert ended in that moment and I have not listened to U2 since. I was not a fan of George Bush's policies either but that wasn't the problem for me. I felt like the excitement that was in the air at the concert had created a kind of 'mob mentality'. I felt that many people in that arena had gotten lost in that excitement and, by doing so, had given their power over to Bono. He had then asked them to do something that his ego wanted them to do and I had a feeling that many of them would actually do it.

I wanted nothing to do with that kind of mind-based power game. I wanted to function in the world from Love not ego. Bono had given me a shining example of what can be done with people who become excited. They can be made to do anything you want them to do. This was a key moment on my journey and I felt grateful to Bono for showing it to me.

From that day forward, I no longer wanted to become 'lost' in either happiness or excitement. I was determined not to give my power away to anyone who may use it to have me do something that their ego wanted me to do. It didn't matter to me whether their intent was well meaning or malicious. I was choosing to be myself in the world, to live my life from Love, and not to be a puppet of Bono, my society, or anyone else.

I then made the choice to remove all of my barriers to Love; including the ones underlying the positive emotions.

I did wonder if I would ever be happy again. I liked being happy and I really didn't like the possibility that happiness was over for me. I needn't have worried. I soon discovered that I could enjoy happiness without becoming lost in it.

I found that the energy of happiness would still arise in me and I could enjoy it whenever it did. I wouldn't 'become happy' and would remain aware of everything around me while enjoying the happiness. Basically, I could enjoy happiness and be Love as long as I did not pursue happiness and did not become lost in it when it arose. This was wonderful news for me. I did not have to give up happiness.

More importantly, I discovered joy. As I went through the process of removing my barriers to Love, I began to spend more and more time abiding in a state of inner peace. I began to feel that inner peace even when emotions such as anger, depression, or happiness arose in the body. Eventually, I also began to feel joyful when those emotions were coursing through the body. I then knew, from my own experience, that joy is not an emotion. Joy is a part of my natural state of being!

At that point, I no longer had any desire to seek happiness or to be happy. I had an inner state of peace and joy that felt far more beautiful to me than any fleeting emotional state. If happiness arises then that is beautiful. I can remain at peace and be filled with joy while it is present in my being. If depression arises then that is equally beautiful. Again, I can remain at peace and be filled with joy while it is present in my being. Inner peace and joy are not dependent on the presence of any temporary emotions.

I was then ready to use every emotional reaction, both 'positive' and 'negative', as signposts indicating that I had either a barrier to Love or a misalignment that needed to be healed. I began to follow every emotional reaction down inside myself in order to heal the source of it. In that way, I have been able to confirm for myself that every emotional reaction is indeed triggered by either a barrier to Love or a misalignment.

****

The Second Signpost: Fear

Where does fear come from?

It comes from inside oneself not outside. Fear can only arise in a person if they have a false belief that is causing them to feel like a part of their false self is under threat. Fear is always created by the ego. Fear and Love cannot co-exist. If I become afraid then I have become identified with a part of my false self and am disconnected from Love.

An external event will result in your feeling afraid when it either triggers one of your unresolved barriers to Love or highlights a misalignment in your life. There is no other source of fear. That is what makes fear a signpost. Whenever fear arises, you are being gifted with an opportunity to either remove a barrier to Love or resolve a misalignment. If you have no barriers to Love and no misalignments then you will not feel fear.

I did not know how to free myself from fear when I first set out on my journey of self-discovery. I didn't know anything about barriers to Love and how to find and remove them. Fear was a constant companion of mine during those early days. For example, I was afraid of what my friends and family were thinking of me. I was also afraid that I was going crazy. I was afraid that I would run out of money and become destitute. On and on it went. I was pretty much in a constant state of fear.

However, I was also fiercely determined to find another way of being regardless of what that cost me. I did my best to simply face my fears head on. That was not always easy. My disenchantment with the corporate world had given me the determination to set out on my journey but it hadn't taken away my fear. It only helped me to keep going despite any fear that arose.

For example, I signed up for a 'Ten Days of Yoga' program at the Yasodhara Ashram in British Columbia. The ashram was a ten hour drive from Vancouver. I love to drive and had felt perfectly calm, and even happy, as I drove across B.C. I remained that way right up until I reached the ashram itself. For some strange reason, an absolute terror came over me as I approached the entrance. That fear overwhelmed me and I was unable to turn in to the ashram. Instead, I drove past it and parked a couple of kilometers away. I was literally shaking with fear as I turned off the car.

I had no idea where the fear was coming from. I took a few deep breaths, got out my journal, and began to write. I slowly calmed down and was eventually able to muster the courage to drive back towards the ashram. I was still feeling afraid as I turned into the driveway but the fear was not as strong as it had been, and I was able to overcome it.

I parked and took a few more deep breaths before getting out of my car. I entered a building and a lady at the reception desk smiled at me. I told her that I was there for the ten day course and she registered me. She then had a friendly man of about my own age take me to my room. As we walked across the grounds, the fear finally abated and I felt fine.

The source of that fear had not surfaced during that whole time. I had simply overcome it by facing it. I had not let that particular fear stop me from doing what I knew, deep in my heart, I was meant to do.

A few days later, I was lying in bed, about to go to sleep, when a 'woman' tapped me on the shoulder and told me that it was *"time to go"*. I was in a male-only wing of a building and the 'woman' did not have a physical body. She simply shimmered and appeared as a 'woman'.

Surprisingly, at least to me, I was not afraid. I accepted what I was seeing and let her words sink in. We had been meditating on death that day and I thought she meant that it was time for me to die. At that point in my journey I didn't know what to do with my life and was not going to return to the corporate world regardless of the cost. I felt disappointed that I was going to have to die but resigned myself to it. If I had to die then so be it. I let go.

The next thing I knew, I had left my body and was 'speaking' to the 'woman' while we 'stood' on a balcony overlooking a lake. Neither of us were in a body! She told me that I had it all wrong and reiterated that it was *"time to go"*. I was confused but she didn't clarify what she meant. We 'stood' on that balcony in silence for a little while and then she took me back to my body.

I was able to fall asleep rather easily after that and woke up the next morning wondering if it had really happened. Had I left my body to talk to an ethereal woman? I was in a bit of a stupor as I left my room to go down the hall and take a shower. When I returned to my room, a five dollar bill that I had left on my desk was standing on its edge. I was even more shocked by the sight of that bill than anything that may or may not have happened the previous night.

I picked up the five dollar note and tried to get it to stand on its edge myself. It took me a few tries before I was able to do it. How could that bill have been stood on its edge? I was in the room alone, and was the only man in the course, so there weren't any other people anywhere around. I looked at the window and it was closed. There was no way that a breeze could have done it. I was stumped.

I then went looking for the man who had initially shown me to my room. I found him near the breakfast area and told him what had happened. He took me over to show me a picture of a woman that was hanging on a wall. He asked me if it had been her. It had.

He then told me that the woman in the picture was Swami Radha and that she had passed away ten years earlier. I was shocked. Swami Radha had founded the ashram, after becoming enlightened in India, and then returning to B.C. She had then passed away.

The realization of what had happened to me began to sink in. Apparently, a dead enlightened master had tapped me on the shoulder and told me that it was *"time to go"*. This was not an everyday occurrence for me. In fact, it was the first time anything like it had happened to me. I was shocked.

Was all of this real? What was going on? I didn't know what to say to this friendly man who was telling me in a matter of fact way that I had received a communication from beyond the grave.

He then told me that the five dollar bill had been her way of reassuring me. Apparently, when something happens that a spirit feels we may have trouble accepting, they give us a physical sign.

I was way out of my depth with all of this. I did my best to let the ramifications sink in. Could I wander around without my body? I had already experienced leaving my body at a Vipassana retreat so this part of the interaction with Swami Radha was the easiest one for me to accept. However, could a spirit 'talk' to me? Could a spirit move a physical object (the five dollar bill)? I did not know. My illusions about what it meant to be human were definitely being threatened. I did my best to accept the possibility that it had indeed happened.

Later that day, I realized that Swami Radha was telling me that it was time for me to go to India. I had been feeling drawn to India for months and had been feeling too afraid to actually bite the bullet and go. I had even been writing in my journal that I needed someone to tell me that it was 'time to go'. She had!

With 'her' confirmation, I decided to go to India. I landed in Delhi three weeks later and, three weeks after that, I was working one on one with a Dzogchen master in a Tibetan Bon monastery. It had been time to go. The student was ready.

I have a feeling that the fear that I had felt when I initially drove up to the ashram had something to do with my 'meeting' Swami Radha. My sense is that 'I' had felt threatened by what may occur at the ashram and had done 'my' level best to protect myself. If I had allowed that fear to stop me from following my inner guidance then I would not have entered that Ashram. I would not have had the mind blowing experience of leaving my body to 'talk' with an enlightened master. I may not even have had the life changing experience of working with a living Dzogchen master.

That experience reinforced my determination to not let fear stop me from following my inner guide.

That story is also an example of the primary approach that I initially used for dealing with fear. I simply took a deep breath and faced it. That direct approach worked for many of my fears but not all. I would not face a fear head on if doing so would result in physical harm. For example, I was not going to face my fear of heights by jumping off a cliff. I didn't mind a bruised ego but I wasn't up for a destroyed body.

I didn't know how to deal with these kinds of fears and accepted that I had to live with them; at least for the time being. I also set the intention to find a way to overcome them and then trusted that my inner guide would eventually show me how.

It wasn't until I learned about this alternative perspective on healing that I learned how to deal with those types of fears. I was told that every fear is based on a lie. A fear is simply a part of the false self, the ego, trying to protect itself. Essentially, fear is my ego's way of trying to protect a lie. If I can find the lie underlying a fear, and let go of that lie, then that fear will dissolve away.

Finding the lie involved allowing myself to feel the fear and then going into an insight meditation. I would ask my inner guide to show me the false belief underlying the fear and then patiently wait for it to do so. Once I saw the lie, I would stop believing it and the fear would dissolve away. This approach worked for me. This was the secondary approach to dealing with fear that I had been looking for.

From that point forward, I had a two-pronged approach for dealing with every fear that arose from inside me. The first prong was to face the fear head on. As long as my facing it would not harm anything other than my ego then I would use that approach. If, after facing the fear, there were no adverse effects from having done so then the fear would typically just dissolve away. For example, I faced my fear of going to India by going to

India. After being in India for a couple of weeks, the fear was gone. This approach typically worked well for me.

However, it did not work in the cases where I believed in a fear so strongly that my ego would subconsciously do everything in its power to prove itself right. I would then create circumstances in my life that ensured that the fear did come to fruition. Fear then became a self-fulfilling prophecy. It would keep recurring no matter how many times I faced it. This is where the second prong came in to play. I dealt with those fears using the same approach that I used for dealing with the fears that I could not face head on because doing so would result in physical harm.

The second prong was the meditative approach described above. One of the surprising outcomes of adopting this meditative approach to healing fear was the discovery that the source of a feeling of fear was not always a specific fear. I found that I could be feeling afraid because of any one of the four barriers to Love becoming triggered, or even because of a misalignment. Fear would arise because I was afraid of:

- something in particular (a specific **fear**);

- having a **belief,** that I was clinging to, be proven false;

- having an **emotional trauma** recur;

- either pursuing a **desire** or having a desire be thwarted; or,

- having to make a change to my life because of a **misalignment** between my chosen life and my soul's journey.

As a result, I had to adjust the meditative approach that I was using to free myself of fear a little bit. Instead of using an insight meditation to find the lie underlying a feeling of fear, I used it to find either the barrier to Love or misalignment underlying that feeling of fear. I would then either remove the barrier to Love or resolve the misalignment.

For example, if the source of my feeling afraid was actually a fear of something in particular then I would continue to sit in meditation and ask to be shown the lie upon which that fear was based. Once I saw the lie, I would choose to stop believing it and the fear would be gone. This process is outlined in exercise '*6. Letting go of a particular Fear* '.

If, on the other hand, the source of my feeling afraid was either a misalignment in my life or one of the other three types of Barriers to Love then I would use the appropriate process for removing it (see exercises '*5.*

Bringing your Life into Alignment with your Soul', *'7. Removing a Belief'*, *'8. Healing an Emotional Trauma'*, or *'9. Letting go of a Desire'*). Once either the barrier to Love or misalignment underlying a feeling of fear was removed then the fear would be gone.

The entire process for healing a feeling of fear is described in exercise *'3. Healing the Source of Fear'*. I use this process whenever I observe fear arising inside the body.

Over time, I have managed to almost completely eliminate fear from my being. This has been an amazing gift for me. Fear no longer overcomes me and I am able to remain in a peaceful and Loving inner space in pretty much every situation. For me, living in a state of inner peace is so much more pleasant than living in fear.

One of the other wonderful benefits of freeing myself from fear has been that fear no longer slows down my journey. In the past, I would be delayed for weeks, or even months, while I summoned up the courage to face a fear head on. That no longer happens. I deal with fear as soon as it arises. I will ether face it head on or use the meditative approach to heal the underlying source of the feeling of fear.

The Fear of Death

There was one particular fear that I could not heal by either facing it head on or using the meditative approach. It was the fear of death.

I had a problem with this fear because it is based on the lie that 'I am the body'. I mentally understood that I was not the body, and that 'I' did not die when the body died, but I still couldn't release the lie. My mental understanding that 'I am not the body' was useless to me. I remained afraid of death no matter how often I told myself not to be. Something inside me was clinging to that fear and was not going to let it go no matter what my mind 'knew'.

I was later told that the vast majority of fears are built on the fear of death. Apparently, I could remove most of my fears in one fell swoop if I could only overcome the fear of death. That possibility only frustrated me even more. I still didn't know how to let go of the fear of death. Therefore, instead of healing all of my fears in one fell swoop, I had to deal with them one at a time.

I set the intention to have my inner guide support me in finding a way to overcome the fear of death and then did my best to patiently wait. Patience was not my strong suit.

It took my guide a few years before it found a way to break through my resistance to letting go of the lie that 'I am the body'. Basically, it had to kill 'me' in order to get me to release it. That's a story for another day.

Trust not Courage is the Antidote to Fear

The key to freeing yourself from fear is trust not courage.

I was slow to learn this. I had been raised to believe that being courageous was the honorable way to be. I believed that I was not a 'real man' unless I was courageous. I even became attached to being perceived as courageous. I reveled in being the one who would not let fear affect him when things became scary or difficult.

Thus, it came as quite a shock to me when I first heard that trust not courage was the antidote to fear. That possibility went against everything that I had come to believe, and blew a huge hole in a part of my identity that I liked.

However, I knew in my heart that it was true. I knew that being courageous didn't take away my fear. It only allowed me to stand and face whatever was coming my way despite the fear. Sometimes facing fear in that courageous way would free me from the fear because it would show me that there had been nothing to fear in the first place. However, that was just a fortunate byproduct. I was really just using courage to repress my fear and, more often than not, the fear would remain with me. Basically, I was not healing fear using courage. I was just ignoring it. I reluctantly accepted that courage was just a mind game.

It was only when I came to fully understand 'trust' that I was able to embrace the possibility that trust was indeed the antidote to fear. However, trust is not an antidote to fear if I put my trust in my monkey mind, your monkey mind, an external God, a belief system, or anything else that is created from the ego. The ego creates fear, it does not resolve it.

Trust only becomes an antidote to fear when trust is put in one's own inner guide. Trusting my inner guide became my primary tool for freeing myself from fear. My inner guide knows which fears I can face head on and which ones I need to take into meditation. If my inner guide asks me to face a fear head on then I trust that I am ready to face whatever is coming my way. I am then able to maintain a peaceful inner space of Love while facing that fear. If my inner guide invites me to use meditation to heal a feeling of fear then I trust that my inner guide will show me the underlying barrier to Love or misalignment.

Trust not courage is the antidote to fear.

That said, I am grateful to courage for having played such an active role in my life. It was courage that allowed me to step out of the corporate world and set out on my journey of self-discovery. During the early days of that journey, I was clueless as to where I was going or what I was doing. I was scared and it was courage that kept me going.

Eventually, I learned to trust my inner guide and that took over my journey. However, it wouldn't have had the opportunity to do so if courage hadn't given me the strength to take my first hesitant steps away from a life that did not serve me. Thank you courage and thank you trust.

****

The Third Signpost: Pain

Pain and illness are signposts.

They are messengers to be heard not things to be cured. Responding to their messages involves delving inside to find and remove the underlying barriers to Love or misalignments. Doing that will release the associated energetic disturbances and the body will then heal itself.

I did not 'believe' this was true when I first heard it. I invite you not to believe it either. Instead of adopting a blind belief, I spent the next few years exploring whether or not pain and illnesses were messengers for me. Whenever a pain or illness, whether physical or psychological, arose in my body, I would use it as an opportunity to hear its message.

I would enter into a meditative state, focus on the pain or illness, and ask my inner guide to tell me the message that it had for me. I would then respond to that message by removing the underlying issue. This process for healing oneself is described in exercise '*1. Healing the Source of a Pain or Illness*'.

I struggled with this process at first. I had difficulty hearing my inner guide and would have to repeat the meditative part of the process a few times before getting an answer. Eventually, I would hear my inner guide and it would indeed show me either the barrier to Love or the misalignment that was creating the pain or illness. I would then remove the barrier or resolve the misalignment and the body would heal itself.

Through healing my own ailments in this way, I found that all of my pains and illnesses were indeed signposts. The more I explored this connection, the more I became convinced that this perspective on healing did work for me.

I now use every pain and illness that arises inside me as a signpost.

Overcoming my own Mind

My greatest obstacle in healing my pains and illnesses was my own mind.

My mind resisted the possibility that this kind of healing approach could actually work. That resistance had me half-heartedly delving inside myself to find the source of my ailments. A part of my ego didn't believe it was possible to heal myself in this way and was trying to sabotage the process. It was only after I started to have results that I was able to overcome my own mind. I was able to let go of the false belief that this approach wouldn't work and that part of my ego dissolved away. I was then able to fully embrace this approach to healing.

Once my mind accepted this approach to healing, it created another obstacle. It got excited about the potential for this kind of healing. It then became so involved in the process that it would jump in with its own ideas of what barrier to Love or misalignment was causing a pain or illness. I would then waste my time trying to heal whatever it was that my mind thought was creating the pain or illness. Invariably, responding to whatever my mind 'thought' was the message would not work. I would remove it and the body would not heal. My mind was essentially clueless in helping me to find what needed to be healed.

Its interference, and the resulting repeated failures, often left me wondering if I was on a wild goose chase. It seemed like I couldn't heal anything and that I was just wasting my time with the whole idea that I could heal myself. I doubted myself and this self-doubt often threatened to derail my journey. Invariably, whenever I felt like giving up, someone would appear to spur me on.

For example, I met a shaman in Australia who did some energy clearing and soul retrieval work with me. During that process, he looked at the reasons for my soul having incarnated and said that one of the reasons was to find a cure to cancer. He then looked me in the eyes and said, "*You already know the cure*".

I was taken aback by this comment. I didn't know the cure for cancer. I wasn't a medical researcher and wasn't sitting in a laboratory actively looking for one. Sure, one of my closest friends did have terminal cancer, and I was hoping to find a cure for her, but I hadn't found one. Or had I? Was this new approach to healing that I was exploring really capable of curing cancer?

His comment, combined with my own determination to find a way to help my friend with cancer, spurred me on.

I persevered with using insight meditation to try and find the messages underlying my pains and illnesses. Eventually, I became proficient at distinguishing between my mind's chatter and the answers from my inner guide. This happened through perseverance and trial and error.

Once I began to hear my inner guide's answer to the message underlying a pain or illness, and acted on that message, I did begin to heal myself. This process actually worked! As long as I acted on my inner guide's response, and not my rational mind's thoughts, I could heal myself.

The key for me was to learn to distinguish between guidance from my inner guide and the ramblings of my rational mind. One thing that helped me to know that it was my guide 'speaking' was that its answer was almost always a surprise. If I had already known the message underlying a pain or illness then I would have acted on it. Of course the answer would be a surprise! I was a little slow to realize that.

I also gradually became proficient at being able to feel the difference inside me between the two sources of the answer. Answers from my inner guide invariably come with a calm energy of 'knowingness' that is not present with the answers that are generated from my rational mind.

I was eventually able to confirm that this healing approach does work for me. I feel deeply grateful to the circumstances in my life that spurred me on when my own mind threatened to derail me. It would have been easy for me to discount this healing approach in those early experimental days. My mind was disrupting the healing process over and over again with its well-meaning, and useless, ideas. Fortunately, I had both the determination to persevere and the prompting of others to continue.

Healing the Body is not always Appropriate

There are two scenarios that I have come across where the healing of a pain or illness is not actually appropriate. In these two cases, despite the presence of an illness, there is no healing of the body that needs to be done.

The first scenario involves an illness or disability whose underlying message is that the soul has lessons to learn from living in a body that has that illness or disability. Those lessons are often around compassion, patience, empathy, and embracing specific senses such as hearing. The healing to be done in these cases is to learn the soul lessons rather than to heal the illness or disability.

The second scenario occurs when a soul has finished their current incarnation and has chosen an illness as its way of leaving the body. This latter scenario arose for my mother who passed away from liver cancer. There was nothing to be done for her other than to manage her pain and be there to support her through the transition. As her son, I felt a great deal of sadness at her passing but I also knew, deep down, that it was her time to go. There was no healing to be done for her body. The only healing that I did with her was to support her in coming to peace with leaving the body.

Other than these two notable exceptions, the body will heal itself when the energetic disturbance underlying a pain or illness is removed.

Preventative Maintenance for the Body

It is possible to remove the source of future ailments before they manifest physically. This is what I refer to as preventative maintenance for the body.

How do you perform preventative maintenance?

You remove your barriers to Love and misalignments before their associated energetic disturbances manifest physically or psychologically. You do that by using the other three signposts (anger, fear, and a non-Loving motivation) to find and remove your barriers and misalignments. You do not have to wait for a pain or illness to manifest before healing yourself.

Illness has become a rarity for me and I attribute that to having done so much preventative maintenance on myself. I have been proactively removing the barriers to Love and misalignments that could have led to disease.

A Cure for Cancer?

I shared the story earlier of a man I met in Peru who had terminal cancer and was given two months to live. He used a plant medicine to help him find the barriers to Love (deep emotional traumas) underlying his cancer. He then spent two weeks healing those traumas. Afterwards, he returned to his doctor and was told that the cancer had shrunk. Within months it was gone.

I witnessed all of this and it helped me to accept the possibility that this approach to healing could be used to heal anything; even a supposedly terminal case of cancer.

I also shared the story of a close friend who was also diagnosed with cancer. She had been given two months to live and had lived for fifteen. In the end, she had chosen not to respond to the message from her cancer and had passed away.

I had sat with her during her chemotherapy and had taken her on trips between treatments. When I had felt drawn to leave Vancouver in order to set out on the next phase of my inner journey, it had been with a heavy heart that I chose to go. I knew that it was time for me to leave but that didn't make it any easier to do so. I told myself that I would do everything I could to find a cure for cancer while I was away.

She was my inspiration for exploring this healing modality. I was very much hoping that it would work for her. I even offered to fly her to India to work with the man in India who first explained this healing approach to me but she said no. At the time, she had been told about an experimental drug and she chose to involve herself in the trial for that drug rather than come to India. I was able to easily accept her choice because, at that point, I didn't know if there was any merit to healing oneself in this way. She took the experimental drug while I explored this healing approach on myself. That exploration opened me up to the possibility that it could work for her.

Later on, I was speaking to her over the phone from Australia and she told me that the experimental drug had not worked. She said that her doctor had tears in his eyes when he told her there was nothing more they could do. I heard a pain in her voice as she shared this story that I had not heard before. My heart broke. I told her that I was coming home and booked a flight back to Vancouver.

Upon returning to Vancouver, I described this healing process to her and asked her if she was open to the possibility that something inside her was causing the cancer. She said that she was and that she had already come to that conclusion herself. However, she also said that she was reluctant to open that door. It scared her and she was hesitant to try this approach. She said that she would like to think about it. I did not push her and simply accepted that she was not ready.

She was moved into a palliative care ward a few days later and her mother, her father, and I began alternating staying up all night with her. She and I had many beautiful conversations during those nights. I felt closer to her than ever before. She then asked me if we could give this healing approach a try. I said "of course" and we agreed to try it that night. I felt nervous about my ability to support her through the process but was also determined to give it my best shot.

We began late that night when it seemed like the whole world was asleep. I guided her into a meditation and had her ask her inner guide to show her the source of her cancer. After a few minutes, she looked up at me and said, "*I know why I have cancer*".

I did too. I had activated my clairvoyant sense by this point of my journey and she had given me permission to look at her energy. As a result, I had been 'reading' her energy while she was asking to be shown why she had cancer. She had then flashed a memory and I had seen it at the same time as she had. It was of a rather horrific, at least to me, event that had happened to her as a little girl. I was shocked by what I had seen.

I looked at her and nodded in response to her comment that she knew why she had cancer. With as much gentleness and compassion as I could muster, I asked her, '*Would you like to do anything about it?*"

She hesitated for only a moment before saying, "*No, I can't do that to my family*".

We both knew that her saying no to healing the trauma associated with that memory meant that she was going to die. I accepted her decision. I knew that healing that trauma would be tremendously challenging. It was her choice whether to embark upon that healing journey or leave the body. She chose to leave and I was not going to try and convince her otherwise.

From that moment forward, I stopped looking for a way to heal her. Instead, I spent as much time with her as I could. I did my best to Love her and to ease her transition out of the body.

I am eternally grateful to her for sharing that part of her journey with me. It was both an emotionally challenging and beautiful time for me. I was looking into her eyes in the moment when she began to pass away. There was a pleading look in her eyes and I immediately called for her mother to come over and hold her as she passed.

The memory of that look in her eyes is as vivid today as the day I saw it. It inspires me to find a way to prevent any other child from having to go through what she went through.

I do feel that she could have cured her cancer. I also feel that this approach could be used by anyone to cure cancer. However, it does require one to:

- have the openness to accept that it could work;

- the ability to go beyond the mind and hear one's inner guide; and,

- the willingness to act on whatever message is received from one's inner guide.

Was that shaman correct? Did I already know a cure for cancer when I was a lost wanderer? Yes, I feel that I did. However, please don't take my word for it. I invite those who feel so inclined to find out for themselves.

The Taripay Pacha - Disease will become a thing of the Past

I do feel that we, as a race, will reach a point where we will fulfill the prophecy of the Q'ero. I mentioned that prophecy briefly in Chapter 2. It is a prophecy that humanity is on the cusp of moving into a golden age called the Taripay Pacha.

In that golden age, we will have dropped our identification with the false self (the mind and body), remembered who we really are (as eternal beings of Divine Love), and become self-healers. We will be removing the barriers inside ourselves to Love long before those barriers manifest physically or psychologically. Disease will no longer exist.

Will this prophecy be fulfilled? Will we move into a golden age and will disease become a thing of the past?

I do not know. It is not up to me. It is up to all of us.

However, I am optimistic that humanity will find its way 'home' and that a golden age will emerge. That is my dream. It is what inspired me to write this book. It continues to inspire me every day to guide people 'home'.

It also gives me hope that what happened to my beautiful friend as a little girl will not have to happen to any more children. I feel that a person who has healed themselves would not consider harming a little child, or any other being, in any way. That is a part of my dream. I would love to live in a world where children, and all other beings, are safe to live their lives without being harmed by someone who is functioning from their own wounded ego.

I feel that together we can create such a world. With every individual who moves beyond their ego, and into Love, we will collectively move one step closer to manifesting that world.

****

The Fourth Signpost: Non-Loving Motivation

Anything that you say or do from your ego is non-Loving. For example, you are being non-Loving if you are:

- espousing an opinion;

- defending a belief;

- trying to convince someone of something;

- attempting to fix or change someone;

- trying to get someone to do what you think is best for them;

- trying to satisfy a desire;

- reacting from an emotion;

- making choices from fear;

- blaming someone for the way you feel;

- competing;

- being manipulative or controlling;

- using force;

- helping someone; or,

- sacrificing yourself for someone.

These are just a few of the many examples of what causes a person to have a non-Loving motivation behind their interactions with others. We will explore a number of the more common causes of a person becoming non-Loving in more detail in Chapter 8. In this chapter, we are going to describe the process for finding and removing the source of ANY non-Loving motivation.

You begin by using mindful awareness (with absolute honesty and integrity) to observe when the motivation for anything that you think, say, or do is coming from your ego. If your motivation is coming from ego then you are being non-Loving.

The process for healing a non-Loving motivation involves a few steps.

- Find a quiet space where you can sit in meditation.

- Visualize the scenario in which the non-Loving motivation arose.

- Allow yourself to feel that motivation arising in you.

- Enter into an insight meditation and ask to be shown the root cause inside you of that motivation.

- Either resolve any misalignment that you discover (using exercise '5. Bringing your life into alignment with your Soul') or remove any barrier to Love that you find (using exercises '6. Letting go of a Particular Fear'; '7. Removing a Belief'; '8. Healing an Emotional Trauma'; or, '9. Letting go of a Desire').

This process is described in exercise '4. Healing the Source of a Non-Loving Motivation'.

Love is the source of all creation. It is the source of all mankind. We are, at our core, simply Love. Our purpose is simply to share the Love that we are with everything around us, with no conditions and no expectations.

7. Insights into Love

Love was a challenging thing for me to embrace during the first forty years of my life. I did not resonate with the conditional love that I grew up with and I rejected it. I was also confused as to how love could be used interchangeably in reference to chocolate, sports, friends, ice cream, family, and lovers. How can all of that be love? I felt like I was definitely missing something.

I eventually gave up on my society's perspective on love. I stopped telling anyone, even my long-term partners, that I loved them. How could I say 'I love you' when I didn't know what it meant? I was pretty sure that it didn't mean 'become mine and do whatever I tell you to do'.

I had then set out on a voyage of self-discovery. One of my primary intentions for that journey was to find a kind of Love that resonated with me. I found it. There is a form of Love that is not given or received. It is something that you become. It is called Divine Love.

How do you become Divine Love?

The energy of Pure Source Awareness, and of the Higher Self, is Divine Love. Divine Love will flow through the mind and body, and out into the world, when a person drops their identification with the false self and allows their Higher Self to function through them. Life then becomes Divine Love in action.

I explored the possibility that such a Love could exist inside me and discovered, much to my delight, that it did. Love would indeed flow through my mind and body when I detached from the false self and fell silent inside. I would then be Love. I would even be able to remain as Love right up until the point when I became triggered back into functioning in the world through my ego once again. Essentially, Love would only disappear when I was back in my ego.

This showed me that the key to becoming Love is to go beyond the ego.

What is the ego? My ego is a set of false beliefs that are called the barriers to Love. They are so called because they disconnect me from Divine Love every time I am triggered into functioning from one of them. The false beliefs that make up my ego are the only barriers that exist to my being able to remain as Love.

It is these same barriers to Love that you are removing on the journey of becoming a self-healer. Removing them both heals you and returns you 'home' to the being of Divine Love that you have always been. That is why the word Love appears throughout the process of becoming a self-healer.

In this chapter, we will be delving deeper into the world of Love. We will explore the qualities of Love, discuss the relationship between sex and Love, and highlight a few common misconceptions about Love. The following topics will be covered:

- Love is awareness;

- Love is limitless;

- Being conditionally loving is not being Loving at all;

- Sex is not Love;

- Becoming lost in sexual desire ensures that no Love will be involved in any subsequent interaction;

- Most men are masturbating into a woman during sex;

- Love making occurs when two people are able to remain connected to an inner space of Love during sex;

- The 'love Dream' (sex plus relationship equals Love) is a lie;

- The 'Romantic Dream' (a prince or princess is going to show up and make you happy) is another lie;

- Loving another does not depend on their Loving you;

- Loving another means to accept their choices regardless of any perceived impact on you;

- Love can be present even when two personalities are clashing; and,

- Loving relationships are an opportunity to learn about oneself not the other.

****

Love is Awareness

I am Loving someone (or something) when I bring my awareness to them without activating my ego. Thus, I am being Loving whenever I bring my awareness to:

- a part of my body without either judging it or wanting it to be different than it is;

- my feelings and thoughts without becoming lost in them and without trying to discount them, suppress them, or change them in any way; and,

- another person without judging them, blaming them for the way I feel, trying to convince them of anything, or wanting them to change in any way.

I began to do this with my body, myself, and other people. I soon discovered the healing power of Love. Divine Love is awareness without the presence of ego. This form of Love is profoundly healing.

Loving my body

For most of my life, I ignored my body unless something was wrong with it. I felt like I had a durable body that would keep going no matter what I did. I took advantage of that. I abused my body with hard exercise, poor food, and lots of alcohol. For the most part, it kept ticking merrily along. Taking care of it was something that I definitely neglected. I was not Loving it.

I eventually decided to change that. I found myself feeling grateful to my body for everything that it allowed me to do. I then set the intentions to start both listening to it and looking after it with regular exercise and healthy food.

When I began to do this, the first issue that popped to the surface was my relationship with junk food. By bringing awareness (Love) to what I was putting into my body, I was Loving myself. By using this form of self-Love, I found that I would often eat donuts, chocolate, or potato chips as my way of avoiding facing an emotional issue that was surfacing. Basically, my body was taking the abuse for my avoiding myself. With that awareness, I then had the choice to either Love myself, by healing any emotional pain that was surfacing, or continue to be non-Loving towards my body. I chose Love.

Loving myself

I also spent most of my life being unaware of how I actually felt. My answer to 'how are you?' was typically either 'good' or 'fine'. In reality, I couldn't have answered that question in any other way because I had buried my emotions so deeply that I had no idea how I felt anymore

Bringing awareness to how I felt meant first allowing myself to feel again. I began to do this. I began to Love myself by bringing awareness to how I was truly feeling in any given moment without judging those feelings, suppressing them, or wanting to change them in any way.

My ego didn't always like what I unearthed from inside me by Loving myself in this way but that didn't matter. I knew that giving myself permission to feel the way I did was Loving myself. I also knew that I wouldn't have to feel the same way for the rest of my life.

Accepting how I currently felt was the first step in healing myself. It opened the door to my being able to remove whatever barrier to Love or misalignment was leading to my feeling that way. I would then be one step close to being Love.

Loving Others

I struggled at first to Love other people. I would get caught up in their judgments of me or their anger towards me and would react from my own ego. Basically, I would respond to their ego from my own ego. It was a challenge for me to remain detached from my ego when everyone around me was seemingly trying to engage it.

I knew that my reacting from ego was being non-Loving but that didn't make it easy to stop. It was only by removing more and more of my barriers to Love that I became better able to remain loving with those who were being non-Loving towards me. However, I was determined to be Love no matter what. I had to find a way to Love others regardless of how they treated me.

I eventually learned that I could Love others by simply listening to them from a silent inner space. I discovered that it was possible to bring my full attention to another person without activating my ego in any way. I would not judge them, would not question what they were saying, and would not suggest that they change themselves or their activities in any way. I would just Love them.

Initially, there were many times when people became angry with me for not responding to them. Therefore, I put an emphasis on learning how to respond to people from a silent inner space rather than from my ego. Speaking from silence is speaking from Love. I spent a great deal of time bringing my awareness to when I was speaking from ego versus when I was speaking from silence. I slowly became able to discern when I was speaking from Love versus from ego. I was then able to remain as Love while having interactive conversations with people. It did not matter whether the other person was speaking from their ego or from love. I could create, and hold, a space of Love between us.

Powerful transformations would occur for both of us in that Loving space. The benefits for me were in my being able to bring awareness to my inner world to see when my ego became activated and wanted to jump in with some kind of opinion, comment, or judgment. I found more of my barriers to Love in this way and was then able to remove them.

For others, the Loving space that I was holding between us gave them the opportunity to find their own answers to questions that they had about themselves. I would listen to them from a silent inner space and allow my Higher Self to ask probing questions that took them ever deeper into themselves. If they allowed themselves to explore deep within then they would invariably find the answers that they were looking for.

****

Love is Limitless

Love has no limits.

The energy of pure Source awareness is Divine Love. Divine Love is limitless. It flows through absolutely everything in this world of form. It is the essence of who you are.

The only thing that is preventing you from accessing this form of Love is your identification with the false. The false has limits.

Identification with the body limits you to functioning in the physical realm within the capabilities of the body. It also instills the fear of death in you which will hold you back from living the life that you incarnated to live.

Identification with the ego limits you in countless way. Your fears prevent you from living life fully. Your beliefs limit you to being open only to what falls within the limits of those beliefs. Your emotional traumas trigger fear and non-Loving emotional reactions such as anger and frustration. Your desires blind you from being open to possibilities that fall outside of those desires.

You are not the body and you are not the ego. The body and ego are limiting. You are limitless.

If you find that anything that you think, say, or do is limiting you in any way then it is not coming from Love. It is coming from a barrier to Love.

****

Conditional love has no Love in It

What is conditional love? It certainly isn't Divine Love.

I am engaging in conditional love when my love for another is conditional upon them either satisfying my desires or behaving in the way my beliefs think they should. For example, I am being conditionally loving when I want someone to either do what I want, change in any way, agree with me, or give up something for me. There is no Love in conditional love. It is a game of the ego.

Heaven forbid that someone who is trapped in a conditionally loving relationship would want to be their own person. No, that is not allowed. If they stop being the way the other person wants them to be then the other will not love them. Conditional love is a prison.

It is a prison that I spent way too much time in. My mother said that she loved me but then tried to turn me into a proper English gentleman. For me, the words '*I love you*' came to mean '*stop living your own life and become what I want you to be*'.

As a result, I did not trust my mother when she said that she loved me. When I heard those words, I would immediately wonder what she wanted from me. That led to my not trusting any woman who tried to love me. Basically, I was totally screwed up when it came to love. For a guy who 'loved' women, and very much wanted to have a female life partner, that sucked.

I wanted to free myself completely from conditional love and that journey began with forgiving my mother. I came to accept that she was doing her best to love me in the only way she knew how. I Loved her and I knew in my heart that she Loved me too. I was able to forgive her because I knew that she was just doing what she thought was best for me. She was just passing her own conditioned beliefs on to me.

In a way, I am grateful to her for teaching me what it was like to be the recipient of conditional love. Because of her, I was able to learn, from my own direct experience, that conditional love has no place in the world of Love. It certainly had no place in my life any longer.

After forgiving my mother, I opened myself back up to the possibility of having a Loving relationship with a woman. I had closed myself off to women for far too long. I was feeling hopeful that I could have a lover in my life without having to step back into the jail cell that was conditional love.

****

Sex is Not Love

Lust was a huge obstacle for me in accessing Divine Love.

I have always had a rather high sex drive, or should I say lust drive. I would invariably start off a relationship with a new lover by having frequent sex. The regularity of sex would slowly begin to taper off as we became comfortable with each other. My lustful feelings towards my partner would have been satisfied and the desire for sex with her would wane.

However, I found that I would still want to look at pornography. This always confused me. The desire for porn showed that I still had a high sex drive but I wasn't that interested in making the effort to have sex with my partner. Porn was so much easier. This pattern of turning to pornography to satisfy my sexual cravings, rather than embracing sexual intimacy with my partner, seemed messed up to me.

Long before discovering Divine Love, I had tried my best to figure out what was going on. I talked to a few of my friends, both male and female, about sex and relationships. They invariably had similar stories to share. It seemed that there were many of us who were experiencing that the regularity of sex in a relationship would taper off over time. I also discovered that I wasn't the only one who was curious about how to avoid that happening.

The only answer that any of my friends had come up with was to experiment with sexual fantasies. None of us had an answer that really worked. Some of my friends even thought that this pattern in a relationship was just 'human nature'. There was nothing that could be done about it and we just had to accept it. I disagreed. I felt that there had to be more to it.

As a brief aside, I have come to realize that the term 'human nature' does not apply to me. Identification with the false self is the prevailing view of what it means to be human. That is no longer me. I am not the false self and I no longer believe that any patterns created by the false self are natural. For me, there is nothing natural about the prevailing understanding of what it means to be 'human'. There is no such thing as 'human nature'. I also feel that the term is used as a clever way for a person's ego to keep that person, and others, trapped in the false.

Okay, back to the world of sex. I had an additional problem with my sexuality that many of my friends did not have. I could not tell my sex partners that I loved them. I equated the word love with 'conditional love' and I did not trust it. I refused to use the word love in reference to a partner. To top that off, I had been taught to believe that it was 'wrong' of me to have sex with a woman that I did not love. As I didn't know how to love a woman, this belief meant that it was wrong for me to have sex.

Needless to say, I did my best to ignore this belief. However, I would always feel guilty before, during, and after sex. I would even feel guilty for having lustful thoughts about a woman. The guilt that I felt when I looked at porn was off the charts. Oh, the shame! For me, sex and guilt were inseparable. I was a mess.

I kept trying to do something about it. The journey of self-reflection that I embarked upon had given me a greater understanding of Love. I had discovered a form of Love that I could embrace. It was not conditional. It was an energy that flowed through me when I dropped my identification with the false self and fell into an inner space of peace and serenity. I was in Love with this kind of Love. This Love, combined with my having forgiven my mother for her conditional love, had finally opened the door to my being able to tell a woman that I Loved her. That was huge for me.

I had then gone to the Osho ashram in India for the first time. I had been tentatively ready to explore my issues around sexuality but was still terribly confused about the relationship between Love and sex. I was pretty sure that sex was not Love but I didn't understand the connection between the two. I had gone to that ashram hoping to find someone who could help me gain clarity on all of this.

Osho himself had been the first one to broach the subject. There was an event called 'white robe' that was held at the ashram every night. It included dancing, a video of an Osho discourse, and a brief meditation. Osho gave a pretty accurate description of my sex life during one of his discourses. He said that,

"Most men are just masturbating into a woman during sex."

I was shocked by his directness. My initial reaction was that it couldn't possibly be true. However, I let his words sink in and I knew in my heart that it was. I had been doing exactly that all of my life. It wasn't that I wanted to masturbate into my sexual partners. No, not at all, I wanted to have Loving connections with the women that I dated. However, I hadn't known how to do that. I didn't know what Love was and believed that sex would allow the relationship to flower into the romantic love that I had seen in fairy tales. It didn't.

There was no Love in my sexual encounters because I didn't know what Love was and I didn't know how to Love anyone. As a result, for me, sex with a woman was solely about physical pleasure. It was no different than masturbation.

It was hard for me to accept that all I had ever done was '*masturbate into a woman during sex'* but it was true. Osho's comment left me feeling even more determined to find a relationship between sex and Love that resonated with me. I wanted to Love a woman not masturbate into her.

I had then gone looking for something in the ashram that could help me understand sex and Love. I ended up taking a course called 'Connecting to Self-Love'. That course showed me how to begin Loving myself. My journey into Love was going ever deeper. I had discovered a form of Love that resonated with me and now this course opened the door to my beginning to actually Love myself. I still hadn't learned about sex but I was enjoying learning about Love.

I next headed off to a place called the Humaniversity in the Netherlands. They taught me how to create intimate and Loving connections with other people. It was there that I experienced how intimacy was created by my openly and honestly sharing my feelings with others without holding anything back. The other person would simply listen to me without judgment or comment. By each of us opening up to the other in this way, we were able to create Loving connections with each other. This was huge for me. I had discovered how to be Loving towards others.

I was making progress. I had discovered a form of Love that resonated with me and had learned how to open my heart up to Loving both myself and others. That was the foundation that I needed in order to take the next step; to bring sex into the world of Love.

The people at the Humaniversity then showed me that I could maintain a Loving connection with someone even when I was sexually aroused! I could do that only by not getting lost in sexual desire. I had to remain connected to the Love that flowed from within me while allowing sexual energy to also flow through the body.

That was hard for me. I had spent my whole life attaching myself to lust and it was difficult for me to remain in a silent inner space when sexual desire began to course through me. I failed at first and that led to my driving at least one beautiful woman away. However, I kept being put in one situation after another where I would be connected to Love and then have sexual desire be triggered. That enabled me to keep practicing the art of remaining mindfully aware even when sexual desire was coursing through me.

My graduation came when I was able to make Love with a woman. I was able to remain connected to Love inside me right up to, and even during, sex with her. Making Love with her was the most beautiful sexual encounter of my life up to that point. I had experienced the connection between sex and Love. Love was far more expansive than sex. Love was a state of being that I could remain connected to as long as I wasn't triggered into functioning from my ego. Sex was a physical act that could be done either outside the world of Love or within it.

In order to bring sex into the world of Love, all I had to do was to remain silent inside and not get triggered into functioning from my ego. I had even managed to do it. I had been able to make Love with a woman. That was a huge breakthrough for me. I had learned that it was possible for me to remain as Love even when one of my biggest obstacles to doing so, sexual energy, was present. I had also experienced a much more beautiful form of sex than simply masturbating into a woman.

Making Love for the first time opened the door to my being able to heal the many issues that I had with sexuality. I had been in the 'safe' environment of the Humaniversity when I first managed to make Love. There had been mutual consent amongst everyone there that having sex was a part of our healing journeys. That consent allowed me to temporarily set aside my beliefs around sex being wrong. I had not then felt guilty about having sex even though my partner and I had both known that it was just for one night.

My next challenge was going to be to make Love back in the 'real' world. All of my beliefs and insecurities around sex, Love, and relationships would then be back in play. I knew that I had a ton of healing to do around my sexuality before I would truly be able to make Love.

What did I know at this point?

Sex is not Love. Sex can be brought into the world of Love but it is not Love. Once I become lost in my sexual cravings for a woman, I cannot Love her. I can only make Love with a woman if I have first created a Loving connection with her. That is accomplished by being open and honest with her about the way I am feeling, listening to her share how she is feeling from a silent inner space, and accepting her exactly as she is. The loving connection must then be maintained throughout any sexual encounter. Satisfying my sexual desire for her becomes secondary to my remaining in a place of Love for her. I will stop at any point, even after penetration, if I feel that the Loving connection between us has been broken.

I finally knew the relationship between sex and Love. Basically, if a Loving connection between myself and a woman naturally flows into a sexual liaison then we can make Love. If I want to satisfy my sexual desire for a woman then I can have sex with her but I cannot make Love with her.

I also knew that, in order for me to be able to remain connected to Love during sex, I was going to have to heal everything around my sexuality that could trigger me into functioning from my ego. I had a long list of triggers to remove. They included:

- my attachment to lust;

- my beliefs that sex was wrong outside of marriage;

- my romantic fantasies of a future life with a woman;

- my fear of rejection;

- my performance anxiety;

- my insecurities around my body and penis size;

- my fear of premature ejaculation; and,

- a memory that I had of being sexually abused by monks in a past life.

I felt like that was a bloody long list. Fortunately, my high sex drive gave me the motivation to want to heal all of it rather than head for the nearest monastery. I was determined to stop getting lost in lust. I wanted a Love life not just a sex life. I wanted to Love a woman and have that Love returned.

I also knew how to get there. I simply had to remove the barriers to Love that were underlying all of my sexual issues. This I could do. I understood the connection between sex and Love. I also knew how to bring sex into the world of Love. That knowledge gave me the ability to bring mindful awareness to any encounter that triggered sexual energy in me. Whenever I was in the company of a woman who inspired sexual energy to flow in me, I would observe my inner reaction and find when my barriers to Love were preventing me from maintaining a Loving connection with her. I would then delve inside to find and remove those barriers to Love.

I finally felt ready to bring sex into the world of Love. I opened myself up to having a Lover in my life again. I also set the intention to stop having sex unless it was part of making Love. I was determined to become Love in every situation; including the ones that involved sexual desire.

All I had to do then was to trust that my inner guide would bring everything into my life that I would need in order to heal my issues around sexuality. My sexual relationships then became a school in which I could find and remove all of the barriers to Love inside me that prevented me from having a Loving connection with a woman.

I was very much looking forward to that part of my healing journey. I did enjoy sex. That said, I was determined not to allow my enjoyment of sex stop me from remaining Loving towards a woman that I found sexually desirable. Love, not sex, definitely came first for me.

Over the next few years, I dated a few women and they were my teachers. They gave me the incredible gift of providing me with opportunities to have my many sexual issues triggered and to then find and remove my barriers to Love. That was a long journey and I fell from grace many times in my relationships with those women. I was not able to remain Loving towards them at all times. I did eventually find the barriers to Love underlying my sexual issues but I know that it was sometimes a painful journey for myself and for the women I dated.

To each of them I would like to say that I am deeply sorry for the times when I became triggered and was unable to Love you in the way that you deserved. I am also profoundly grateful to all of you for sharing a part of your journey with me. You gave me the opportunities that I needed in order to heal my sexual issues. Thank you.

After it was all said and done, I had discovered how to bring sex into the world of Love, had healed my sexual issues, and was able to make Love with a woman. Sex became a sacred event for me. It was an activity to be undertaken within the world of Love not outside of it.

****

The 'love Dream' is a Lie

The 'love Dream' is the idea that sex plus relationship will equal Love. It does not. The 'love Dream' is a lie.

Unfortunately, I bought into this lie hook, line, and sinker. I grew up believing that I could discover Love through a relationship with a woman. I had then done my best to enter into committed relationships with the women that I had been sexually attracted to. Love had not flowered. It had not flowered the first time, the second time, or even the third! For me, the 'love Dream' was a cruel lie.

The 'love Dream' is a false belief. It was an easy belief for me to drop. I had wasted the first half of my life thinking that eventually I would get a relationship 'right' and would discover Love. It had not worked and I was finished with looking for Love outside of myself. I chose to simply stop believing in the 'love Dream' and it was gone from my life.

The beautiful part of letting it go was that I was then free to Love everyone; not just my sex partners. If Love was available inside me then I could share that Love with everyone. I just had to become it first.

****

The 'Romantic Dream' is a Lie

The 'Romantic Dream' is popularized in fairy tales. In this dream, we are told that we just need to wait for the 'right' partner to appear, to fall in love with him or her, and then life will be beautiful. 'Romantic love' will supposedly save us from all of life's miseries. It is a lie.

I had been a rather naive child. I had fallen for this lie as well.

I realized that the romantic dream was bollocks long before I actually let it go. Unfortunately, I was strongly attached to having my princess show up one day and make me happy. That would have been so much easier than going inside and healing the true source of all of my pain and suffering; the barriers inside me to Love. Thus, I clung to the 'Romantic Dream'.

My grip on the 'Romantic Dream' began to loosen when I discovered that Love has no limits. The romantic dream is full of limits. The romantic dream is basically saying that, '*I will give you my power if you give me yours*'. I will give you the power over my happiness if you will give me power over yours. Talk about setting limits.

My playing that power game with another person would usually work for a little while. The gain that I got from giving a woman my power – typically sexual gratification and companionship – would feel so good that I was willing to give my power away for at least a little while. However, eventually the gain that I was getting from being with a woman would stop feeling so good. I would then grow to resent her for taking my power away (even though I had freely given it to her) and I would tire of being with her. Our relationship would then become a loveless and resentful one.

That type of relationship definitely wasn't what I was looking for. I was looking for Love. I knew that pursuing the romantic dream was not going to work and that it was time for me to drop my childish fantasies. It was time for me to grow up, take responsibility for my own life, and become the Love that I was seeking. That process included my blowing up the 'Romantic Dream'.

I tried to blow it up. I really did. However, I still struggled to let it go. I had a deep sadness inside me that had been there for most of my life.

That sadness would surface with a vengeance whenever I allowed myself to accept that the romantic dream was not going to work for me. I would then cling to the dream in order to pull myself out of the sadness. I was stuck. I was going to have to heal that sadness before I could drop the romantic dream.

I did exactly that. I knew that the sadness was being sourced from either barriers to Love or misalignments inside me. I decided to drop the romantic dream, let myself feel sad, and delve inside to find and remove the underlying causes of the sadness. The depth of the sadness was almost overwhelming. Facing it was a long and painful journey.

I quickly discovered that the main issues underlying my sadness were related to self-worth and self-Love. There turned out to be multiple layers to those issues. I was able to easily remove the barriers to Love that were created during my upbringing around these issues. Doing so enabled me to accept myself as I am. I stopped comparing myself to others and became comfortable with being me. I embraced self-Love. I no longer needed anyone else to validate my existence. That process removed a great deal of the sadness that I had been feeling but there was still a deeper layer that I had not yet reached.

That deeper layer seemed to be coming from the very core of my being. I spent a great deal of time exploring the source of this sadness and found that it came on strongest when I contemplated the idea of becoming some kind of spiritual guide. I would then feel desperately sad. I felt like there was no way that I could become a guide for anyone. I knew very little about spirituality and was barely keeping myself above water. How could I guide anyone else? In my mind, I was definitely not worthy of being my own guide let alone anyone else's.

The sadness would deepen. It would only lift when I tried to deny the possibility of my becoming a spiritual guide. I was stuck. In essence, I was feeling drawn down a path, becoming a spiritual guide, that I did not feel worthy of following. I tried to hide from the sadness but there was nowhere to run. No matter where I went, I was constantly receiving reminders to head down that path.

For example, the enlightened master that I worked with in a Tibetan monastery once said to a friend of mine that *"Bruce has potential"*. That comment triggered overwhelming sadness in me. I interpreted his words to mean that maybe I was meant to find my own way 'home' and then become a guide of some kind for others. Regardless of what he actually meant, I did not feel worthy of his words.

Another time, a seer from Thailand told another friend of mine that I was going to start a spiritual movement one day. Me? I knew nothing about initiating spiritual movements. How could I possibly do that?

One of my most shocking moments came when a shaman from Australia said that I was going to find a cure for cancer. He then told me that I had already found it. I was shocked by his words. I was very new to this form of healing at the time and had not yet realized its potential. His words about my providing the world with a cure for cancer felt like a huge weight being dropped on my shoulders. The sadness deepened.

On and on it went. Wherever I went in the world, I would meet spiritually aware beings who were all guiding me towards something that I was both deathly afraid of and did not feel worthy of.   The sadness was never very far away. I could tell that I had a huge barrier inside me and I didn't know how to remove it. I did my best to live with the sadness and asked my inner guide to help me heal it.

I looked at where my resistance could be coming from. I did not resonate with the idea of gurus and disciples and was not going to go down that path. I also did not resonate with organized religion and did not feel drawn to become a priest, shaman, or anything else within a religious hierarchy. I didn't know what to do and simply trusted that my inner guide would show me how to overcome this issue.

Healing that layer of sadness turned out to be a long and often emotionally painful journey. The first step in healing it was to find a definition of a spiritual guide that resonated with me.

A spiritual guide is one who has connected to their own inner guide and can support another in connecting to theirs.

I could do that! If I could support a person in connecting to their own inner guide then they will be able to access their own answers. They could find, inside themselves, everything that they would need to find their own way 'home'. They would not need an external guru or religion. I could then simply Love and support them as they learned to trust and follow their own inner guide.

This understanding of what it is to be a spiritual guide opened me up to the possibility that one day I could accept becoming a spiritual guide. The sadness remained. It would still flare whenever I contemplated that possibility. I was still blocked.

It was only when I started to relive past lives in which I had been a spiritual guide, and failed spectacularly, that the deeper healing began. I will provide a full description of those lifetimes, and the associated healing journeys, in a future book. I will present a brief summary here.

In one lifetime, I was stoned to death and relived the feeling of having every stone hit my body. It was a brutal experience to relive dying that way as I again felt every stone hit me. After dying in that lifetime, I went to what happened immediately afterwards and discovered that I had been furious about being stoned to death. I felt like I had been doing the best I could and that it had been unjust for me to have been killed. The trauma of that experience had left me with a deep fear of ever becoming a spiritual guide again.

I was able to heal that trauma. The lessons that I was to learn from that lifetime were patience and humility. I had not been humble in that lifetime and had pushed people beyond where they were ready to go. My ego had gotten in the way of Love. I embraced those lessons, forgave the souls of the people who had killed me, forgave myself for having failed as a spiritual guide, and opened up to the possibility of becoming a spiritual guide once again.

That healing journey did alleviate some of the deep sadness, but not all. I went through a few more healing journeys around past lives. In one, I had been a monk who was killed by Vikings on the island of Iona. I had wanted to fight back but the head monk, my father in this lifetime, had been insistent that we did not fight. He had been the first one killed by the Vikings and I had then tried to fight back. I had tackled one of the Vikings and, as I had done so, I realized that my father had been right. There was no point in fighting. I had then allowed myself to be killed. The lesson from that experience was that there is no value in fighting violence with violence. I embraced that lesson.

It wasn't just learning the lessons from past lives that I had to go through in order to free myself of the sadness. At one point on my journey, I felt drawn to work with a shaman in the Amazon. He helped me to let go of the fear of death. He guided me into such a reduced state of physical being that I felt like I was going to die. I could not hold on any longer and let go.

I was later told that my body had shut down for twenty minutes. Apparently, the person with me could not detect any breathing or heartbeat during that time. My experience of that time period had been of having my awareness shift into another dimension in which I felt deeply Loved. I had then returned to the body. After that experience, I was no longer afraid of physical death.

I was also shown, during that same night, that I had incarnated in this lifetime to find my way 'home' and to then be a stepping stone for others to do the same. I then knew, from the depths of my being, that I had incarnated for exactly that purpose. I felt ready to embrace being a spiritual guide.

I was still not quite able to go there. There was still something inside me that was standing in the way. On and on it went. I was learning all of the lessons from the many lifetimes in which I had played the role of spiritual guide. I was also overcoming any fears that would prevent me from becoming one in this lifetime. However, I was still blocked and sadness still remained.

The final step in my healing journey came when I was working with a shaman in the Andes of Peru. He supported me in accessing a feeling of grief that was profound. It was so strong that I felt like it would kill me if I allowed myself to fall into it.

We were doing a ceremony in an Incan site at the time. I was sitting beside an ancient fountain while feeling the tip of that grief and also feeling unable to let myself fall fully into it. I was stuck. The shaman had then walked over to me, looked me in the eye, and said, "*Do you trust me*". I looked up and said "*Yes*". He then simply said, "*Let go*". I did. I allowed myself to fall into the grief.

It did overwhelm me. I fell into the fountain, held myself in the fetal position, and wailed. I was recalling a lifetime in which I had made decisions as a spiritual leader that had resulted in many, many people dying. I felt responsible for their deaths and the grief was too much for me. I was inconsolable. I just lay in the fountain, held myself, and cried from the depths of my being.

I didn't know how to free myself from the grief and didn't try to. I just let myself cry and cry and cry. I was then gifted with something remarkable. Many of the souls of the people who had died due to my mistakes appeared before me. They radiated Love towards me and they forgave me. I felt overawed by what I was witnessing and simply let their forgiveness sink in. I felt so deeply grateful to them for appearing in one of my darkest moments.

With their forgiveness, I was able to gather myself together and leave the fountain. The shaman took me over to a quiet part of the site and I shared with him what had happened. He helped me begin the process of forgiving myself. In that lifetime, I had been doing what I had thought was best but I had been coming from ego not Love. I had not allowed Love to make the decisions. Instead, I had become impatient, had imposed my own wishes on the situation, and had chosen from ego.

I embraced the lesson from that lifetime. It was that any decision I make from ego is non-Loving and can cause pain, and even death, for myself and others. The alternative is to remain patient and allow Love to decide. After embracing that lesson, I was able to forgive myself for being responsible for the deaths of so many and healed that emotional trauma. The energetic shift inside me from that healing journey was profound. It took many months for it all to sink in and for me to come to peace with that journey.

The sadness was then finally gone. I had accepted the possibility of my becoming a spiritual guide, had healed my fear of becoming a guide, and had embraced the lessons that I had learned from my many failed attempts to guide others in past lifetimes. I was no longer afraid of becoming a spiritual guide.

However, I did not yet feel ready to guide anyone. I had come to realize that the only way that 'I' could guide others was by first going beyond the false self and becoming Love. At that point, Love would guide others not me. 'I' could become a spiritual guide but only if 'I' got out of the way and allowed Love to function through me.

This realization allowed me to finally drop my issues of self-worth. 'I' was not worthy of being a spiritual guide and never would be. The false self could not guide anyone. However, 'I' could move beyond the false self and allow Love to guide others through me. Love would then be living me and Love would be a spiritual guide for myself and others.

Would 'I' become a spiritual guide one day? I didn't know and it no longer mattered. That was not up to me. It was up to Love.

The deep sadness that I had felt for most of my life was finally gone. I had healed my issues of self-worth and self-Love. I could even feel a deep sense of inner peace and even joy.

I was then ready to let go of the romantic dream. I no longer needed the false hope that it offered. I dropped it; at least for the most part.

I say 'for the most part' because the imprint that it had left on me was very deep. It would occasionally rear its ugly head. It would do so whenever I was struggling to face an emotional pain that was surfacing. If I could not face it then I would be triggered into functioning in the world through my ego once again. The thought of finding a lover to make me happy, rather than face one more emotionally challenging journey, would pass through my mind. That approach seemed so much more pleasant to my ego than actually facing the emotional pain.

However, I was done with playing ego games. I was able to ignore any romantic fantasies that arose because I knew that they were based on a lie. I was not going to find happiness, inner peace, or Love through a romantic dalliance. I would only find the Love that I was seeking by removing my barriers to Love.

The romantic dream no longer held any control over me. It had actually become an ally for me on the healing journey. I began to use it as a signpost. Whenever romantic fantasies began to pass through my mind, I knew that my false self, my ego, had been activated. It was then using the romantic dream to try and protect itself from having to face an emotional issue that was surfacing. I was done with letting the false self run my life. Rather than succumb to any fantasies that arose, I would delve inside to find and remove the barriers to Love underlying the emotional issue that those fantasies were trying to protect my false self from.

The lie that was the romantic dream had lost its hold over me.

I shared the details of my journey in overcoming deep sadness with you in order to highlight the process. If you are facing your own deep sadness then you will have to find and remove your own underlying barriers to Love. Those barriers may be similar to the ones that I faced or they may be completely different. The only way to find out is to delve inside yourself and remove the barriers to Love underlying your sadness.

You do not have to remain a prisoner of sadness and you do not have to hold on to the lie that is the romantic dream.

****

Loving Another Does Not Depend on their Loving You

I can Love someone regardless of whether or not they Love me. As long as I do not want anything from another person, including their Love, then I can remain connected to Love. I can then embrace them with that Love.

The only thing that can prevent me from being able to Love another is to become triggered into functioning from my ego. If that happens then I will be disconnected from Love and will be non-Loving with myself and everyone else.

What can trigger me into functioning from my ego? My barriers to Love. Thus, I can Love others, regardless of how they feel about me, as long as I am not reacting from a barrier to Love.

The greatest barrier that I faced in being able to Love others was my desire to have them Love me. If I became lost in that desire then I would be thrown into my ego and would become needy and clingy. I would then do or say things in the hopes of gaining their Love. I would not be Loving myself or them.

This desire for the Love of others is common. It stems from the feeling of being separated from whom we really are; Love. Whether or not we realize it, most of us feel that we are lacking a connection with something and we are looking for it. The something that we are looking for is Love. This thirst for Love is what drives us to seek Love from the outside world. Unfortunately, that is a futile quest. Love can only be found within.

This external search for Love is keeping us trapped in the games of the ego. The very act of seeking Love is disconnecting us from the Love that we are looking for. We have two choices. The first is to continue this search and thereby guarantee that we do not find Love. The second is to turn inwards and embark upon the journey of becoming Love.

I made the choice to turn inwards and to stop wasting my time looking for Love from others. I set the intention to let go of any desire to have others Love me. I then used mindful awareness to observe when I desired Love from another. When that desire arose, I would delve inside to find and remove the barrier to Love that had been triggered.

This process was effective for most of the people in my life. I wasn't overly attached to receiving the Love of either strangers or the vast majority of my friends. Letting go of any desire that did arise to have them Love me was no problem. However, I struggled to let go of the desire to have both my family and a potential life partner Love me. Even though I knew that my wanting them to Love me meant that I could not Love them, it was still hard for me to let go of that desire.

With my family, I spent many months working on just being myself around them so that I could Love them. I then observed what happened inside me when I shared what was going on in my life with them. In this way, I discovered that I had a deep fear of losing their Love and that fear was driving me to want them to Love me. That fear was also preventing me from being absolutely honest with them because I didn't want them to see the ugly sides of myself that I was still working on. I was afraid that they wouldn't Love me if they saw everything. As a result, I was essentially hiding parts of myself from them.

I was caught in the paradox of being non-Loving towards them in order to avoid losing their Love. I was going to have to free myself of this fear of losing their Love. I chose to face the fear head on. I slowly exposed more and more of myself to them. I gradually allowed them to see all of me. I became open and honest with them. I was Loving myself and them.

An amazing thing happened along the way. The fear of losing their Love disappeared and my desire to have them Love me also faded away. It turned out that Loving myself, and them, was enough. I no longer needed them to Love me. I was free to Love them regardless of how they felt about me.

My Loving them also opened the door to the possibility of my having much more Loving connections with them than I could ever have had while I was hiding. My father in particular took this opportunity to form a Loving bond with me. We now have a friendship that is open, intimate, and mutually Loving. I had discovered that my Loving others invites them to return that Love. They may or may not do so but at least the door is open.

And then there were my Lovers. They were my greatest teachers in learning to remain connected to Love regardless of how they felt about me. I very much wanted my Lovers to Love me. However, I knew that my getting lost in that desire would stop me from Loving them. What to do?

I chose to use my relationships with potential life partners as fertile hunting grounds. I was determined to find and remove every barrier to Love that was preventing me from Loving the beautiful women who came into my life. I did my best to bring mindful awareness to every moment of our interactions so that I could 'see' when I was becoming non-Loving by wanting them to Love me. My intention was to then delve inside to find and remove the barriers to Love that were triggering that desire.

It wasn't quite that easy. I would like to be able to say that I would catch myself becoming triggered before I said or did anything from my ego but that would be a lie. I failed many times to catch myself before I fell from grace (became non-Loving). I would invariably feel terrible after being non-Loving and would apologize. I would then go inside to find and remove whatever barrier to Love that had triggered me into my ego.

With practice, I slowly became able to catch myself being non-Loving as it was happening. I would then stop the interaction, apologize, and return to a Loving inner space. When next alone, I would delve inside to remove whatever barrier to Love had been triggered.

Eventually, I reached the point where, for the most part, I could feel myself being triggered into my ego before it actually happened. I would then watch the thoughts and emotions flowing through the body while remaining in a Loving space with my partner. When I was next alone, I would remove the barrier to Love that had been triggered.

The final hurdle that I had to overcome in being able to remain Loving towards a woman came when a partner 'cheated' on me with another man. I found it extremely difficult to remain connected to Love in that scenario. 'I', my ego that is, was hurt by this event and I went through a series of emotions. The feeling of anger towards my partner and the other man came first. That was soon followed by my feeling needy, wanting her to come back, depression, and finally resignation. That was not a fun ride. The emotional pain was strong. I did my best to learn the lessons from that experience and to forgive them but my effort to do so was half-hearted. 'I' was feeling hurt.

The emotional pain did eventually subside and I opened myself up to having another Lover. And then it happened again! I had obviously missed my lessons the first time around. I felt determined to learn them this time so that I wouldn't have to go through this story again. I accepted that the anger I felt towards this second Lover for 'cheating' was sourced from inside me. I delved inside to find its source. I discovered that I still wanted my Lover to take away my desire for Love by Loving me. I had not let go of that desire completely. As a result, I had been clingy, needy, and had not fully opened my heart to them.

I learned my lesson this time around. I knew that I could not find the Love that I was seeking through a woman. I embraced that lesson and truly accepted that I could only find Love by becoming it. I felt gratitude to this second woman for having cheated on me. She was giving me a powerful lesson. I forgave her, and her new partner, and sent them both Love. I also forgave the first woman who had cheated on me, and her partner. Lastly, I forgave myself for being needy in those relationships and for effectively driving those two women into the arms of other men.

I have not had to go through the experience of having a woman cheat on me again. That feels to me like confirmation that I have truly let that desire go.

Through this diligent use of mindful awareness, I was eventually able to remove the vast majority of the barriers to Love that were preventing me from Loving a woman. I was no longer seeking their approval or their Love. I was Loving them regardless of how they felt about me.

I was not an easy person to live with during that inner journey and I feel deeply grateful to the woman who shared it with me. I would like to take this opportunity to thank them. You were my teachers. You gave me the invaluable gift of reflecting my barriers to Love back to me. Thank you. I am deeply grateful for every moment that we shared. I would also like to apologize for all of the times when I failed to Love you. You deserved to be the recipient of Love rather than the non-Loving energy of my ego and I am sorry for failing you.

I am no longer looking for anyone to Love me. I am now able to Love everyone regardless of how they feel about me.

That said, I also know that I am not perfect. It is likely that I still have a few barriers to Love that have not yet been triggered. Those barriers will eventually surface. When they do, I will apologize if I become non-Loving, will own the emotions that arise inside me, and will delve inside to find and remove the underlying barriers to Love.

****

Love can Exist when Two Personalities are Clashing

Love can exist between two people even if their personalities are clashing.

I am not my personality and neither are you. Our personalities are both false. The interaction of my personality with yours has nothing to do with Love. If I do not become my personality then I can remain connected to the inner space of Love regardless of any disagreement between my personality and yours. We can then Love each other even though our personalities are in conflict.

A clash of our personalities can then be used as a healing opportunity. Our personalities are made up of our barriers to Love. Any clash of our personalities is actually a clash between one of my barriers to Love and one of yours. From my side, I can perform an insight meditation to ask my inner guide to show me the barrier to Love inside me that has become engaged in the conflict. I can then remove that barrier to Love and thereby dissolve one more part of my false self. You can also perform an insight meditation to find your barrier to Love.

In this way, every conflict that arises between two personalities can be used as a healing opportunity for both parties.

****

Creating Loving Relationships

After developing a deeper understanding of Love, I felt finished with anything that did not serve Divine Love. For example, I felt done with:

- codependent relationships;

- conditional love;

- sex solely for physical gratification;

- the love dream;

- the romantic dream; and,

- letting my personality get in the way of loving myself and others.

I felt inspired to pour all of my energy into creating Loving relationships with everyone in my life.

So, that begs the question, what is a Loving relationship?

For me, a Loving relationship is one in which my intention is to interact with another person from an inner space of Love. I hold the intention to accept them exactly as they are and to not try and change them in any way. A Loving relationship is an opportunity for me to learn about myself not the other.

What am I learning about myself?

I am learning about what causes me to fail to interact with that other person from an inner space of Love. I call this falling from grace and it is only my barriers to Love that can cause me to fall. Therefore, if I do fall from grace then I have an opportunity to heal myself. I begin that process by feeling gratitude to the other party for highlighting an unhealed part of my false self and apologizing to them if I have acted out from my emotions in any way. I will then own my emotions, as being sourced from inside me, and will follow them down inside myself to find and remove the barrier to Love that triggered them.

Cultivating Loving relationships

I cultivated Loving relationships with everyone in my life; regardless of whether or not they knew it. That effort greatly accelerated my healing journey because my relationships were a literal minefield of barriers to Love. The process that I followed for creating Loving relationship involved: setting the intention to have Loving relationships; accepting that the relationship was an opportunity to learn about myself; using mindful awareness to observe when I was being non-Loving; and, removing the barrier to Love that caused me to be non-Loving. This process is described in '*Exercise 30. Creating Loving Relationships*'.

My relationships with strangers and friends were the easiest for me. There weren't many barriers to Love being triggered by those relationships and so it was relatively straightforward for me to remain Loving in them.

It was much more difficult for me to remain Loving in relationships with my family and with my Lovers. These were the relationships that I had the most conditioning around and hence the most barriers to Love. For example, I had roles that I would easily fall back into, beliefs about the way I was supposed to be around these people, unresolved emotional wounds, and, of course, many issues around sexuality. I embraced these relationships as opportunities to heal myself.

It took a great deal of determination and self-observation to heal most of the barriers inside me to my being able to remain Loving with my family. I now feel that my relationships with them are primarily Loving. Again, I am under no illusions about being perfect. There may well be more barriers to Love that will surface in the future. I will deal with those barriers as they arise and, in the meantime, will enjoy being able to Love my family.

And then there were my Lovers. These relationships were definitely the most challenging ones for me. I entered into the dating arena in a very different way than I had done in the past. I was no longer simply looking for either companionship, someone to Love me, or for sexual gratification. I was entering into a relationship with a Lover in order to learn how to remain Loving towards them always.

I did my best to bring mindful awareness to my interactions with a Lover at all times. I was constantly tuning in to my motivation for everything I did and said while with her. I wanted to be aware of when I was being non-Loving towards her. It turned out that I was being non-Loving far more often than I cared to admit. I had to be brutally honest with myself about my true motivation for everything that I said or did. That was the only way I was going to find and remove my barriers to Love. I felt like I was in an advanced school of learning about myself and my ability to remain Loving.

There were so many different barriers to Love that were being triggered. For example, I wanted them to Love me, wanted them to satisfy my sexual cravings, cared about their opinion of me, was sexually insecure, was attached to the romantic dream, wanted them to make me happy, and so much more. For a while, the barriers were being triggered faster than my ability to remove them. I was failing, often spectacularly, to Love the woman that I was with. I just kept apologizing for my failures and kept working on myself. Over time, I was able to heal many of the barriers to Love that were arising.

As I mentioned earlier, I feel deeply grateful to the women who were my teachers during that time. They were my mirrors. They showed me the obstacles inside me to my being able to Love them regardless of anything that they said or did. The lessons were often brutal for me to learn and I am sure that my failures were not pleasant for my Lovers to experience. However, the gift of freeing me to become Love was immeasurable. Thank you again for sharing a part of your journey with me. I am deeply grateful to each of you for your reflections. I am also sorry for everything that I said or did that hurt you in any way.

I eventually became able to enter into Loving relationships with everyone in my life. That does not mean that I am able to be Love always. There are still occasions when I fall from grace. When that happens, I delve inside to find and remove the barrier to Love that caused me to fall. My relationships continue to be a school for healing myself and becoming Love.

I have also begun to enter into Loving relationships with all sentient beings not just with people. Every person, tree, and animal is my teacher. They are all showing me the barriers inside me to Love.

Creating Mutually Loving Relationships.

A mutually Loving relationship is one in which both parties hold the intention to interact with the other from an inner space of Love. In these relationships, there is an acceptance that both people are learning about Love and that neither is perfect.

In a mutually Loving relationship, if I fall from grace and become non-Loving then I will own my emotions and not blame the other party for how I feel. Instead, I will delve inside to find and remove the barrier to Love that was triggered. Similarly, if the other party becomes non-Loving then I am not going to take anything they say personally. I am going to do my best to continue Loving them by remaining connected to my own inner space of Love. I am also going to support them in healing, at their own pace and in their own way, the barrier to Love that caused them to fall from grace.

****

Summary of Love

The love that we are all seeking is Divine Love. It is not something that you can give or receive. It is something that you become by removing all of the barriers inside yourself that you have built against it.

Love is not for the faint of heart. Love is a sacred fire. It will burn away all of the illusions that you hold about both yourself and the world. Love is a flame of transformation. It will transform you from being a prisoner of the false to being Love. You will be like the phoenix rising out of the ashes.

The self-healing journey is a destructive one. It will destroy your ego and return you 'home' to Love. Love is who you are.

In the next chapter, we will explore a number of insights and accelerators for your self-healing journey. They may apply to you and, if so, will guide you in avoiding the pitfalls that can delay your journey 'home' to Love.

I cannot speak until I have nothing to say.

8. Non-Loving Motivation

We can interact with others from either Love or ego but not from both. We are disconnected from Love whenever we become triggered into functioning from our ego. There is no Love in anything that we think, say, and do from ego. Thus, to function from the ego is to be non-Loving.

This realization provides a huge opportunity for self-healing.

By bringing awareness to our motivation for everything that we think, say, and do, we can observe when we are being non-Loving. We can then choose to find and remove the barrier to Love that is causing us to function in that way. The motivation behind our thoughts, words, and deeds thereby becomes another indicator of when healing work is needed.

That healing can be accomplished by sitting in meditation, visualizing the scenario in which the non-Loving motivation arose, allowing yourself to feel that motivation, and asking your inner guide to show you its source. The source will either be a misalignment in your life or a barrier to Love. The process for healing the misalignments or Barriers to Love underlying your non-Loving motivations is described in exercise '*4. Healing the Source of a non-Loving Motivation*'.

This chapter provides a description of a few non-Loving motivations that people commonly use. They include:

- Defending or espousing a Belief;

- Wanting to satisfy a Desire;

- Judging Others;

- Judging Yourself;

- Caring about the Opinions of others;

- Speaking from ego;

- Sacrificing Yourself (which is egotistical not Loving);

- Playing the Victim role;

- Succumbing to an Addictive Craving; and,

- Becoming Attached to Rational Thinking.

****

Defending or Espousing a Belief

If you are either defending or espousing a belief then you are being non-Loving. Every belief that you hold is a part of your ego and every belief is false.

I struggled to accept the possibility that every belief was false when this was first said to me. My mind raced off to find examples of beliefs that were 'true'. For example, I believed that if I jumped off a cliff then I would die. Wouldn't I? What about gravity? Isn't gravity real? I also believed that the sky was blue and that trees were green. Aren't they? Examples like this 'proved' to my mind that some beliefs were true not false.

It wasn't until I realized that my level of consciousness affects the way I perceive the world that I understood the limiting nature of beliefs. For example, if I identify myself with the ego and body then I am limiting myself to the mind/body level of consciousness. I will then believe things like 'the sky is blue' and 'gravity will make me fall if I jump off a mountain'. If I cling to those beliefs then I am locking myself into the mind/body level of consciousness. I will remain trapped in the false and will not awaken to who I really am.

Beliefs only hold the illusion of being true while we remain identified with the false self (the mind and body). Every belief is actually false when viewed from the perspective of who you really are. The sky is not blue and trees are not green. It is only your body and mind that sees them that way. You will 'see' their true nature when you go beyond the false. Holding onto beliefs is a game of the false self.

I invite you to be open to the possibility that every belief that you hold is false.

If you are functioning from a belief then you are caught up in the games of the ego. You are being non-Loving towards yourself and others. For example, you are being non-Loving whenever you are:

- stating an opinion;

- defending an opinion or belief;

- caught up in thinking that either you are right or another is wrong;

- trying to convince somebody of something; or,

- stating something as though you think that it is actually true.

In every one of these cases, you are functioning from a non-Loving motivation. They are all signposts indicating that you have a barrier to Love (a conditioned belief) that needs to be removed. You can remove that belief by sitting in meditation and asking to be shown the belief underlying your non-Loving motivation. You can then ask to be shown the lie underlying the belief. Let go of that lie and you are free of the belief. This process is outlined in exercise '*7. Removing a Belief*'.

****

Wanting to Satisfy a Desire

Another common way in which you can be triggered into being non-Loving is to become lost in desire. You will be non-Loving whenever you want:

- a certain outcome to either happen or not happen;

- someone to either do something or stop doing something;

- somebody to change something about themselves or their behavior; or

- to acquire, get rid of, or hold on to something.

By bringing awareness to when you are acting from a desire, you can then find and heal the barrier to Love underlying that desire. You do this by sitting in meditation and asking to be shown how you feel you will benefit from satisfying that desire. You then find and remove the misalignment or barrier to Love underlying that perceived benefit. This process is described in exercise '9. *Letting go of a Desire*'.

****

Judging Others

I was a highly judgmental person during the first forty years of my life. Passing judgment on others was a common pastime among my peers and I thought that it was 'normal' to behave in that way. I even thought that being judgmental could be humorous.

It was only after I discovered that every judgment of another is a judgment of myself that I began to use my judgments as signposts in healing myself. I began by owning my judgments. Every time I found myself having a judgmental thought about another, I would ask myself *"why do I feel that way about myself"*. I would then delve inside to see if I really did feel that way about myself. Low and behold, when I was completely honest with myself, I found that I did. My judgments of others were indeed all false. They said nothing about the other person and a lot about me.

Love does not judge. It is only when I am functioning from a barrier to Love that I can judge someone. It is my ego that judges others not the being of Love that I am. Thus, I know that I have a non-Loving motivation whenever I am being judgmental. I then have an opportunity to find and remove the underlying barrier to Love.

It doesn't matter if the judgment is positive or negative. I could think that someone is either an angry and mean person or an admirable person. Both judgments are false. All I am really saying by making those judgments is that I feel that I have qualities that I feel are mean and other qualities that I find admirable. Neither of those judgments have anything to do with the other person. They are just statements of how I feel about myself.

Whenever I caught myself being judgmental, even if it was just a thought that I keep to myself, I would delve inside to find and remove the barrier to Love that was triggering it. I did that by owning every judgment as my projection. I would apologize to anyone that I had said something judgmental to and then take the judgment into an insight meditation. I would ask to be shown the barrier to Love underlying the judgment and I would remove that barrier. The judgment would then be gone and I would have healed one more part of my false self. I would be one step closer to becoming Love. This process is described in exercise *'25. Healing your Judgments of Others'*.

I recommend that you use your judgments of others as opportunities to heal yourself. Being judgmental is a non-Loving game of the false self.

****

Judging Yourself

I was my own worst critic. I judged myself constantly. I would say things to myself like 'my feet are ugly', 'I am a hairy beast', 'I hate my man boobs', 'I am a jerk when I get competitive', 'why did you say that?', and so on. It was like having a bully inside my head that was just waiting to jump all over me.

I did my best to ignore my inner bully but it affected the way I lived my life. I was afraid to do or say things because of what 'I' thought about myself. My inner bully was constantly being non-Loving towards me.

It was time to look at myself with the eyes of Love rather than the eyes of my self-abusive inner critic. There is a barrier to Love underlying everything that we criticize ourselves about. Removing those barriers will remove that inner critic. I did this by using mindful awareness to observe when I was judging myself. I would then delve inside to find and remove the barrier to Love that had triggered me into being judgmental. That enabled me to begin accepting myself exactly as I am.

Removing those barriers to Love didn't change my actual physical appearance. Removing them only stopped me from judging my appearance. I could then choose, from a Loving inner space, whether or not I felt drawn to change that part of me. For example, I judged myself for being chubby and found that my desire to be attractive to the opposite sex was creating that judgmental thought. After removing that barrier to Love, I felt drawn to explore the cause of my being overweight. It was due to my using food to avoid facing issues that were surfacing. I then faced those issues and the weight fell away.

Over time, my inner critic did fall silent. Ding, dong, the bully is gone. I now have a Loving, rather than judgmental, relationship with myself. I recommend that you create a Loving relationship with yourself as well. This process for healing your judgments of yourself is described in exercise '*26. Healing your Judgments of Self*'.

Being Proactive in Healing your Judgments of Self.

You do not have to wait until a judgmental thought pops into your head before healing your judgments of yourself. You can be proactive in finding those judgments.

There is an exercise that you can use to bring awareness to the way you judge yourself. It involves having you stand up in front of others and tell them everything that you like and don't like about yourself.

I did this exercise and found it extremely difficult to express the way I truly felt about myself in that way. However, I persevered and it gave me a list of all the ways in which I judged myself; both positively and negatively. I took that list into a series of meditations and, for each item on that list, I asked to be shown the barrier to Love that was triggering it. I then removed that barrier.

****

Caring about the Opinions of Others

"Care about what others think and you will always be their prisoner." Lao Tzu

I spent most of my life trying to live up to the expectations of my parents and my society. I worked hard to do what they told me would bring me success and happiness.

I eventually managed to achieve everything they said to do. I should have been happy but I wasn't. I was miserable. I discovered that, for me, trying to live a life based on what others thought did indeed make me their prisoner.

A Rumi quote came to me while I was at a meditation retreat in Rishikesh, India. It summed up my situation rather well.

"For years, copying others, I tried to know myself.
From within, I couldn't decide what to do.
Unable to see, I heard my name being called.
Then I walked outside."

Upon hearing that quote, I felt that my leaving the corporate world and setting out on my inner journey had been my way of 'walking outside'. I was finished with copying others and was ready to walk outside. I felt pleased with myself for having had the courage to do that but I still felt lost. I was outside. Now what?

The above quotes from Lao Tzu and Rumi both resonated strongly with me but they also failed to provide me with a roadmap for what to do once I was 'outside'. How did I break free of the opinions of others? Where did I go once I was outside? Of course, if they had told me what to do then they would have been going against their very words. Still, I wanted to know. What did I do once I was outside? What was the alternative to adhering to the false promises of my society?

In my case, I had stepped outside without having a clue as to where I was going. My desire to know what to do next on my journey was my first great challenge in dropping the opinions of others. If I had no one to tell me what to do then how would I know what to do? What was the alternative to abiding by the opinions of others? It was scary to be stepping out into the big, bad world with no direction and no guidance.

By saying no to my society's way of life, I had unwittingly taken the first step in letting go of the opinions of others. I had turned my back on all of the guidance that I had been given during my early years. I was ignoring the opinions of everyone in my society about how I should live my life. That included my teachers, friends, family, co-workers, corporate leaders, marketers, politicians, law enforcers, religious leaders, members of the media, and everyone else who believed in the way of life that my society espoused.

I knew that their frame of reference did not work for me. It had actually been relatively easy for me to stop caring about what they thought of how I was 'supposed to live life'. I had taken the first step. I had broken out of the prison that was my society's opinion of the 'right' way to live.

However, I didn't know what the next step was.

I spent the next few years mostly stumbling around in the dark. Fortunately, there were a few people, such as His Holiness and a woman who taught me about spiritual tools, who came into my life and guided me in finding my own way rather than pushing me into adopting theirs. I felt like I desperately needed their guidance and it was hard for me not to care about what they thought of me.

I felt blessed to have met His Holiness in particular because he didn't hold any opinions about me; at least none that he shared with me. There was no need for me to care about his opinion because he didn't express one. He didn't criticize me and he didn't praise me. He just guided me. I Loved the example that he set of how to Lovingly support another person in finding their own way. I felt like I had found someone who was focused solely on guiding me onto my own path rather than pulling me onto his. How lucky was I?

The woman who taught me spiritual tools was a little bit different from His Holiness. For the most part, she taught me a set of tools that would prove invaluable in my finding my own way. For that, I am deeply grateful to her. However, she did hold opinions of me and she did share them with me. At the end of the final session that I was to have with her, she said "*I never thought you would get this far.*" I was devastated. How could she not believe in me? How could she not believe that I could learn the tools that I needed to find my own way? Her words felt like a knife to the gut. I knew in my heart that she had meant those words as praise but they had cut me to the core. I walked away from her that day feeling like I was done working with her.

In effect, my ego had been bruised by her words because I cared deeply about what she thought of me. Her not having complete faith in me had hurt 'me' because her opinion mattered to my ego. I left her practice a week or two later and didn't see her again for two years. By that time, I had let go of caring about her opinion of me. I was then able to interact with her from an inner space of Love and gratitude rather than from a bruised ego. This example showed how I still cared about the opinion of others.

My next big breakthrough in letting go of caring about the opinions of others came when I stopped identifying with the roles that I was playing in life. For example, I had identified myself with being a 'spiritual seeker'. I had then been trying to live up to the images and assumptions of what I thought it meant to be a spiritual seeker. I cared about what the people in spiritual communities thought of me because I thought that they were also 'spiritual seekers'. Their opinion mattered because they were my validation as to how well I was playing that role. I was able to let go of caring about their opinion of me as soon as I stopped identifying with that role.

With concerted effort, I have, for the most part, been able to free myself of the opinions of everyone. I found that the most challenging people in my life to do that with were my family, the people who have asked me for support on their own journey, and my guides.

In the case of my family, I had to stop identifying myself with being a 'son', 'brother', or 'uncle'. That was difficult for me to do because those roles had become deeply ingrained. However, I was able to accomplish it because I knew that the only way that I could Love them was to break free of identifying with my roles. I still play the roles of brother, son, and uncle but I am not identified with any of them.

The people who asked me for guidance and support on their own healing journey were another challenge for me. I had to stop identifying myself with being a 'guide', 'teacher', 'mentor', or anything else, and simply Love them. Only then could I stop caring about what they thought of me. This was especially difficult with those who wanted me to be their teacher or mentor and tried to put me on a pedestal. That would invariably lead to them wanting to tear me down.

I had to learn how to stop people from putting me up on a pedestal. A friend showed me the way to do that when he simply said that, "*They can only put you on a pedestal if you let them*". I let those words sink in and I knew that he was right. A part of my ego had liked being put on a pedestal. I removed the barriers to Love underling my desire to be put on a pedestal. I have not had a problem since. I simply ignore any efforts that others make to put me on one. That's their game not mine. I'm not getting up there.

My guides were the final challenge that I faced. They were the beings who showed up, either in a body or not, when I most needed guidance in navigating my journey. It was only when I was able to completely trust my own inner guide that I became truly free of their opinions. By trusting that my inner guide was guiding me 'home' to Love, I was able to stop looking towards others for that guidance.

I was finally free. I no longer cared about the opinions of anyone else. I had taken back my life and was no longer a pawn in someone else's game.

I did not find the answer as to what to do now that I was 'outside'. Instead, I was simply okay with being outside. I had turned my life over to my inner guide and was simply trusting that it knew the way 'home'. 'I' no longer needed to know what to do. I was simply living in the Gap and flowing with life.

Caring about the Praise that I receive from others also makes me their Prisoner.

People's opinions of me included both their criticism and their praise. If I cared about either of them then I was their prisoner.

I was easily able to stop being a prisoner of critics. I was able to simply ignore most criticism because I knew that another's judgment of me was a reflection of them not me. If I found myself caring about their criticism then I would know that they were "pushing one of my buttons". I had a barrier to Love inside me that was being threatened by their words. I would then delve inside to find and remove that barrier. This process worked well for me. I was able to use my inner reaction to the criticism of others as a way to heal myself.

However, I didn't realize at first that my enjoying the praise of others also made me their prisoner. My ego liked praise and it took me a little while to catch on that praise was actually an insidious trap. I liked receiving praise and so I would do or say things from my ego in order to receive more of it. Identifying myself with the praise that I received was causing me to strengthen my false self. As soon as I realized this, I began to break free of praise.

My either enjoying praise or seeking it throws me into my ego and causes me to be non-Loving towards myself. Thus, whenever I felt myself enjoying praise I would delve inside to find the underlying barrier to Love. I would then remove that barrier. Similarly, if I found myself seeking praise then I would find and remove the underlying barrier to Love. Eventually, I learned to graciously receive the praise of others, while ignoring it.

****

Speaking from Ego

A poem flowed out of me while I was meditating on a beach in Bali. It invited me to question my motivation for speaking.

Talking to hear your own voice,
That is not beautiful.
In silence, beauty emerges.
No words are needed.
Then words have meaning.

After receiving that poem, I began to pay attention to my motivation for speaking. Much to my dismay, I found that my motivation was invariably ego-based. I was speaking either to tell someone something, to convince someone I was right, to defend myself, or even to fill the silence. In essence, I was speaking to hear my own voice and it was not beautiful.

Worse yet, it was non-Loving. That left me wondering if it was possible to both speak and be Loving. I certainly hadn't been able to accomplish that for the first forty years of my life.

By this point on my journey, I did know that I could become Love by falling completely silent inside. My mind would then be quiet and I would be aware of everything that was happening inside me and all around me. Love would be flowing through me. I would be Love. However, I would become disconnected from that silent inner state every time I opened my mouth to speak. In essence, the very act of speaking was disconnecting me from Love.

I didn't know what to do about this. I hadn't yet learned that it was possible to speak from silence and so speaking was activating my ego. I didn't like that. I wanted to be Love. If the only way to be Loving was to keep my mouth shut then I felt strongly drawn to do exactly that. Unfortunately, not talking to anyone didn't seem to be a practical approach to living life amongst people in today's world. Words are currently the primary means of communication and I still felt drawn to interact with people. What to do?

To speak or not to speak, that was my question. I wanted to live a life from an inner space of Love and was confused as to what role, if any, words could play in my doing so. I began to speak less frequently which meant interacting with people less and less. I soon began to avoid people unless absolutely necessary.

I also closely observed what happened inside me whenever I so much as wanted to speak. What I discovered was that words were both disconnecting me from Love and creating a separation between me and what I was experiencing. As soon as I began to speak about what I was experiencing, I was no longer experiencing it. For example, by describing a tree as being a Cypress or an Oak, I was lost in my conditioned mind. I was no longer experiencing life through the essence of who I am. Instead, the false self was simply talking about it.

Again, what to do? I was confused. I knew that I was activating my conditioned mind whenever I chose to allow words to pass across my lips. That, in turn, was disconnecting me from Love and causing my interactions with others to be non-Loving. Furthermore, I was no longer experiencing life and was simply one more actor on the stage of life.

The question remained, 'How could I interact with others in a Loving way when my use of words was preventing me from doing so?'

Unfortunately, the answer to that question was not the one I was looking for. For the time being, I couldn't. I could only connect to Love, and experience life, when I allowed myself to remain in an inner state of peaceful awareness. In the early stages of my journey, I could only do that when I was either alone in nature or in meditation. I wasn't yet capable of remaining connected to Love when I was in the presence of others let alone when I was in conversation with them.

In the meantime, any desire to speak would disconnect me from Love. I felt like I understood what Lao Tzu meant when he said, in the 'Tao Te Ching', that,

"Those who know don't speak. Those who don't know speak."

To me, 'those who know' are those who know that we are eternal beings of Love. Why speak if doing so is going to disconnect us from the Love that we are. There is nothing to be said. Why speak? Why not simply remain silent and be?

That was a tempting option for me. I found myself empathizing with monks who took vows of silence. I seriously considered taking one myself. However, I had already tried the step of heading off to a monastery and had discovered that the monastic life was not for me; not in this incarnation anyway.

That eliminated the monastic option but not the reclusive one. I did consider the option of disappearing from the world. I even sought out a cave in the Himalayas and found one near the town of Bageshwar, India. Bageshwar is on the Hindu pilgrimage route to Mt. Kailas and people have been meditating in the nearby caves for thousands of years. If there was any place in the world to live in a cave then that was it.

By the time I actually reached a cave, I had become pretty certain that I was not going to spend the remainder of my days as a recluse. Something inside me simply knew that I was going to spend this lifetime amongst people. However, I had come all this way so why not at least give it a try?

The cave that I was directed to had a small entrance about three feet high. I got onto my knees, hunched over, and made my way into the cave. It was a little damp in the cave but not too bad. There was enough room inside for me to either sit comfortably or to lie down flat. It was dimly lit because of the light coming through the entrance and the airflow wasn't too bad. All in all, I felt like it could work.

I sat on a rock in the center of the cave. The rock was smooth and seemed rather well shaped for my bottom. The thought passed through my mind that people had likely been sitting on this rock for thousands of years. It had probably been worn into this rather pleasant shape. I closed my eyes and fell into a meditative state.

I felt peaceful, relaxed, and completely at ease in that cave. I felt like I could easily have chosen to live out my days with that as my home. However, it was not meant to be. During that meditation, I confirmed, from somewhere deep in my being, that this type of existence was not for me; at least not this time around. After that beautiful meditation, I crawled out of the cave, stood up, thanked the cave for being there, and then walked away. I returned to the world of people. A reclusive life was not for me.

That left me with only one option. I was going to have to find a way to remain Loving while speaking. I wasn't even sure if that was possible but I had to try. For me, the only acceptable way to interact with people was to do so from an inner space of Love. There may come a day when we are all telepathic but that day hasn't yet come. Words are still a necessary part of our world. Thus, I felt that the only choice left to me was to learn how to remain as Love while speaking.

Why Speak?'

I had a conundrum. I felt drawn to interact with people and was determined to become Love. I also felt that words were necessary for me to be able communicate with others and that words blocked Love. What to do? I chose to focus on the question of 'why speak?'

I was determined to free myself of all non-Loving motivations for speaking. I was able to do that by using mindful awareness to observe my motivation for speaking and to remove the barriers to Love underlying any non-Loving motivations. Unfortunately, all of my motivations for speaking seemed to be non-Loving. I struggled to find any reason to speak.

My first real hint that it was possible to have a Loving motivation for speaking came while I was attending a Satsang in India. The Satsang was being led by a man named Devageet. He caught my attention when he said, *"say what you mean and mean what you say"*.

I perked up when I heard those words. They very much intrigued me because he was telling me that I could actually speak. I felt very curious as to what he was getting at.

My understanding of the ensuing discussion was that a person would be saying *"what they mean"* when they expressed their truth about either the way they felt or what they had experienced. Their current feelings and their current understanding of their experiences were their truth. If a person were to say anything else then they would be simply spewing out the contents of their ego.

Exactly! I had already watched myself constantly opening my mouth to regurgitate my ego. It seemed like that was all I ever did when I spoke. I liked where this conversation was going. Devageet seemed to be both confirming what I already knew about speaking from ego and giving me reasons to speak.

First of all, he was telling me that speaking about the way I currently felt was a valid reason for speaking. This strongly resonated with me because I had already learned that Loving myself included openly and honestly expressing the way I currently felt. Speaking about my feelings did disconnect me from Love but it also helped me in finding and removing my barriers to Love. I can do that by speaking about my feelings in order to explore how I truly feel deep down. I can then remove the barriers to Love that are triggering those deeper feelings. I had already used this technique on my journey and it had proved invaluable.

I loved this possibility. I had my first reason for speaking. I could speak about the way I currently felt. Doing so would disconnect me from Love but it would also enable me to find and remove more of my barriers to Love.

The second reason that Devageet gave me for speaking was to share the truth of my experiences. The intention for doing so would be to open a door for another person to see through the limitations of their own rational mind. That may then inspire them to remove their own barriers to Love.

The challenge for me would be to remain Loving while sharing my experiences. I could only do that by accepting that everyone has their own unique journey to follow. My experiences, and the lessons that I learned from them, apply only to me. They may not have relevance for another. All I can do is tune into my inner guide and listen to it when it suggests that I share the story of an experience with another person. I do not need to know why I am sharing the story. If the lessons from my experience resonate with another then that may open a door for them to do their own healing. However, that is their business, not mine.

I embraced this second reason for speaking. I was open to anything that I could do to support others in removing their own barriers to Love. I then began to share the stories of my experiences with others, but only when I felt inspired to by my inner guide to do so. I would not know at the time of sharing if my doing so was actually supportive. However, I often received feedback from others that my experiences did open doors for them. I had a second reason for speaking.

I began to freely express the truth about the way I felt and to share my experiences. I found that my doing so was invaluable in supporting myself and others in becoming Love. However, I also soon came to realize that even my 'truth' was false.

I discovered that the 'truth' about how I was feeling in a given moment was really only my current 'truth'. I would no longer have those feelings once I removed the underlying barriers to Love. In essence, the 'truth' about the way I felt wasn't true outside of the illusory world of my personality. The feelings would be gone once the part of my personality that was creating them had been removed.

I also discovered that even the 'truth' about my experiences, and the lessons that I learned from them, was false. Those events were experienced by my false self. My perception of both the experience and the lessons that they were bringing me was coming from that false self. The 'truth' of what 'I' had experienced and what it had meant to 'me' fell away when I went beyond the false. The events had happened in my reality but my perception of them was false.

In this way, I learned that my 'truth' is only true within the imitations of the false self. It has no validity outside of the false. As I began to move beyond the false, I realized that 'truth' is a state of being not something to be stated.

However, I did find that sharing my 'truth' was invaluable part of my healing journey. It supported me in breaking free of the illusions of the false and returning Home to Love. It also seemed to support others in doing the same.

Speaking my 'truth' in a world where few are focused on Becoming Love.

I found that it was easy for me to practice speaking my 'truth' when

I was living in a spiritual community in India. I found it much harder to do so after I had returned to the western world. I was then back in an environment where people were more focused on the external world than the internal one. I often felt like I was the only one who wanted to become Love.

It seemed like I couldn't go anywhere without someone trying to draw me into an ego-based conversation. I struggled with how to respond. Initially, it felt rude for me not to engage and so I would speak from my ego in order to match them. However, I found that this approach was soul destroying for me. It meant that I was not being Loving towards myself.

I was getting lost in the desire to be polite. That desire caused me to repeatedly disconnect from Love and to engage in conversations of the false selves. Eventually, I was able to drop that desire and accept that I simply couldn't play the personality game anymore. However, that left me even more confused about how to converse with people. I wanted to engage with them but not at an ego level.

I didn't know what to do and found myself withdrawing from people. I became reclusive for extended periods of time. However, there was something inside me that kept telling me to engage with people. And so I did.

It was a mighty struggle. I felt like I had a completely opposite motivation for speaking than everyone around me. I wanted to speak only when it would support me, or others, in moving closer to Love. Everyone else seemed to want to speak in order to engage their ego and disconnect themselves from Love. In other words, I felt like I wanted to destroy my personality while everyone else wanted to enhance theirs. This situation was not conducive to smooth discussions. I was left with very few conversation partners and felt like I was all alone amidst a sea of people.

At times, I did try to engage people at the level of destroying the personality. That was a mistake. I soon discovered that my doing that was being incredibly non-Loving towards them. If someone doesn't want to have their personality destroyed then my attempting to do so was just plain cruel. I quickly learned that lesson. If a person is choosing to remain identified with their ego then I feel that the Loving thing for me to do is to simply leave them alone and remain silent.

From then on, I would only support a person in becoming Love if they explicitly invited me to do so.

My desire to converse with people was waning. I did not feel drawn to engage in ego-based conversations. I also did not feel that it was appropriate for me to engage with people at the level of destroying the false unless they specifically invited me to do so. As a result, I began to remain silent regardless of who I was with. I even became comfortable doing so.

A magical thing then happened. I began to Love them. By remaining silent in their presence, I was able to maintain that silent inner space that enabled me to become Love. I was no longer being drawn into my ego. I then began to feel completely relaxed and at ease with people. I was remaining in a state of Love regardless of what they were doing. I was being silent and therefore Loving.

Silence can Speak

By choosing to remain silent regardless of who I was with, I then discovered that silence can speak. Words began to flow out of me that were coming from that silent inner space and not from my ego. Those words were infused with Love. This was a very cool thing for me to observe happening. Invariably the words that came from silence were supporting others with where they were at in their lives. There was no ego-based motivation behind them at all. 'I' was not speaking them, silence was.

This was a huge breakthrough for me. 'I' had learned to allow silence to speak through me. I did not need to have a reason for speaking anymore. I could simply get out of the way and allow silence to speak, if and when Love felt inspired to do so.

I came to love silence. Years later, I came across the following quote from an unknown author and simply said 'yup'.

> *"If you're going to speak then be sure that what you say is more profound than the silence you are breaking."*

Other reasons that I found for speaking

I had made the choice to free myself of any ego-based desire to speak. I was doing that by bringing mindful awareness to the motivation underlying my desire to speak. If the motivation was non-

Loving then I would remove the underlying barrier to Love. Through this process, I found three other scenarios (other than speaking the truth about my feelings and sharing my experiences) in which my speaking did not indicate the existence of an underlying barrier to Love.

Firstly, I learned how to speak from silence. The words that emerged from inside me when I was resting in a silent inner space were coming from Love. There was no ego-based motivation behind them.

Secondly, I found that there were times when it was appropriate to use humor as a way to lighten the tone of a conversation. I will now do that but only when I have first tuned into my inner guide and it gives me the guidance that the seriousness of the conversation is no longer serving me or others. I will not use humor to be derogatory towards anyone and I will not use humor as a way to avoid myself. I will only use it when guided to do so.

Lastly, I discovered that I still needed to use words in order to make logistical arrangements related to following my inner guide. There was no underlying barrier to Love when I was speaking with this intent.

Thus, I found that there were just five reasons for me to speak. I would allow myself to speak when I was:

- speaking from silence;

- expressing my feelings in order to support myself in removing my barriers to Love;

- sharing my experiences in order to support others in removing their barriers to Love;

- speaking when my inner guide has invited me to use humor to lighten the tone of a conversation; and,

- speaking in order to make logistical arrangements related to following the guidance of my inner guide.

If I speak for any reason other than those listed above then my motivation is non-Loving. I then have an opportunity to find and remove the underlying barrier to Love.

Observing my motivation for speaking greatly assisted me on my healing journey. It showed me where I was strongly attached to my false self and enabled me to rapidly find and remove many of my barriers to Love. I highly recommend that you use your motivation for speaking as an indicator of when you are being non-Loving.

****

Sacrificing Yourself is Egotistical Not Loving

Why is sacrificing yourself egotistical?

I was raised as a Christian. I was taught to believe that sacrificing myself for others was a beautiful thing to do. I chose to do it myself. My older brother was killed in a car accident when I was thirteen. His death devastated my mother and she became deeply depressed. I then decided to stop being a rebellious son who wanted to live his own life and instead become what she wanted me to become. I felt like I had essentially sacrificed living my own life in order to make life easier for her.

Hadn't that been an act of Love? No. It had been an act of my ego. It was non-Loving towards myself and her. Oops.

Sacrificing oneself is egotistical because it puts the other person under a debt of obligation. It is only the ego that would do that to another person. Love would not do that. Basically, if I feel that I am making a sacrifice for you then, knowingly or not, I will be putting you into my debt.

This came as quite a revelation for me. Upon hearing it for the first time, I reflected on the role that sacrifice had played in my life. I could think of many examples of how sacrifice created debt. For example, I was often told things like:

- look what I gave up for you;

- Jesus sacrificed himself for you so you must …..; and,

- I sacrificed my dreams to give you the life that…. .

In each of those situations, the person saying it was trying to get the other to do what they wanted. They were using the story of how they sacrificed themselves to make the other one feel indebted to them. It didn't take me long to accept that sacrificing oneself is a non-Loving act of the ego.

There is an alternative to sacrificing oneself and that is to function from Love. If I freely give of myself to others, without asking for anything in return, then no indebtedness is created. I am simply being of service from a silent inner space of peace and Love.

I can actually do the exact same thing from either a sacrificial or Loving space. If I feel that I am sacrificing myself then I am coming from ego and am putting the other person into debt. There is no Love whatsoever in my actions. On the other hand, if I perform the same action from a silent inner space then it is a Loving act. I am simply being of service and will not be asking for anything in return. Personally, I would rather be a Loving person than play the ego game of sacrificing myself.

After realizing that sacrificing myself was non-Loving, I set the intention to stop doing it. I then brought mindful awareness to whenever I had the feeling that I was sacrificing myself in any way. If I found myself feeling sacrificial then I would immediately stop whatever I was doing. If I could then shift myself into an inner space of giving freely of myself then I would resume doing it otherwise I would not. Regardless of whether or not I continued on with my actions, I would later take that feeling of sacrifice into a meditation in order to find and release the barrier to Love that was triggering it. Thus, the feeling of wanting to sacrifice myself became another useful signpost on my healing journey.

I will make you a deal. Don't sacrifice anything for me and I won't sacrifice anything for you. I will Love and support you on your journey, without asking for anything in return, and I will accept any Love and support that you freely give to me.

****

The Victim Role is the Ego Seeking Attention

Playing the victim role is a cry for attention that is often accompanied by self-deprecating thoughts. Those thoughts literally drain the life force energy right out of you.

I explored this perspective on the victim role for myself. I had played the 'woe is me' card quite a few times in my earlier years. I had done it to get attention (usually in the form of sympathy) and hadn't realized just how self-destructive it was. In recalling the times when I had felt like a victim, I could remember having thoughts such as 'I am a loser', 'I know nothing', and 'I can't help anyone because I can't even help myself'. Those were definitely self-deprecating thoughts. When I allowed myself to feel what it was like to say 'I am a loser', I could feel myself slump down in my seat. It felt like my energy was literally draining away. Playing the victim role did drain my life force energy. Who knew?

It didn't take me long to accept that my playing the victim role was egotistical, non-Loving, and self-abusive. It clearly didn't serve me. It may have gotten me some fleeting attention but the cost was too high; being non-Loving and abusive towards myself. It was definitely time to stop. I set the intention to let go of playing the victim role once and for all.

I would then bring mindful awareness to whenever I felt like I was 'playing the victim role'. I knew that any action that I took from that feeling would be non-Loving. Whenever I observed the victim feeling arising inside the body, I would know that I was craving attention. I would then delve inside to find and remove the barrier to Love that was triggering that craving. This process is described in exercise '27. *Letting go of Playing the Victim Role'*.

****

Succumbing to an Addictive Craving

Succumbing to an addiction is a non-Loving thing to do to oneself. An addictive substance provides you with a false substitute for what you really want.

I discovered at an early age that I had what was considered to be an addictive personality. Shortly after graduating from high school, my father sent me to a career counselor. He had done so in order to help me find the 'right' career. I really had no idea what to do with my life at that point and felt grateful to my father for this gift.

The counselor gave me a battery of tests and then asked me to return a week later to hear the results. I spent that week looking forward to hearing what career I would soon be embarking upon. I was more than a little disappointed when he told me that I had a strong intellect and that I would be best suited to an engineering field. I already knew that I could do well in a field such as engineering but I had no passion for it. I had been hoping for something else; something that would light a fire inside me. Engineering didn't.

In retrospect, I feel that those tests were an evaluation of my rational mind not me. A test of my rational mind was not going to find anything that would inspire me. I would only find inspiration by going beyond the rational mind. I waited another twenty-five years before I finally found a way to go beyond the mind and discover that inner fire.

After the counselor had passed on this disappointing news about engineering, he told me that he had included a different kind of test in my package. This test assessed a person's tendency towards becoming addicted to substances. He then told me that I had scored the highest total he had ever seen. He warned me to be very careful of developing addictions.

Woohoo! At least I had scored high on something. I smiled to myself at his warning. I also took it to heart. I had already begun to use alcohol as a way to numb my feelings of being lost in the world and I knew that I was on a slippery slope. I kept his warning in the back of my mind throughout my adulthood.

I did my best to avoid drugs and gambling. For the most part, I was successful. However, I did allow myself the luxury of indulging in alcohol, desserts, and escapist activities such as movies, television, skiing, and porn. Those activities seemed relatively 'harmless' to me. Even so, I would take the extra precaution of dropping things like alcohol for a few weeks at a time just to be sure that I wasn't addicted.

It was only when I began to heal my barriers to Love that it became clear to me that my addictive cravings were coming from a desire to avoid myself. I also knew that I was just temporarily escaping from my feelings by drinking alcohol, watching TV, and watching porn. Those activities didn't change the way I felt about myself and my life. They only gave me a temporary reprieve at best and often left me feeling worse afterward. My addictions were indeed a false substitute for actually facing the way I truly felt inside.

I was able to accept that my cravings were coming from barriers to Love and that I could use those cravings as healing opportunities. However, I found it difficult to muster the determination to actually break free of my cravings. I was rather attached to my addictions and didn't see them as being all that harmful.

It wasn't until I was in India and working on healing myself that I began to feel like it was time for me to take my cravings seriously. Devageet reminded me that I was just avoiding myself by succumbing to my addictions. I knew that he was right. I also felt like he was telling me, in his own gentle way, that it was pointless to keep working on myself if I was going to keep succumbing to my addictions. I would just be avoiding my deeper issues by doing that.

It was time for me to decide whether or not I was going to take my journey 'home' seriously. Was I going to go all the way down the rabbit hole or was I just going to keep dancing around the surface? Deep down, I had long since made that choice. I was going to go as far down the rabbit hole as I could possibly go. However, my mind had been holding me back. It was time to break the grip that my mind had over my life.

Up until that point, I had been rather lackadaisical about using my cravings as signposts. My mind didn't want to have to face itself and I had been letting it win. I had been giving in to my cravings far too often for my liking. No more. I felt determined to use my cravings as the messengers they were rather than succumbing to them. Whenever I felt myself craving something, I would delve inside myself to find the feelings that I wanted to avoid. I would then find and remove the barriers to Love that were triggering those feelings. This process is described in exercise '28. *Freeing Oneself from Addictive Cravings*'.

Healing the underlying root of my addictive craving was often a challenging journey. My cravings were invariably being triggered by feelings that my mind really didn't want to face. As a result, I would still occasionally succumb to my cravings. Each time that I caved in, I would be reminded that giving in to my addictions was not the answer for me. I would have temporarily relief from my feelings but would then usually feel worse. Not only would the feelings underlying the craving be stronger, I would also feel guilty for having succumbed.

My determination to heal myself kept growing stronger. Eventually it grew to the point where giving in to my addictive cravings was a far worse choice than facing the emotions that my mind wanted to avoid. I was then able to use all of my addictive cravings as opportunities to heal myself.

Craving Something versus Feeling Drawn to it.

There is a difference between craving something and feeling drawn to that same thing.

A craving is triggered by your ego when it wants to avoid the feelings that are arising from inside you. It is your mind's attempt to have you use an addictive substitute as a false substitute for actually facing yourself.

On the other hand, feeling drawn to something is guidance from your inner guide. Following that guidance will provide you with an opportunity to learn about yourself and will move you one step closer to living the life that you incarnated to live. In essence, a craving is from the ego while feeling drawn to something is coming from Love.

There were times on my journey when I felt drawn to watch a movie and other times when I craved the opportunity to watch a movie in order to avoid myself. I found that I would tend to feel empty after watching a movie when I was giving in to a craving. On the other hand, I would often gain valuable insights into my journey when I watched a movie that I felt drawn to. There would be something in the movie that I needed to see or hear.

For example, I felt drawn to watch the movie 'La Bamba'. I was surprised by that choice because I was focused on my inner journey and 'La Bamba' didn't seem to be aligned with that. However, I trusted my inner guide and so I watched it. I was enjoying the movie when one line jumped out and hit me right between the eyes. The line was, *"to live is to sleep, to die is to awaken"*. That resonated strongly with me and it left me feeling even more determined to awaken.

I made the choice to allow myself to be drawn to a movie but not to give in to my cravings to watch one. It took practice for me to learn the difference between craving something and feeling drawn to it.

I spent many hours meditating on the underlying source of my various cravings. In that way, I slowly became able to feel the difference inside me between when I was craving something and when I was being drawn to that same thing. A craving came with a feeling of longing and had the energy of a functioning ego. Feeling drawn to something came with a calm feeling of just knowing that I was being guided towards it.

There was a fine line in this distinction for me. My mind would often try to convince me that I was being drawn to something when I was actually just craving it. Through trial and error, I eventually became proficient at feeling the difference.

****

Addicted to Rational Thinking

The strongest addiction that I had to break free from was my addiction to rational thinking.

I didn't even know that I was addicted to thoughts for most of my life. Even when I discovered that going beyond the rational mind was a big part of the journey 'home' to love, I still hadn't put two and two together. I hadn't made the connection that one of the biggest things that was preventing me from going beyond the rational mind was my addiction to the thoughts that it generated.

I was raised in a society that revered the intellect. I was taught, from a very early age, to intellectualize the world around me. It was drilled into me that using logic was the best, and only reasonable, way to function in this world. I bought into that conditioning completely. I would:

- label everything I saw (such as an oak, ash, or cypress tree);

- try to figure out how things worked;

- solve puzzles;

- debate points;

- have an opinion;

- compare things;

- define things;

- understand things;

- devour books that intellectualized spirituality; and,

- basically use logic to run my life.

I could have put many more things on that list. The ways in which I rationalized life seemed never ending. I was completely addicted to rational thinking. It was quite a challenge for me to break free of this addiction. Doing so meant that I had to accept the possibility that the thoughts being generated by my rational mind had no credence whatsoever.

That was not easy for me to do. I had a high-powered intellect that had enabled me to thrive in a society that was devoted to intellectualization. Was that such a bad thing? The only problem that I had with being materially 'successful' was that I had been miserable. I had been literally soul sick. However, I had been able to use my intellect to figure out how to play the greed game and had been good at. I therefore liked the idea that I could use that same intellect to be successful at the spiritual game. Yup, I was rather delusional.

My intellect was both a blessing and a curse. It was a blessing in that it helped me to 'succeed' in the western world. It later also enabled me to understand the more esoteric views of the human experience that were held by the various cultures that I explored. Lastly, it helped me to discover how to remove the barriers to Love, become a self-healer, and return 'home' to Love. In essence, it played a huge role in my being able to find the doors that would lead me 'home'.

It was also a curse. I had used my rational mind to find the way 'home' and then 'thought' that I could actually use it to return there. I couldn't. My rational mind could not go beyond itself. Instead, it just kept getting in the way. For example, I would think that I had already let go of a barrier to Love when all I had done was mentally understood it. I hadn't taken the step of feeling it to heal it. The journey home to Love is one of following one's feelings and inner guidance not one's rational thoughts.

There were many more examples of how my rational mind would get in the way. It would block my insight meditations by guessing at the answer to what I was meditating on. I would then follow that answer only to discover that it was invariably wrong. One of my favorite ways in which it got in the way was to imagine what a 'spiritual' experience was supposed to be like and then have me try and have that experience. I wasted a great deal of time in this way. It took me a while to realize that any effort by my mind to try and experience something that was beyond the mind was a guarantee of failure.

On it went. My rational mind would enjoy something like astral travel and think that I could gain more value from trying to repeat that experience over and over again. I wouldn't. From astral travel, I gained experiential confirmation that I was not the body. Doing more astral travelling did not enhance that insight. It took me a while to learn to embrace an experience when it happened, learn the lesson, and move on. My mind didn't always want to move on. It liked playing with these new experiences. It was like a cat playing with a ball of string.

In order to overcome my addiction to rational thinking, I had to cultivate trust in my inner guide. I needed to trust that my inner guide would bring the experiences into my life that would allow me to learn my lessons and remove my barriers to Love. My inner guide not my intellect needed to be in charge of my self-healing journey.

That said, my rational mind was very useful in getting me to the precipice of returning 'home' to Love. It helped me to understand the human experience and to discover the way 'home'. However, at that point it became an obstacle. My attempts to use it to actually become Love prevented me from doing so.

This was a core issue for me. My addiction to rational thinking was very strong. I actually believed that my thoughts were true. I was constantly getting lost in intellectualizing both my experiences and the world around me. I would then be disconnected from Love. I cannot be lost in rational thinking and be Love. The two cannot co-exist inside me. Unfortunately, I was addicted to rational thinking. That addiction was blocking me from becoming Love and it was strong.

After realizing that rational thinking was an addiction, I became fiercely determined to break free of it. I knew that every rational thought was non-Loving. It did not matter what I was talking about or how well-meaning I was. I could be talking about peace on earth, the woman I Loved, non-violent ways to communicate, puppies, a golden age for humanity, or even Divine Love. Regardless of the topic, if I was speaking from the rational mind then there would be no Love flowing through me. I had to break free of this addiction. Only then could I even consider bringing any Love into the world.

I felt like I then understood what Eckhart Tolle was pointing at when he said that,

"Spiritual awakening is awakening from the dream of thought." (4)

It was time for me to wake up from the dream of thought. I had begun to cultivate trust and now I needed to also remove the barriers to Love that triggered me into functioning from my rational mind. I did that by using mindful awareness to observe when I was getting lost in intellectualizing life rather than living it. It was overwhelming at first. It seemed like there was a constant stream of thoughts arising in my monkey mind. I felt like there was no way I could deal with them all.

I had to find a way to focus on the core thought streams that were causing me to become non-Loving. I chose to step back from individual thoughts and to instead bring awareness to when I was generally interacting with another person from my rational mind. If I was identified with any rational thoughts that were swirling through my head then I knew that I was being non-Loving.

Whenever I found myself engaging in a conversation using rational thinking, I would stop. I would then take that thought stream into a meditation. I would replay the conversation in my mind and ask to be shown the barrier to Love that had triggered me into rational thinking. I would then remove that barrier to Love. It worked. I found that I could remove my barriers to Love by focusing on bringing awareness to when I was lost in rational thinking rather than focusing on individual thoughts. This process is outlined in exercise '29. *Breaking the Addiction to Rational Thinking'.*

My addiction to rational thinking was an insidious one for me. It took me years to break free of it and I still find myself occasionally falling back into the non-Loving world of rational thought. Fortunately, that is now a rare event rather than the state of being that it was. I feel like I have woken up from the dream of thought.

There is an alternative to rational thoughts: Loving thoughts.

I have spent many years bringing mindful awareness to my thoughts. Through that journey, I have discovered that my thoughts arise from one of two sources; either my rational mind or Love.

When I first began to observe my thoughts, they were almost exclusively coming from my rational mind. Using meditative techniques, I was able to gain distance from these thoughts and to simply watch them rather than become lost in them. Gradually, the steady stream of thoughts from my rational mind began to fall silent. Eventually, there were moments when my mind was no longer cluttered by rational thoughts and I was able to rest in a silent inner space. Those moments were beautiful. They were few and far between at first but slowly grew to become a more common occurrence in my life. I cannot begin to tell you how great a relief that was.

As my rational mind began to fall silent, I discovered that there was another source of thoughts. These other thoughts were coming from beyond my rational mind and had a completely different energetic feel to them. They would arise when my rational mind was inactive and I was in a deeply peaceful and silent inner space. 'I' was not thinking these thoughts. They were simply emerging from within. They were also infused with Divine Love.

I would later discover that these loving thoughts were referred to as divine inspiration. I loved that term: divine inspiration. I could work with that. The divine that I feel they are coming from is the divine within, not some external divinity. The divine within is Love and could either be my Higher Self or Source. I cannot prove that and I would not try to do so. If I try to prove anything then I am back to functioning from my rational mind and all subsequent thoughts would be non-

Loving. All I can say is that I somehow 'know' that divine inspiration is sourced from the divine within.

Regardless of what label is given to the source of these Loving thoughts, they have a completely different feel than rational thoughts. They are Loving. When I allow Loving thoughts to flow through me and out into the world, a Loving space is created. That space invites others to become more Loving. That space does not fight with the rational minds of others.

Rational thoughts, on the other hand, are inherently violent. They are stemming from a desire to defend or strengthen the false self. They come with an energy of conviction. Any rational thought that I send out into the world is a challenge to the rational minds of others to either agree or disagree with me. My friends are then those whose rational minds are aligned with mine and my enemies are those whose minds are not. Conflict is rarely far away.

I made the choice to drop my addiction to rational thinking. I wanted to become Love not be violent. I began to cultivate my ability to remain in an inner state of peace and silence. I did this through healing myself of the barriers to Love that were preventing me from abiding there. Once in that silent inner space, I am then able to choose to respond to the Loving thoughts that arise from divine inspiration. I have chosen to become Love rather than be rational.

Rational Thoughts retain a small role in my life

It is no longer appropriate for me to become identified with my rational mind. For me, the rational mind is simply a tool that allows my higher self to exist in this world of form.

That tool has not been destroyed by my journey of becoming a self-healer. It is only the personality that has been destroyed. I still have a rational mind. However, I know that I am not that mind and I am not any thoughts that arise within it.

Once I broke my addiction to rational thinking, the role that rational thoughts played in my life was greatly reduced. For example, I will not, under any circumstances, use rational thinking as a means for making any choices about my life. I will not rationalize who to date, what to do, when to take action, where to go, or how to interact with another person. Doing so would be non-Loving towards myself and everyone else. Instead, I tune into my inner guide in every moment and simply allow it to guide me. I am not living life, Love is living me.

That said, I still use rational thinking in two limited scenarios. In both scenarios, I am not identified with those thoughts and do not believe that they are 'true'. I use rational thoughts:

- as a small part of the process of doing something 'practical' (like fixing a leaky roof or looking after the logistics related to following my inner guide); and,

- to support others in breaking their addiction to rational thinking.

When I am faced with doing something practical, I will first tune into my inner guide for guidance. I will not simply jump in with my rational mind and try to figure out what to do. I will act on any inspiration that comes from my inner guide. If I feel inspired to read a manual and follow its directions then I will do so. Rational thoughts will arise while following those directions and I will act on those thoughts. It would look, from the outside, like I was being rational but I am not. Throughout the process of doing something practical, I am constantly tuning in to my inner guide and following its guidance.

I will also use rational thoughts to support others in breaking free of their addiction to rational thinking. For example, the rational mind can be used to debate both sides of the same question. It is possible to use logic to arrive at two completely opposite conclusions. If I find that a person is using logic to avoid themselves then I may feel inspired by my inner guide to show them the futility of living life based on logic.

I will then use rational thought to arrive at two contradicting conclusions to the same question. While doing this, I will be infusing the words with Love and will not be believing anything that I am saying. In reality, I am expressing Loving thoughts disguised as rational ones.

I first came across this latter use of rational thinking in India. I was attending a nightly meditation that included a video of a discourse by Osho. One evening, Osho led us through a beautiful examination of the spiritual journey and came to a conclusion that deeply resonated with me. I went to bed that night feeling content. The next evening, he led us through another beautiful examination of the spiritual journey and came to a conclusion that completely contradicted what he had said the previous night. I was confused and angry.

After that second discourse, I walked over to a cafe, sat with a few others, and ranted about Osho. How could he do that? How could he say one thing one night and then completely contradict himself the next? I felt like he didn't know what he was talking about and wondered what the hell I was doing listening to such drivel.

One of the people who I was with then stood up, put his hand on my shoulder, and said *"he's doing it on purpose"*. I didn't understand what the person meant by that. What was Osho doing on purpose? A woman then added that Osho was showing us how the mind could be used to justify anything, and that trusting the rational mind was a fool's game.

I fell silent at that statement. I didn't know what to say. I hated the possibility that she could be right because, at that time, I was strongly identified with my mind. I had spent my whole life bowing down to the God called intellect. My mind recoiled at the idea that I had been so badly misguided. I soon got up and returned to my room. There, I allowed myself to stew in my own discontent.

Over the next few weeks, I came to realize that Osho had actually given me a gift during those two evening discourses. He had shown me that it was futile for me to try and live life with my rational mind in charge. That realization was one of the main factors in my being able to drop my addiction to rational thinking and to turn my life over to my inner guide. I had been shown the futility of trying to use the mind to explain life. Thank you Osho.

He had also shown me a rather powerful way of using rational thoughts to break another person's addiction to rational thinking.

Life is a journey to be enjoyed not a struggle to be endured.

9. Insights and Accelerators

This is your healing journey and the pace at which you move through it is up to you. There are three primary factors that will influence the speed of your journey. They include:

- your choice of how fast you wish to have your inner guide bring healing opportunities into your life;

- your mastery over finding and removing the barriers to Love that arise in your mirror; and,

- your ability to avoid the distractions that can slow down, or even derail, your journey.

The first factor is yours to set. You may feel determined to move through your journey as quickly as possible. In that case, you can invite your inner guide to bring issues into your life at a fast and furious pace. On the other hand, you may find that you are feeling overwhelmed by everything that you have been facing and feel drawn to either slow the journey down or even take a break. You can! At any time, you can simply ask your inner guide to either speed up or slow down your journey. Your inner guide will bring healing opportunities into your life at whatever pace you choose.

Personally, I chose the fast and furious approach. That choice led to my having a rather challenging journey. I was not gentle with myself and, at one point, my body literally shut down for three weeks. Oh well, all's well that ends well. Actually, it isn't over. All's well so far.

We are going to focus on the second and third factors in the next two chapters of this book.

The second factor is your ability to heal the barriers to Love that you find in the mirror that is your life. In this chapter, we will be exploring a few insights that can assist you in gaining that mastery, and some accelerators that you can use to be proactive in healing yourself.

The third factor involves avoiding the distractions that can slow down, or even derail, your journey. Simply becoming aware that something is a distraction is often enough to prevent it from derailing you. We will discuss a few of the common distractions in chapter *'10. Distractions'*.

****

Accelerating Your Ability to Heal Yourself

The healing of one barrier to Love creates space inside you for the next healing opportunity to appear in your life. If you become bogged down with healing one barrier then your overall healing journey can be delayed.

This happened to me on my journey. I often found that a lack of clarity on both what was happening inside me and how to heal the issues that were arising, would delay me for days, weeks, and even months. Eventually, I would gain that clarity, mainly through trial and error, and be able to heal myself. That process was frustrating. I often felt that it would have been rather helpful to have had someone provide me with some insights on what was happening inside me rather than struggle to figure it out on my own.

This chapter contains a few common insights that will hopefully help you to avoid 'spinning your wheels' the way I did. It also contains a few ideas on how you can be proactive in accelerating your journey.

The insights and accelerators that we will discuss are listed below.

- How to know when the healing of an issue is complete.

- Only you can Heal yourself

- Receiving a Wake-up Call.

- A Misalignment between your Chosen Life and the Life you incarnated to Live.

- Forgiving someone Heals you not them.

- You have to go from Feeling (not thinking) to Being.

- Be honest with yourself about the way you feel.

- Feeling Stuck is an Indicator of Fear.

- Healing Depression - the failure to Accept 'What is'.

- Breaking Free of Guilt.

- Practicing the Art of Listening.

- Take back your Power.

- Stop Trying to take the Power of Others.

- Live Life without engaging in Power Games.

- Heal the Source of Loneliness.

- Stop Identifying with the Roles that you play.

- The Rational Mind imposes False Limits.

- Freedom is a State of Being.

- Living in the Gap is Freedom.

- Use Imagination to Accelerate your Self- Healing Journey.

- The Therapy Trap.

Please take only what resonates with you. These insights and accelerators are common issues that many of us have to face on our healing journey. Some of them will apply to your journey and others will not. Only you will know.

****

How do I Know When Healing is Complete?

One of the challenges that I faced in healing myself was to know when the healing of a particular issue was complete.

How do I know if I have completely healed a barrier to Love? How do I know when all of the misalignments and all of the barriers to Love underlying a signpost have been healed?

It was often difficult for me to know when I had healed everything associated with a particular issue. This was particularly relevant for healing my emotional traumas because there were often many layers of emotions to be healed for one emotional trauma.

The one surefire way for me to know was to find out if the signpost that had pointed me at the barrier to Love in the first place was still there. Did I still feel the fear, emotional reaction, pain, or non-Loving motivation when I recalled the external event that had triggered the signpost? In essence, I would know that the healing of a barrier to Love was complete if the signpost was gone.

Thus, whenever I felt that healing might be complete, I would return to the signpost to see if it was still there. If I could still feel the signpost then I would know that there was more healing to be done. However, I would not know what was left to be healed. The barrier to Love that I had been working on may need more healing or I may have finished with that barrier and have a second barrier to Love that I needed to find and remove.

This confusion led to my occasionally wasting my time trying to heal a barrier to Love that I had already healed. For example, when the signpost was a pain or illness, I wouldn't give my body enough time to heal itself and would continue to try and remove a barrier to Love that was already gone. I also wasted my time trying to remove a barrier to Love that was healed when there was a second barrier to Love associated with the same signpost, and I didn't know it. Because the signpost was still there, I would think that I hadn't finished healing the first barrier to Love.

Eventually, I developed a process of tuning in to see if the healing was complete that did work for me. Once I felt that I had healed a particular barrier, I would visualize the external events that had caused the signpost to arise in me. If the signpost was gone then I would know that the healing was complete. If the signpost was still there then I would know that there was more healing to be done. I would then use insight meditation to ask to be shown, once again, the barrier to Love or misalignment that was triggering the signpost.

If I was shown the same barrier to Love that I had already been working on then I would know that I had not completely healed it. I would then continue the healing journey with that barrier to Love. On the other hand, if I was shown a different barrier to Love or a misalignment then I would know that the previous barrier had been healed and that it was time for me to move on to the next one.

After healing each subsequent barrier to Love or misalignment, I would again visualize the external events that triggered the signpost and repeat the process. I would do this until the signpost was gone. Only then would I know that everything related to that signpost had been healed. This process became my primary way for knowing when the barriers to Love and misalignments underlying a signpost had been completely healed.

Over time, I also learned to feel subtle shifts in my energetic body when healing occurred. I eventually became proficient at feeling the energetic disturbances in my energy body. I could then feel them be released when I healed a barrier to Love or misalignment. I would literally feel my energy shift and begin to flow freely. I would then know that I had healed something. However, I would not know if the healing was actually complete.

If I felt an energetic shift for a barrier to Love that was a fear, belief, or desire then the healing would typically be complete. This is because there is usually only one energetic disturbance underlying each of those barriers. However, I found that the healing of an emotional trauma was much more complex. There were often two or more energetic shifts required to complete the healing of a trauma. The first energetic shift would occur when the emotions that were stored alongside the memory of the original traumatic event were released. The second energetic shift would occur when the false beliefs taken on at the time of the trauma were let go. Thus, feeling an energetic shift take place was not enough to show me when an emotional trauma had been healed. To top it off, emotional traumas also often had multiple layers of emotions that needed to be healed.

How could I know when the healing of an emotional trauma was complete? I ended up adopting an inner child visualization technique for confirming that the healing was complete. I would visualize myself as the boy that I was when the trauma first occurred. I would then visualize myself sitting next to the boy and asking him if he was okay. If he was okay then I would give him a hug and invite him to merge back into me. If he merged back in then I would know that the trauma had been healed. If he didn't then I knew that I had more healing work to do. I would then do a cyclical process of healing a layer of emotions and repeating the visualization technique until he merged back into me.

I ended up with a three-pronged approach for knowing whether or not the barriers to Love and misalignments underlying a signpost had been healed.

1. I would tune in to see if I could feel when an energetic disturbance was released. If I could feel it release then I would know that a part, if not all, of a barrier to Love or misalignment had been removed.

2. If the barrier to Love was an emotional trauma then I would

repeatedly perform the inner child visualization until the traumatized part of me merged back into me.

3. Once I felt that a barrier to Love or misalignment may have been healed, I would check to see if the signpost was gone. If it was gone then I would know the healing was complete. If it was not gone then I would start the healing journey all over again in order to either finish healing the barrier to Love or misalignment that I had been working on or to begin healing the next one.

****

Only You Can Heal Yourself

Everyone is a healer and the only one they can heal is themselves.

You are the only one who can accomplish any true healing for yourself. Healing occurs when the barriers to Love and misalignments inside you are removed and the energetic disturbances that they created are released. Only you can remove those barriers and misalignments. No one can do it for you.

That said, I do feel that highly aware beings, such as His Holiness, can temporarily heal other people. They can remove an energetic disturbance and can support a body in coming back into a healthy state. However, if the barrier to Love or misalignment that created that energetic disturbance is not removed then the energetic disturbance will recur, along with any associated pain or illness. The only way to truly heal a disease or illness is to remove its source; the barrier to Love or misalignment that caused it.

I was told a story of a woman whose 15 year old boy was diagnosed with cancer. She was desperate to find a way to cure him and took the boy to see Sai Baba in India. Sai Baba apparently has the ability to heal others. She was able to gain an audience with Sai Baba and asked him if he could heal her son. In reply, Sai Baba looked at the boy and told him that he could remove the cancer but that the boy would not then receive the message that the cancer was bringing him. He asked the boy if he wanted him to remove the cancer. The boy said no.

Every physical and psychological ailment has a message for you. That message is a gift. True healing occurs when you hear the message and take the appropriate action. Only you can take that action.

****

Receiving a Wake-Up Call

As discussed earlier, it is possible to create a misalignment between the life that you are choosing to live and the life that you incarnated to live.

I invite you to open yourself up to the possibility that your soul incarnated to learn a set of soul lessons and to fulfill a soul purpose (see chapter *'10. Distractions'* for more information on a Soul Purpose). Your inner guide, or soul, is bringing experiences into your life that will give you the opportunity to learn those lessons and to fulfill that purpose.

If you are using your rational mind to direct your life, rather than listening to your inner guide, then you may be living a life that does not allow you to learn your lessons. In other words, your chosen life may not be in alignment with the life that your soul incarnated to live.

If this is the case then your inner guide may eventually resort to giving you a wake-up call in order to get your attention. My inner guide has done this for me on at least three occasions that I am aware of.

A 'wake-up' call is a message from a person's soul telling them to stop living the life that they are currently living and to start living the life that they incarnated to live. A 'wake-up' call typically comes in the form of a major life event such as a bankruptcy, the death of a loved one, a personal health scare, or a spiritual awakening. The person then makes a fundamental change in their life (heeds the call) and comes into alignment with the life they incarnated to live.

My first wake-up call occurred when I had an allergic reaction to antibiotics that scared me half to death. I spent a number of weeks in bed with severe joint pain. It was so debilitating that I was unable to move even a finger without being in agony. I also had swelling everywhere in my body, including in my neck. I vividly recall the terror of being driven to emergency with my throat swelling shut. I felt like I was going to die.

I was deeply shaken by that event. It took me a few weeks to physically recover and I spent that time questioning what I was doing with my life. I seriously considered making a change. I went for psychological counseling and briefly looked into finding a new career. The counseling that I found didn't resonate with me and I soon gave up on it. I also didn't know which way to turn career wise and the temptation of staying in my existing job was too strong for me to resist. I gave up on the job search and returned to corporate life. I ignored that 'wake-up' call.

The second 'wake-up' call happened while I was in the outback of

Australia. I was standing in the middle of the desert surrounded by the most profound silence that I had ever experienced. I then fell silent inside and experienced an inner peace that felt absolutely magical. I felt like I was being shown what life could be like. I came away from that experience feeling determined to find a way to feel that way always. That was my second 'wake-up' call and I turned my life upside down in order to respond to it.

The subsequent inner journey has not been an easy one and I have often wondered if I was losing the plot. Was I reading something into the experience in the outback that just wasn't there? Throughout my journey, a part of me had really wanted verification that throwing away a stable life in order to try and find my own way in the world was a worthwhile endeavor. I doubted myself and often struggled to keep putting one foot in front of the other.

Fortunately, my determination not to return to a life that I could no longer live was stronger than that doubt. Equally fortunately, I regularly came across inspiring words that left me feeling that finding my own way was a worthwhile endeavor. For example, I read a quote from Socrates that was like a balm for my tortured soul.

"The unexamined life is not worth living".

Exactly! I felt like I had spent my first forty years living an unexamined life and I agreed that it had not been worth living. I was more than ready to examine my life.

The words of Clarissa Pinkola Estes later came to me and they became like a lifeline for me.

"When a great ship is in harbor and moored, it is safe, there can be no doubt. But that is not what great ships are built for." (5)

I knew that I would have been safe remaining in the safe harbor of my corporate life. I could have worked for about fifteen more years, had a comfortable retirement, and then passed on. Life would have been 'safe'.

However, I had not incarnated to live a safe life. I had incarnated to live my life. I knew in my heart that remaining safely moored in harbor was not for me. I simply couldn't do that. Instead, I made the choice to 'set sail'. I went out in search of my own way in the world. There were many dark days on the subsequent inner journey and I leaned on the quote about great ships many times for inspiration. To this day, I remain deeply grateful to Clarisa Pinkola Estes for her words.

I was eventually able to embrace the decision that I had made to leave my society behind and to go 'walkabout'. I had left a 'safe' and 'unexamined' life in order to seek out my own life. And I was okay with that.

I came to feel that there was indeed such a thing as a 'wake-up' call, and that I had received two of them. The first one had been a frightening allergic reaction that had almost killed me. The second one had been a kind of spiritual awakening. I feel that both were messages from my inner guide telling me to stop living my chosen life and to begin living the life that I incarnated to live. Fear hadn't worked on me but Love had.

My third wake-up call came in the form of flesh eating disease.

I had returned to Vancouver after leaving the monastery where I had been studying with an enlightened master. I wanted to see my family and to work as a consultant in order to raise money for my next adventure. After a few months of being back in Vancouver, I had felt drawn to 'set sail' again. I had then struggled with the question of where to go.

I had been told about a Mexican shaman, by another guest at the monastery, and I wanted to seek out that shaman. All of my guidance was telling me to go to Thailand but I didn't want to go there. I thought that Thailand was a place for partying and prostitutes and I wasn't into either. I refused to listen to that guidance. I really wanted to study shamanism and, even though I had been told the shaman in Mexico was not taking on any new students, I still wanted to go and find him. I booked a flight to Oaxaca and began telling all of my friends that I was going to go walkabout in Mexico.

Shortly after booking that flight, I woke up one morning with a very sore ankle. It was red and I could barely stand. I hobbled over to a nearby clinic. The doctor there drew a circle around the red spot on my ankle and told me to take a taxi straight to the nearest emergency. He said that he would call ahead to tell them that I was coming. I didn't know what was wrong with my leg but I could tell from his response that it was urgent.

Instead of taking a taxi, I called a friend who lived nearby and she drove me to the hospital. They were waiting for me. They took me straight in and hooked me up to an IV drip of antibiotics. It was only then that I was told that I had flesh eating disease. I was scared. I thought that I might lose my leg or even die. I called my family to tell them what was going on and then did my best to remain calm. Fortunately, the doctors caught it in time and I didn't lose my leg.

I wasn't able to walk properly for the next few weeks and there was no way that I could go walkabout in Mexico. I didn't get on that flight. Instead, I remained in Vancouver recovering. I used that time to reflect on my next step in life.

It was clear to me that my wanting to go to Mexico had been coming from my ego not my inner guide. When I tuned into my inner guide and actually listened, I knew that Thailand was my next destination. I had learned my lesson. I was ready to follow my inner guide no matter what it asked of me. I also felt drawn to visit Bali and so I booked a flight to Thailand with a four week layover in Bali on the way.

I was then back in the flow of life. Bali turned out to be the place where my inner guide revealed to me, through poetry, what my inner journey was really all about. I then went on to Thailand where, instead of partying and having sex, I met a woman who taught me how to regress back into my past lives so that I could heal some deeply held traumas. That healing was a necessary part of my journey.

As a side note, I do not recommend delving into your past lives unless you feel strongly drawn to do so. I certainly wouldn't do it out of curiosity. Why? Because it can be an extremely painful journey both emotionally and physically. I feel that most healing can be done through the events of this lifetime and that it is not necessary, except possibly for a few core issues, to open up the door to past lives. Dealing with one's current lifetime is usually more than enough.

In my case, I had a few core issues that required me to relive my past lives. It was one of the most challenging things that I have done on my journey. I relived the traumatic events from those lives and felt all of the emotional and physical pain that I had felt at the time. Those traumatic events had created barriers to Love inside me that carried over from lifetime to lifetime. Those barriers were preventing me from allowing myself to be visible in the world in this lifetime. They were effectively blocking me from once again becoming some kind of spiritual guide. I had to remove those barriers to Love in order to live the life that I had incarnated to live.

In retrospect, I feel that I was guided to Thailand in order to heal those issues because I would not have been able to proceed with my life if I had not done so. Healing them had been so important to my journey that my inner guide had resorted to using flesh eating disease to make sure that I went there. The flesh-eating disease had been a gift. It had been a strong message that I had a misalignment between the life I was choosing to live (going walkabout in Mexico) and the life that I had incarnated to live (heal my barriers to becoming some form of spiritual guide).

I had tried to ignore my inner guide and the result had been a rather unpleasant 'wake-up' call. From that point forward, I have always done my best to follow my inner guide.

I feel grateful for having received all three of these 'wake-up' calls. I feel that they triggered me into bringing my life into alignment with the life that I incarnated to live. They also left me feeling that the message underlying a pain or illness could indeed be a misalignment between one's chosen life and the life they incarnated to live. Therefore, I added the possibility of such a misalignment to the process of becoming a self-healer.

I recommend that you simply remain open to the possibility that you too could receive a 'wake-up' call. With that openness, you will be able to respond to your 'wake-up' calls by resolving whatever misalignments exist in your life. If your 'wake-up' call comes in the form of a disease then you may even be able to heal that disease by resolving the misalignment.

****

Forgiving Someone Heals You Not Them

The journey of healing my deepest emotional wounds was often an extremely challenging one.

It was invariably shocking for me to recall a traumatic event. I had chosen to bury those events deep inside myself for a reason. It was often too difficult for me to actually face an emotional trauma when it first surfaced. I would need to return to the memory a few times before I could accept the possibility that it may have happened. This delay would leave me struggling with an open emotional wound. Eventually, I would begin to accept that the event may have happened and only then could I begin the healing journey.

My next big challenge came when I needed to forgive the other people involved. The emotions associated with the trauma were often so strong that I could not forgive them. When this happened, I would repeatedly set aside time to sit quietly, recall the event, allow myself to feel the associated emotions, and attempt to forgive. In many cases, I would end up beginning the healing process by 'pretending' to forgive. Pretending wouldn't actually accomplish any healing but it would open the door to my being able to forgive for real on another day. Eventually I would be able to forgive, while feeling the emotional pain, and I would have begun to heal that wound.

This process of repeatedly having to feel the pain from a traumatic event was not pleasant. I quickly became determined to find a way to streamline that process. Two realizations helped me to minimize the number of times that I had to recall an emotional trauma before healing it.

The first was the realization that *my inner guide will only surface an emotional trauma when I am ready to face it.*

No matter how shocking and excruciating the emotional pain associated with a traumatic event felt, I was ready to face it and heal it. That realization helped me to overcome any resistance I felt to allowing myself to recall a traumatic event and to feel the associated emotions.

The second realization was that *my forgiving someone heals me not them!*

This was a huge realization for me. Why hadn't anyone told me this before? I thought that forgiving someone was about setting them free of any guilt they may be harboring. It wasn't. It was about setting me free of the emotional pain that I was holding onto because of something I felt they had done to me. As long as I refused to forgive someone then the only person who suffered was me. Until I forgave them from the depths of my emotional pain, that pain would remain locked inside me and I would remain its prisoner. The only way to free myself from my own inner pain was to forgive everyone that I felt any animosity towards.

My resistance to forgiving others came from my wanting them to suffer for what I perceived they had done to me. That resistance fell away as soon as I realized that forgiving someone freed me, not them, from suffering. I was then able to forgive others more easily and to heal my emotional traumas much faster than before.

That realization also meant that it didn't matter if the other person knew that I had forgiven them. I could forgive someone in the privacy of my own room and it would be just as healing for me as forgiving them in person. Even if I did forgive them in person then their response to my forgiveness was none of my business. It was theirs.

I found that forgiving someone in private was usually the more appropriate approach for me. Any desire of mine to forgive someone in person was typically coming from my wanting to see if they were remorseful before actually forgiving them. Wanting to satisfy that desire was being non-Loving towards both me and them. It only delayed my healing journey and kept me imprisoned in my anger and pain.

I now choose to forgive people immediately upon realizing that I am harboring animosity towards them. I may later choose to tell them in person that I have forgiven them but only if it feels like my doing so would be Loving towards them. Their response to knowing that I have forgiven them is their business not mine.

I have been able to greatly reduce the time that I spend healing each of my emotional traumas through:

- trusting that I am ready to face any emotional trauma that is surfacing; and,

- realizing that forgiving someone heals me not them.

The huge benefit to me is that I now spend less time having to live with the emotional pain that surfaces along with each emotional trauma. I am able to quickly heal the trauma and release that emotional pain.

****

You have to Go from Feeling (not Thinking) to Being

The self-healing journey enables you to remove your barriers to Love so that you can return 'home' to who you really are. You cannot do that using your rational mind. You need to use your feelings because they are your signposts. You have to go from feeling, not thinking, to being.

Your rational mind is the source of the vast majority of your thoughts and you have to go beyond your rational mind in order to become Love. In fact, it is only your identification with your rational mind that prevents you from being Love. Your rational mind cannot take you beyond itself. Only your inner guide can do that. It is your inner guide, not your rational mind, that is going to lead you through the self-healing journey.

Your inner guide will support your healing journey by:

- bringing the circumstances into your life that will give you the opportunity to heal yourself;

- showing you the barriers to Love underlying your signposts;

- guiding you in aligning your life with the life you incarnated to live; and,

- leading you 'home' to Love.

The language of your inner guide is your feelings. Tuning into what you *feel* divinely inspired to do is to listen to your inner guide. Becoming aware of your *feelings* will show you when you have an opportunity for self-healing. Following your *feelings* down inside yourself to find and remove the underlying barriers to Love is the way to heal yourself. Your feelings not your thoughts are what you follow in going from being lost in the false self to being Love.

Giving precedence to my feelings over my thoughts was not an easy task for me. I spent the first forty years of my life treating the intellect as though it was the be all and end all. I had gone to university for an engineering degree and an MBA. I had then become a roaring success in the intellectual world of big business. I 'thought' that I could solve any problem using my intellect. I also believed that, if science couldn't prove it then it wasn't true. Rational thinking had been my way of life.

And then I had received a 'wake-up' call in the outback of Australia. That call showed me that there was something beyond the intellect and that an amazingly beautiful sense of inner peace existed in that space. I had then set out on a journey of self-discovery. I wanted to find a way of living in that space at all times and in all situations.

I started out by voraciously reading everything that I could find on the topics of self-help, Love, spirituality, philosophy, and anything else that came my way. I was like a sponge. I used my intellect to explore every possibility. That exploration began to open doors for me. Through it, I discovered a Love that I could become and was able to create a process for both healing myself and finding my way 'home' to that Love. My intellect was invaluable in getting me to the point where I could begin to heal myself.

However, it couldn't take me any farther. It could not heal me. For example, I couldn't use my mind to practice mindful awareness. Mindful awareness cannot be done from inside the mind because it involves observing the functioning of the mind and body. I also couldn't use my mind to cultivate self-Love. Self-Love is about excepting the way I *feel* not about accepting the way I think I feel. The language of self-Love is "I feel" not "I think". In order to heal myself, I had to learn trust my inner guide rather than my rational mind.

My rational mind was actually a hindrance in healing myself. It delayed my self-healing journey in the following ways.

- My rational mind made it difficult for me to fall silent inside and hear my inner guide. I would get caught up in the thoughts of my 'monkey mind' rather than patiently waiting to receive guidance from my inner guide.

I also struggled to tell the difference between when my thoughts were coming from my inner guide versus from my rational mind. As a result, I spun my wheels for weeks and months at a time while trying to intellectually figure out what to do rather than simply falling silent inside and waiting for my inner guide to show me.

- My rational mind would interfere with my ability to actually follow the guidance that I received. Even when I was able to hear my inner guide, my rational mind would want to know why I was feeling drawn to either go somewhere or do something. If it didn't like the idea of doing whatever it was then it would jump in with all kinds of logical reasons as to why I shouldn't do it. I would then be stuck between my mind's reasoning and my inner guide's guidance.

This inner battle between my rational mind and my soul caused many dark nights of the soul. The only way through those dark nights was to continue doing my best to follow my inner guide and to patiently wait for the dark night to lift.

- My rational mind would get in the way of my being able to retrieve answers from my inner guide during an insight meditation. It would jump in with what it thought was the answer. Once in a blue moon, it would actually have a lucky guess and give me the answer that I needed but most of the time it wasted my time by having me chase down its wrong answers.

- My rational mind's efforts to mentally forgive people had me thinking that I had healed something when I hadn't. Early on in my journey, I didn't know that healing would only occur if I forgave someone while actually feeling the emotions that I felt towards them. Instead of doing that, I would mentally forgive someone for a perceived slight and would think that I had healed that issue. I hadn't. I had to feel it to heal it.

The self-healing journey clearly showed me that I was going to have to free myself from identifying with my rational mind. It didn't matter if I could quote every beautiful word ever said by the Buddha, Christ, Mohammed, Osho, Marvin the Martian, Lao Tzu, and every other being that has passed through this beautiful planet of ours. Nothing would change. I would remain identified with the false self and would be incapable of healing myself and of bringing any Love into the world. I could not think my way to being.

I became determined to free myself from my own rational mind.

My attachment to functioning in the world through my rational mind definitely delayed my self-healing journey. However, I was eventually able to drop my attachment to intellectual knowledge and to turn my journey over to my inner guide. Doing that greatly accelerated my journey.

I highly recommend that you focus on cultivating your ability to listen to your inner guide over your rational mind. If you can trust your inner guide then your healing journey will also be accelerated.

Please be patient with yourself. It is unlikely that you will be able to drop all of your attachments to functioning in the world through your rational mind overnight. I suggest that you simply set out on your healing journey. You can then use the self-healing process to practice functioning in the world with your inner guide in charge rather than your rational mind.

I also invite you to give more credence to the way you feel than to what you think. You may even want to do an exercise that I found very useful on my own journey; eliminate the words 'I think' from your vocabulary. Instead of saying, "I think ....', say 'I feel .....'.

I remain grateful to my rational mind to this day and still use it as the beautiful tool that it is. Yes, it was a hindrance to my actually being able to remove my barriers to Love and heal myself. However, it helped me to understand what was possible. For that, I am deeply grateful. Also, please remember that the self-healing journey is not about destroying the rational mind. It is about emptying it of the ego so that it can then be a servant to Love. My rational mind is still in place and is now acting on divine inspiration, for the most part, rather than rational thought. I say for the most part as I am still removing the remnants of my ego from the shadows of my mind.

****

Be Honest with Yourself about the Way You Feel

If you want to become a self-healer then it will be necessary to give yourself permission to feel the way you do. If you deny the way you truly feel then you will remain a prisoner of your barriers to Love and you will not heal yourself.

You will need to be absolutely honest with yourself about the way you feel. You will have to accept when you feel shame, lust, jealousy, guilt, and so on in order to then be able to find and heal the underlying barriers to Love. Your feelings are your best friends in becoming a self-healer. If you resist the way you feel then you will only slow down your healing journey. Thus, another way to accelerate your journey is to embrace self-Love and accept the way you feel at all times.

That was often a struggle for me. I didn't like to admit to myself that I was angry, jealous, ashamed, or lustful. Throughout my upbringing, I was taught to think of those kinds of emotions as wrong or even sinful. I was conditioned to suppress them as deeply as possible.

Denying the way I felt had therefore become my modus operandi. That denial had made me an acceptable and highly 'successful' member of my society. However, it had also resulted in my having toxic energy floating around deep inside me just waiting to emerge in the form of an emotional outburst or even a disease. In order to heal myself, I was going to have to allow those suppressed feelings to surface and to be brutally honest with myself at all times about the way I felt.

I didn't find much support in doing this from the people around me. My friends and family were from a society that said things like "*you shouldn't get angry*", "*there's no reason to be jealous*", "*don't be sad*", or "*the only way to get over a woman is to get under a woman*". My conditioned mind was very good at running those kinds of statements through my head whenever I felt any of the so called negative emotions arising.

In order to be honest with myself about the way I felt, I had to ignore both my own mind and the well-meaning words of everyone around me. I had to give myself permission to feel the way I did no matter how nonsensical those feelings may have seemed to myself and others. If I felt angry, jealous, or sad then that's the way I felt. My feelings were, and still are, my 'truth'.

One simple 'trick' that helped me to let myself feel the way I did was to drop the word 'should' from my vocabulary. For example, I found that my ego would jump in and tell me that I shouldn't feel angry. My ego always then came up with some ego-based reason why I shouldn't feel the way I did. For example, it would often say either that it was wrong to feel angry or that the situation didn't merit anger. However, it didn't matter whether or not my ego thought that I should or shouldn't feel angry. If I felt angry then I felt angry. My feelings were all that mattered.

Unfortunately, I would often find myself agreeing with my mind that a given scenario shouldn't make me feel angry. I had to learn to simply accept that, if a scenario made me feel angry then it made me feel angry. No amount of rationalizing was going to change the way I felt inside. The only way that I was going to free myself of that anger was to accept the way I actually felt. Only then could I delve inside to find and heal the barrier to Love that was triggering those feelings. If I either denied my feelings or convinced myself that I shouldn't feel the way I did then I would remain a prisoner of the false self.

I was able to accelerate my healing journey by eliminating the word 'should' from my life and being honest with myself about the way I felt. I highly recommend that you do the same for yourself.

****

Feeling Stuck is an Indicator of Fear

I often felt completely 'stuck' on my journey.

Feeling stuck involves having no direction in life and not knowing how to find a direction. It is a feeling of being lost with no way out.

The times when I felt stuck were dangerous ones for me. They were intensely frustrating and I would often struggle to avoid feeling like everything that I was doing with my life was pointless. My mind would scream at me to 'give up' and go back to a 'normal' life. A battle would then rage on between my mind's wanting to give up and my inner determination to find my way home no matter the cost. The cost seemed rather high during those painful periods.

I would often remain 'stuck' for days, weeks, or even months at a time. I had no idea what to do about this feeling of being stuck when it arose. I would either just ride it out or make a decision, any decision, in order to try and shake things up. Invariably, I would end up having to face a seemingly endless period of frustration and despair. It sucked.

And then I was told that the feeling of being stuck comes from fear. I wondered if that could be true. I reflected on the times in my own life when I had felt stuck. Had I actually been afraid of doing something during those times? I had. I realized that my feelings of being stuck had invariably been caused by one of two fears:

- the fear of facing an emotional wound that was surfacing; or,

- the fear of following the guidance of my inner guide.

The first of these, the fear of facing an emotional wound, came from my knowing that I was going to have to feel the deep emotional pain associated with that wound. I was often reluctant, and even afraid, of allowing myself to do that. As a result, I would avoid facing it and would feel stuck.

There were two things that helped me to overcome this particular fear. The first was the fierce determination that I felt to find my way 'home' no matter what came my way. The second was a definition of pain and suffering that strongly resonated with me.

Pain is the short term result of facing yourself and suffering is the long term result of not.

I didn't want to suffer any longer and I was determined to face whatever surfaced from inside me regardless of any associated emotional pain. I knew that the only way for me to free myself from that pain was to face it and to then heal the associated emotional wound. The combination of my inner determination and my desire to end my suffering meant that the fear of facing an emotional wound rarely kept me feeling stuck for very long. I would simply jump in and face the emotional pain.

On the other hand, the fear of following the guidance of my inner guide often kept me feeling stuck for extended periods.

For example, I had felt strongly drawn to go to India but was afraid of going into such uncharted waters on my own. My ego's fear of going to India was stronger than the feeling of being drawn to India and so the fear had won that day; and many other days. That fear prevented me from going to India for many months. I spent that time constantly feeling lost and stuck. Another example came when I felt drawn to visit the Osho ashram in India. For many months, my fear of what people would think of me if I went there prevented me from going.

There are many more examples from my journey where fear had stopped me from following my inner guide. It was clear to me that my being afraid of following my inner guide was the main source of my feeling stuck.

This was a wonderful thing for me to realize. Now that I knew that fear was underlying my feelings of being stuck, I could overcome it. All I had to do was find the fear, free myself of the barrier to Love underlying that fear, and then either face the emotional trauma that was surfacing or follow the guidance of my inner guide. The feeling of being stuck would then fade away. This process is described in exercise '*8 – Freeing yourself from feeling Stuck*'.

Since realizing that fear underlies the feeling of being stuck, I have rarely felt stuck for long.

****

Healing Depression – the Failure to Accept 'What is'

What is depression and how do I heal it?

I faced a number of bouts of depression on my self-healing journey. In my society, I was taught to handle depression by either pulling myself out of it, taking pharmaceuticals, or waiting for it to pass ("*time heals all wounds*"). None of those approaches were very effective for me.

I am not a fan of pharmaceuticals because I feel that they will just numb me rather than heal me. Thus, I did my best to avoid that approach. That left me with the two options of either pulling myself out of depression or patiently waiting for it to pass.

I tried pulling myself out of depression many times and found that I could usually do it for sadness but rarely for depression. On the rare occasions when I was actually able to pull myself out of a depression, I would only stay out of it for a little while before sinking back in. I came to feel that pulling myself out of depression was a temporary solution at best and that it was really just a futile attempt to avoid it.

That only left me with one option; waiting for it to pass. That did seem to work for me but it would often take weeks and even months for the depression to lift. I would be absolutely miserable throughout that time. I would also resort to distracting myself with things like alcohol, partying, skiing, movies, and porn. Basically, that option for depression meant that I had to endure weeks of suffering intermingled with bouts of self-abuse. I didn't particularly like this option either.

Where did that leave me?

Basically, it left me with no effective options for healing depression.

My society didn't seem to have an approach that I could embrace. I was resigned to feeling that I was just going to have to suffer through my bouts of depression while doing my best to patiently wait for them to pass. I wanted to find another way to deal with depression but didn't know where to look.

My not knowing how to handle depression became an increasingly pressing issue for me as I walked my own path 'home'. Depression initially hit me pretty hard in the immediate aftermath of my choosing to leave the corporate world. I refer to that period for my life as my 'year long summer of discontent'. Eventually I did come out of that depression but it was a long and painful ride. I then faced a few other bouts of depression and they were all, invariably, rather debilitating. My healing journey would basically be put on hold until after the depression had passed. I really needed to find a way of healing the source of depression rather than simply waiting it out.

I then came across the idea that meditation was known as 'The Great Medicine' and that it could be used to heal depression. Supposedly, I could consciously allow myself to go into a breakdown and meditation would help me break through to the other side. I was game for anything and decided to give this approach a try. Whenever depression hit me, I would sit in silent meditation and let the depression grow stronger and stronger inside me. I would sit in meditation for days on end. All the while, I was doing my best to patiently wait for the breakthrough.

It didn't work. I would still be depressed for interminable periods of time. Eventually, the depression would simply begin to lift and I would become functional again. I felt like I was still missing some key piece to the puzzle.

I was in India when I was finally given that missing piece. I was told that psychological pain is the gap between 'what is' and 'what you want it to be'.

If this was true then I finally had the answer to healing depression. It meant that my bouts of depression were coming from my wanting things to be different than they were. The solution to depression was then to accept whatever it was that I wanted to be different than it was.

I was elated when I first heard this statement. I knew in my heart that it was the key that I had been looking for. I had been trying to break through depression using patience and meditation, and it had not been working. Now I had another way. Instead of trying to silently meditate my way through depression, I could instead delve inside to find out what it was that I was refusing to accept. If I could then accept it then the depression would lift. I had been so close! I had been sitting in meditation for hours trying to break free of depression rather than sitting in meditation and asking to be shown what it was that I was resisting.

Could this be it? Could this be a way for me to heal depression? I was excited about giving this new approach a try. If it worked then I wouldn't have to spend days, weeks, and even months feeling depressed any more.

From that point forward, whenever I felt depressed, I would use insight meditation to find whatever it was that I was resisting. I would sit in silence, allow the feeling of depression to grow stronger inside me, and ask my inner guide to show me what I was refusing to accept. I would then accept whatever it was. I would often have to remove some kind of fear or other barrier to Love before I could actually accept it but accept it I would. I then discovered, much to my delight, that the depression would lift. This approach worked! I had found a way to heal depression. Woohoo. This process for healing depression is described in exercise '17. *Healing Depression'*.

It took me a few false starts before I was able to master this technique for healing depression. In the beginning, I struggled to hear my inner guide and found myself sitting in depression for extended periods of time. That was not fun.

I also found myself wanting to get out of the depression so badly that I would listen to the answers that my rational mind came up with rather than waiting for my inner guide. I then wasted time trying to accept what my rational mind thought I was resisting. The depression wouldn't lift because my rational mind didn't know what I was resisting. Its input was all just guess work. I had to learn to patiently wait for my inner guide to show me the answer.

With practice, I became proficient at using this process to rapidly heal any depression that arose in me.

This was an immense breakthrough for me on my self-healing journey. Depression had temporarily derailed my journey many times over. No more. My relationship with depression had changed from it being something that I had to endure to it being something that I could use as a healing opportunity.

A Cautionary Note

I would not recommend that you adopt this approach unless you have both cultivated a mastery over mindful awareness and have support from people who have mastered this approach for themselves.

Why do I say that?

This meditative approach to healing depression is a challenging one. It asks you to sit in an insight meditation and allow the depression to grow stronger inside you. You then have to patiently wait for your inner guide to show you whatever it is that you are resisting. Depression can be an overwhelming emotion and this process may require you to allow the feeling of depression to almost consume you before you will be shown what it is that you are resisting. That can be too much for a person to handle on their own.

The most challenging part of this process for healing depression is allowing yourself to sit in depression and let it grow stronger and stronger. That is not a fun ride. However, it is a necessary part of the process of finding the source of your depression. Why? Why do you have to feel the full strength of your depression before you will see whatever it is that you are resisting?

It is because your ego is trying to protect you from something that it perceives as a huge threat. It is your ego that is refusing to accept 'what is' and your ego is not going to let go of that resistance without putting up one hell of a fight. Your ego will likely do its best to convince you that the resistance is in your best interests. It will also do everything that it can to block you from seeing what you are resisting. In order to find the source of your depression, you are going to have to find a way past ego's resistance.

I eventually discovered that the best way to break through my ego's resistance was to stop fighting with it. I did that by sitting, or sometimes walking, in silence and allowing the depression to become intensely strong inside me. Basically, I was surrendering to my ego's resistance. With nothing to fight, my ego would eventually 'give up' and my inner guide would then be able to show me whatever it was that I was resisting.

This would sometimes take many days. All the while I would be sitting, or walking, in depression and asking to be shown whatever it was that I was refusing to accept. It would eventually work. I would see whatever it was that I was resisting. I could then remove the part of my ego, the barrier to Love, that had been in resistance and accept whatever it was 'I' had been resisting. The depression would then lift.

For example, I was in Vancouver the last time depression hit me. I gave myself the luxury of spending two days walking around the city in silent meditation. I was not fighting the depression. I was letting it become stronger and stronger while asking to be shown whatever it was that I was resisting.

On the second afternoon, I was walking across the Cambie Street Bridge when I stopped and looked over the side. The depression was so intense that my mind wanted me to jump over the edge. I was amazed at how quickly my mind had gone from being at peace with life to wanting it to end. That spiral downwards had taken less than two days. Fortunately, I had cultivated the ability to use mindful awareness to simply watch the antics of my own mind rather than succumb to it. With that ability, I was able to simply smile at the craziness of my own mind and walk on.

That evening, I saw what it was that I had been resisting, removed the barrier to Love that had put me into resistance, accepted 'what was', and the depression lifted. I would not have been able to do that without having the ability to watch my mind rather than identify with it. If I had been identified with it then the risk of jumping off that bridge would have been high.

That is why this is not an easy process. It requires you to be able to sit in ever deepening depression without being consumed by it. Mindful awareness enables you to do that. Mindful awareness gives you separation from the emotions flowing through you and allows you to hear your inner guide even when depression is coursing through you.

Thus, I highly recommend that you cultivate mindful awareness before attempting to use this process on yourself. I also recommend that you only use this process when you have twenty-four hour a day support from someone who has mastered this process for themselves.

Depression can have a debilitating effect on a person's life. However, with mindful awareness and support, you can use this process to heal depression. Doing so will greatly accelerate your healing journey.

****

Breaking Free of Guilt

Guilt is a toxic energy to hold inside oneself. Holding onto guilt will prevent you from:

- learning the lessons from your life;

- having Loving interactions with others;

- giving heartfelt apologies to those you may have hurt; and,

- releasing any anger that you feel towards yourself.

Furthermore, the barriers to Love underlying your guilt will have created energetic disturbances in your energy body. Those disturbances may lead to pain or illness if you do not release them.

Guilt is highly toxic.

I was once told that there are only two enemies of man; guilt and fear. I recommend that you free yourself from both.

My own journey into guilt began when I was invited to scream out everything that I felt guilty about during an intense therapy session. It all came spilling out. I felt guilty for:

- the little white lies that I had told throughout my life;

- using women for sexual gratification;

- throwing my anger at my mother and others;

- calling off a wedding one week before the wedding date;

- stealing a bar of chocolate when I was a child;

- impregnating a woman who then chose to have an abortion; and,

- so much more.

I yelled all of this out during that session and felt deeply sad afterwards. The abortion was especially tough for me. I knew that the guilt over that incident was eating away at me and that I needed to find a way to heal it.

In another session, I was asked to state everything that I did to avoid feeling guilty. Again, my list was rather long. For example, I would:

- often visit my parents out of guilt not Love;

- do things for girlfriends that I did not want to do;

- hide my naked body because I had been taught that it was wrong to be seen nude; and,

- avoid speaking the truth about the way I felt about someone in order to avoid feeling guilty if I was to hurt them.

These two sessions opened my eyes to the influence that guilt was having on my life. I felt guilty about many things and was letting guilt affect the way I interacted others. I wondered if there were other ways that guilt had been impacting me throughout my life.

The one thing that jumped out at me was the way my mother had used guilt to manipulate me. She had used it to either get me to do the things she wanted me to do or to train me into becoming a 'perfect English gentleman'. For example, she would say "Big Boys don't cry" and that would leave me feeling guilty if I did cry. She also told me that it was a sin to lust after a woman and that it was wrong to be seen naked. Those kinds of statements left me feeling guilty as hell if I either found a woman sexually attractive or, heaven forbid, allowed someone to actually see me naked. She had used guilt to brainwash me and I had fallen for it hook, line, and sinker.

To make things even worse, I had adopted her approach. I was ashamed to admit to myself that there had been times when I had also used guilt to get others to do what I wanted. I did not like what my mother had done to me and hated to think that I had done the same to others. That had to stop.

I also felt that guilt was blocking me from being able to have intimacy in my life. I had discovered that intimacy with others comes from being open and honest about the way I feel in every moment. However, my fear of feeling guilty would not always allow me do that. For example, I would not express how I felt to a woman if there was any lust arising in me. Instead I would feel guilty about feeling lusty and would try to ignore the woman. Also, I would not tell someone how I really felt about them if I thought that my words might hurt them in any way. I didn't want to feel guilty.

I was sick and tired of functioning in this way. I wanted to have Loving interactions with people not guilt ridden ones. Okay, so guilt was playing a rather huge role in my life. I:

- was feeling guilty about many actions from my past;

- was avoiding doing things that could leave me feeling guilty;

- had been brainwashed using guilt;

- had used guilt to get others to do what I wanted; and,

- could not create intimate relationships with others because of my fear of feeling guilty.

Wow. I had a lot of work to do if I was going to free myself from guilt.

The first step was clearly to let go of all the guilt that I felt over my past actions. That would free me from the toxic energy that I was carrying around inside myself. The second step was to make a commitment to myself to stop doing or saying anything just to avoid the possibility of feeling guilty. If I could do that then I could stop letting guilt control my choices in life, let go of my brainwashing, and create intimate connections with others. The final step was to avoid doing anything that would result in my taking on board any new guilt.

Freeing Oneself of Guilt Step 1: Let go of Guilt over Past Actions

I had a 'list' of items that I felt guilty about from the therapy session in which I had screamed everything out. Simply becoming aware of those items was enough for me to let go of a lot of them.

Awareness was my starting point for letting go of guilt. I recommend that you also bring awareness to everything that you feel guilty about. There is a useful exercise for doing exactly that. It is a group exercise that is done separately by men and women.

Two circles of chairs are set up; one for men and one for women. The chairs are positioned in a tight circle so that people's foreheads would be almost touching if they were to lean forward. The men sit in one circle of chairs and the woman in the other. Each group then leans forward in their chairs so that their heads are almost touching. One person from each group then starts by whispering one thing that they feel guilty about. They speak softly so that only the people in their circle of chairs can hear them. After the first person has spoken, the person to their left whispers one thing that they feel guilty about and on it goes around the circle. The group then keeps going around the circle again and again until everyone has expressed everything they feel guilty about. None of what is said in this exercise is spoken about again. This exercise is described in exercise '*18. Expressing Guilt out Loud*'.

This exercise brings awareness to all of the things that we feel guilty about. It also invites people to express those things out loud and it is deeply healing to let out our guilt in this way. Expressing what we feel guilty about in front of others will liberate you from a great deal of your guilt. However, there will likely be a few items that you still feel guilty about even after doing this exercise. There were for me.

For those items, I found that I could heal them by:

- apologizing from the depths of my heart to all those that I had hurt;

- learning the soul lesson that my past actions had to teach me; and,

- forgiving myself.

This process is described in exercise '*19. Letting go of Guilt over a Past Action*'.

For example, I did this with the guilt that I felt over the woman I impregnated and who had an abortion. In my mid-twenties, I had briefly dated a beautiful, raven haired, woman from Vancouver. We had a wonderful sexual chemistry between us, but little else. It soon became clear to me that we were not compatible as long term partners. I was thinking about ending the relationship when she told me that she was pregnant and that the baby was mine.

I was shocked and scared by her news. I didn't want to be a father at that point in my life and I didn't feel like the woman and I had any future together. I didn't know what to do.

We were sitting at a table next to a small café in a downtown shopping mall when she told me. I was on a break from work and would have to go back shortly. I knew that I had to say something and I did my best to be both supportive of her and honest about the way I felt about the pregnancy. We talked about our options.

From the way she had told me about the pregnancy, I had the distinct impression that she wanted me to tell her that I would marry her and that we would have the baby together. I couldn't bring myself to do that. I didn't love her and couldn't see myself spending the rest of my life with her. Instead, I told her how I felt about her and that I did not want to live with her or get married. I did offer to provide financial support from a distance if she chose to have the baby.

She was clearly upset by my reaction to the news and my heart broke. I really didn't know what to do. She then told me that she wasn't sure if she wanted to have an abortion. She had already had one abortion and her doctor was not happy about her being pregnant again. He had told her that abortion was not a form of birth control.

There wasn't anything left to say at that point. After a few moments of silence, she stood up and told me that she was going to think about whether or not to have the baby. She said that she would let me know what she decided. She then left.

I was in a daze. I did my best to calm my turbulent emotions and then headed back to work. I felt very unsure of what I really wanted. Did I want to provide financial support to her and the baby? Did I want to be a part of the baby's life? Did I want her to have an abortion? I am not proud to admit that I was hoping that she would choose to have an abortion. I was feeling very selfish.

She called me later that same day and told me that she had decided to have the abortion. She also said that she didn't want to see me anymore. She was clearly upset and I didn't know what to say. I felt sure that I had hurt her deeply by not offering to marry her. Before I could speak, she asked if I would pay for the abortion. I said that I would be happy to. I was in shock at how fast everything was moving. She closed off the conversation by saying that she would let me know how much it cost and then hung up.

I felt terrible and my first thought was that I hadn't even asked her if she wanted me to go with her when she had the abortion. I was not happy with myself. I had not treated her very nicely throughout this whole process. More than that, I was denying a child the opportunity at life. Oh God, what was I doing? My heart was aching.

And I did nothing about it. The part of me that just wanted this to go away was stronger than the part of me that wanted to do the 'right' thing.

She called me a few days later to tell me how much the abortion would cost and we met one last time for me to give her the money. That was our last encounter and I again didn't offer to go with her. By then I had the feeling that she didn't want anything to do with me. I didn't hear from her about how the abortion went. She was gone from my life.

I felt riddled with guilt over this episode in my life for many years afterwards. I felt guilty towards her for the way I had treated her when she gave me the news, for actually hoping that she would have an abortion, and for not offering to go with her when she had it. I had not been loving or supportive throughout the whole process and I didn't like myself very much.

However, the guilt that I felt towards her paled in comparison to the guilt that I felt towards the aborted soul. I knew in my heart that I had denied a soul an opportunity at life and I was devastated by that knowledge. I felt like a selfish bastard. Many times over the intervening years, I had sent her and the unborn child my deepest apologies but nothing had changed. The guilt had kept eating away at me.

This guilt had surfaced with a vengeance when I yelled out everything that I felt guilty about in that therapy session. It was the one thing that I felt the most guilty about. Expressing it out loud did nothing to take away the feelings of guilt. I knew that I had to heal it and I finally had the tools with which to do so.

I took the memory of the abortion into a meditation and felt desperately sorry for what I had done. I could feel the guilt building and allowed it to grow as strong as it wanted in me. I found myself falling into deep despair at the magnitude of the guilt that I was carrying. I even felt a physical pain in my heart that I had clearly been trying to live with.

I then started to flash through memories of my relationships with other women. I could see how my fear of repeating a similar 'mistake' had been impacting my interactions with them. I was a mess when it came to relationships with women.

I let myself fall ever deeper into the despair and guilt. The physical pain in my heart grew stronger. It was an excruciating journey but I stuck with it. I felt like I deserved to be punished and was almost glad to be suffering so much.

I was sitting in this stew of emotional and physical pain when something very strange happened. I had my eyes closed and was looking inwards. I then saw a 'vision' of a dark snake-like being crawling around inside me. I recoiled at this image and it took me a moment or two to grasp what I was seeing. It was like I was looking into a 'room' inside me with objects in it like a fridge and furniture. The snake-like thing was crawling out from behind the fridge.

I was too shocked by what I was 'seeing' to question what the heck was happening to me. I fixated on watching this repulsive thing moving around inside me. As the shock died down a little bit, I started to feel strangely happy to have discovered that it was there. I had the feeling that it somehow represented the guilt that I was carrying. I did my best to relax and simply watch it crawling around inside that room.

As I did so, the feeling of grief deepened and the physical pain in my heart became insanely intense. It felt like my heart was on fire. It was all I could do to remain present with the pain. It was a brutal ride. I was a physical and emotional wreck. I stuck with it. The level of sorrow that I felt for what I had done was consuming me. From the depths of all of that pain, I sent the woman and the unborn child a heartfelt apology. The apology came from the very depths of my being and I almost cried out in anguish as I sent it out.

I was still observing the snake-like thing and watched as it scurried out of me after I had apologized. The image of it and of the room that it had been in then disappeared. I felt an amazing sense of relief to have that thing out of me and my abdomen released a tension that I hadn't even known I was holding.

I began to cry. I felt like something inside me had let go when I had made that heartfelt (literally) apology. The tears seemed to be washing away the feelings of guilt and despair. I cried it all out and even the pain in my heart began to dissolve. The tears slowly came to a halt and I eventually sat up.

I was amazed by what had just happened. I was certain that the dark being inside me had somehow represented the guilt that I had been carrying. I had the feeling that it was specifically connected to the child. I felt like I had freed myself from the guilt by sending out that apology and that the snake-like thing leaving me was symbolic of my letting go of the guilt. I was free of that source of guilt.

However, my healing journey for that abortion wasn't over just yet. I was still feeling deeply angry with myself. The apology had released the guilt but not the self-flagellating anger. I knew that I would suffer endlessly if I didn't forgive myself for everything I had done. I didn't want to. I felt like I deserved to suffer for my horrible mistake. I just sat there feeling both relieved to be free of the guilt and very angry at myself for having screwed up so badly in the first place.

After a few minutes, I decided to at least try and forgive myself. I went through the motions of uttering words of forgiveness. I wasn't actually forgiving myself, and was wondering if there was any point in continuing, when I felt a strong urge to learn the lesson from that episode with the abortion. I continued to sit in meditation and shifted my focus to asking to be shown the lesson that I was to take away from this event. I soon started to clearly see that I had made two mistakes. I had allowed sexual desire to rule my actions during the actual sexual encounter and had allowed fear to drive me from then on.

I had been more than happy to have sex, regardless of any potential consequences, because I was inflamed with desire. I hadn't really cared about taking the added precaution of wearing a condom. When my sexual partner had later told me that she was pregnant, I had let my fear of what may happen if she didn't have an abortion drive my interactions with her. I had been incredibly selfish and unloving.

I felt that my lesson in all of this was to acknowledge that,

> *If I chose to have sex with a woman then I am choosing to accept that I must respond from a place of Love and compassion towards her no matter what comes out of our sexual encounter. If she becomes pregnant, upset, jealous, or anything else then I must respond with Love.*

I embraced that lesson. I set the intention to always respond with Love towards a woman no matter how she reacted to having sex with me. As I set this intention, I could feel the anger that I was holding towards myself begin to loosen. I was then able to forgive myself.

The healing journey for the abortion was complete. I had finally been able to let go of the guilt that I had been carrying and my whole being felt different. My abdomen felt lighter, my heart felt bruised but open, and I felt like a weight had been lifted off my shoulders. I was exhausted. I treated myself very gently after that journey.

I was also both amazed at the process that I had just gone through and deeply grateful that it had happened. I did not question the 'vision' that I had seen and just accepted that it was somehow part of the healing journey. The memory of the abortion has remained with me to this day but the guilt and anger at myself are both gone.

I went through a similar process with everything from my past that I still felt guilty about even after expressing it out loud. It was not always pleasant for me to face my guilt but doing so left me feeling lighter and more at peace with myself.

I spent most of my life feeling guilty and it was a tremendous relief to free myself from it. More than that though, I feel that my holding onto guilt for so long had:

- prevented me from learning the lessons from my life;

- impaired my ability to have loving interactions with others;

- stopped me from giving heartfelt apologies to those that I had hurt; and,

- blocked me from releasing anger that I felt towards myself.

Healing my guilt over my past actions was an extremely liberating thing to do for myself. It also enabled me to learn many of the lessons that I had incarnated to learn.

Freeing Oneself of Guilt Step 2: Stop doing things just to avoid feeling Guilty.

I was then free from guilt over my past actions but not from allowing guilt to affect my interactions with other people. It was time for me to stop doing or saying things just to avoid feeling guilty.

There were four different scenarios that I had to address. I had to:

- stop doing anything out of obligation;

- stop allowing others to use guilt to manipulate me;

- stop using guilt to manipulate others; and,

- stop lying about the way I feel in order to avoid feeling guilty.

I will discuss each of these four scenarios in turn.

(i)   Stop doing anything out of obligation.

The only reason that I would do something out of obligation would be to avoid feeling guilty if I didn't do it.

Unfortunately, when I did something out of obligation I was not being Loving. Consciously or subconsciously, I would feel resentful towards those I felt obligated to and the resulting interaction would invariably be unpleasant for all concerned. I wanted to have Loving interactions with people and knew that my doing anything out of obligation would prevent me from being able to do so.

For example, I spent many years going to my parent's house for Sunday night dinner out of obligation not Love. By the end of the evening, I would usually be feeling angry towards my mother and would not be Loving towards her. I didn't like myself when I did this and didn't know what to do about it. Even my brothers noticed and would ask me why I was so angry with our mother. I didn't know. I badly wanted to heal this issue of mine.

I started to play with not doing anything if I felt obligated to do it. I would then take the feeling of obligation into an insight meditation. I would visualize the scenario that made me feel obligated, allow that feeling of obligation to grow stronger inside me, and ask my inner guide to show me the real reason for my feeling that way. The root cause was invariably something like anger, jealousy, fear, or a false belief. I would then follow that feeling down inside myself to find and remove the barrier to Love underlying the feeling. The feeling of obligation would be gone once that barrier had been removed.

I would then visualize myself doing what I had previously felt obligated to do. If I felt drawn to actually do it then I would do so the next time that the opportunity arose. I would then be doing it from a place of Love not obligation. On the other hand, if I didn't feel drawn to do it then I wouldn't.

This process for letting go of obligation is described in exercise '20. Freeing Yourself from Feeling Obligated to do Anything'.

In the case of visiting my parents, the feeling of obligation came from my deep-rooted anger towards my mother. I healed that anger and the feeling of obligation was gone. I was then free to choose, from a loving inner space, whether or not I felt drawn to go for Sunday night dinner with them. On most occasions, I would choose to go and was doing so from a Loving inner space. I then began to enjoy having dinner with them.

I now use any feeling of obligation that arises as an opportunity to heal one more barrier to Love. If I feel obligated to do something then I won't do it. Instead, I will delve inside to find and heal the root cause of that feeling. Once the feeling is gone then I will then choose whether or not I feel drawn to do whatever I had previously felt obligated to do.

(ii)   Stop allowing others to use guilt to manipulate me.

My mother had been a brilliant practitioner in using guilt to manipulate me. She did this both to get me to do what she wanted and to have me become what she wanted me to be; a proper English gentleman.   As a result, I had come to mistrust her and was constantly on guard against her trying to manipulate me.   That mistrust had carried over into my relationships with all women. I did not trust them and would not let them into my heart.

I wanted to heal this mistrust and the feeling of resentment that I held towards women. I knew that the only one who could make me do anything in life was me. It was me who had chosen to become what my mother wanted me to become. She had used guilt to try and push me in a certain direction but it was me who had made the choice to become that proper English gentleman.

I knew that blaming anyone for the way I felt was just a way for me to avoid taking responsibility for my own life. There was a big lesson in all of this for me. That lesson was to always be true to who I am no matter what anyone else says or does. It was time for me to take responsibility for the choices that I made in my life and to stop blaming others. I accepted that it was me who had given up on me. I embraced the lesson of always being true to myself no matter what anyone else thinks, says, or does.

I was then able to forgive my mother for her manipulation and to forgive myself for having given up on me. I was then free of both the anger towards my mother and my mistrust of women. It no longer mattered if they tried to manipulate me into doing something, I was only going to do what I felt drawn to do.

I was free of my fear of others manipulating me through the use of guilt. I was free to be me. I was also free to Love women.

(iii)   Stop using guilt to manipulate others.

During that healing journey, I had clearly seen how damaging it had been for me to have my mother use guilt to manipulate me. Her doing so had strongly affected the way I lived my life and how I interacted with women. I felt that there was nothing Loving about using guilt to manipulate anyone.

I also knew that that I had picked up the habit of using guilt to get others to do what I wanted. I did not want to play that game anymore. I sent a silent apology to those that I had manipulated in the past. I also set the intention to stop using guilt, or any other tool, to try and manipulate others.

(iv)   Stop lying about the way I feel in order to avoid feeling guilty.

I had a pattern of not being completely honest with people for fear of feeling guilty if they were hurt by anything I said or did. I had become a 'nice guy' who always tried to say and do the 'right' thing. In other words, I was a pathological liar that could not be trusted.

This was pointed out to me by a woman at a healing program that I attended. She spent one lunch hour trying to get me angry. She succeeded but I wouldn't show it. She said all kinds of nasty things to me and I just kept doing my best to be 'nice'. I said all the 'right' things even though I was seething inside. Eventually, she stood up and said, *"This is why I don't trust you, you won't tell me you're angry even when you obviously are."* She then stormed away.

I was shocked. I had thought that being a 'nice guy' was the 'right' way to be. I was now being told that my being a 'nice guy' meant that I couldn't be trusted. Was this true?

I looked into this issue deeply and realized that it was. My being a 'nice guy' did indeed make me untrustworthy. It had basically turned me into a liar. I was not telling people how I really felt because of fear. I was afraid of what they may think of me and I was afraid of hurting their feelings. I was hiding from myself and others. It was definitely time for me to drop the nice guy persona.

The challenge for me in letting go of being a 'nice guy' was that I still didn't want to hurt anyone. Fortunately, I had come to realize that I didn't have to feel guilty for expressing the way I felt as long as I expressed myself in a Loving way. I could do that by stating how I felt:

- without blaming others for my feelings;

- without asking anyone to change; and,

- with owning that the source of my feelings was inside me.

It was time for me to drop the 'nice guy' facade and start being honest with myself and others. I then began to express myself openly and honestly, and the walls between myself and others came tumbling down. I began to have beautiful, intimate, and Loving connections with people for the first time in my life.

I am deeply grateful to the woman who told me that she could not trust me because I would not tell her that I was angry even when I was. She gave me a tremendous gift that day. She broke me of playing the role of the 'nice guy' and that freed me to begin Loving myself and others.

Freeing Oneself of Guilt Step 3: Stop taking on Board any new Guilt

I was working hard to free myself from the guilt that I had felt over my past actions and the last thing I wanted to do was to take on any new guilt.

I knew that the way to avoid taking on guilt was to always interact with others in a Loving way. As long as I am coming from Love then I am not responsible for another person's emotional response to me. I do not then have to incur any new guilt for my words or actions.

I set the intention to always interact with others from an inner space of Love. What does that mean? What does it mean to always interact from an inner space of Love?

I can either interact with someone from Love or from ego. I cannot do both. If I am interacting with someone from ego then there is no Love present in my thoughts, words, or deeds. For example, if I am either espousing a belief, expressing an opinion, wanting to be right, seeking to satisfy a desire, trying to avoid a fear, or lashing out from an emotional wound then I am interacting from ego. I have fallen from grace and am functioning from a barrier to Love. I will then take on new guilt if another person's ego or body is hurt in any way by my having interacted in that way.

On the other hand, I will not take on any new guilt if I interact with others in a Loving way. I can do that by:

- sharing the way I feel without blaming the other and without wanting the other to change;

- being playful in a way that does not disparage anyone or anything;

- sharing my experiences when I both feel inspired to do so and am not attached to how the other person responds;

- remaining silent inside and out; and,

- performing a creative act from a silent inner space.

I am not perfect and I do not always manage to interact with people from a Loving inner space. When I do fall from grace, by becoming non-Loving, then I will apologize, learn the lesson that the event is teaching me, heal the barrier to Love that triggered my fall, and forgive myself for being non-Loving.

That is the end of the description of the three-step process that I used for freeing myself from guilt. I have a feeling that it would also work for you. Regardless of the process that you choose for freeing yourself from guilt, I highly recommend that you do so. Guilt is toxic.

****

Practice the Art of Listening

The art of listening involves listening to others from a silent inner space.

From that inner space, there is no desire to respond to anything that the other person says. You simply remain present and listen to them without becoming defensive, without judgment, without getting lost in your thoughts, and without thinking of how to respond to what is being said. You are listening from an inner space of Love and you are creating a Loving environment for others.

You are also giving yourself the opportunity to accelerate your self-healing journey. While practicing the art of listening, you are not to take anything that the other person says personally. It does not matter if the person likes or dislikes you. How they feel about you is a reflection of their inner world not a reflection of you.

However, they may say something that triggers an emotional reaction in you. If that happens then you are being shown that a barrier to Love inside you has been triggered. You then have the opportunity to heal that barrier to Love. The process for doing so is described in exercise '*2. Healing the Source of an Emotional Reaction*'.

In this way, practicing the art of listening, while owning your emotional reactions, can accelerate your healing journey.

****

Take Back Your Power

Arguably the greatest power struggle going on in the world today is between individuals. This is a struggle that many are not even aware of. It has arisen because people have become lost in the ego and have fallen into the pattern of playing power games with each other. If you are going to become a self-healer then you are going to have to walk away from the ego-based power games.

The societal reflection of those power games can be seen in the battles being played out between countries, religions, corporations, cities, and even sports teams. If individuals stopped fighting over power then the societal battles would also end.

What do I mean by power games?

We all have an internal source of power that provides us with both self-confidence and the ability to make decisions regarding the direction of our own lives. Unfortunately, we are constantly giving our power away to nations, religions, corporations, elders, competitors, the things that we identify with, and anyone we consider to be superior to us in any way. The result of giving our power away is that we allow others to make decisions for us, we do non-Loving things at the bidding of others, and we suffer from issues of self-esteem, self-confidence, and self-worth.

What is this power that we are fighting over?

It is an inner power that arises when we abide in a state of being, or level of awareness, that enables us to remain true to ourselves in every situation. Standing in one's own inner power is an act of self-Love.

Power is very different from force. Force arises when we attempt to manipulate and control another into doing our bidding rather than allowing them to follow their own will. Using force to manipulate others is a violent act of the ego.

This distinction between power and force is described in great detail in the book 'Power versus Force' by David Hawkins.

Lao Tzu also describes the difference between power and force in the following quote from the 'Tao Te Ching'.

> *"Knowing others is intelligence; knowing yourself is true wisdom. Mastering others is strength; mastering yourself is true power. If you realize that you have enough, you are truly rich."*

Mastering others is a display of force. Mastering yourself, meaning your own ego, is true power. I highly recommend that you stop using force to pursue ego-based goals and instead step into your own inner power.

You do that by ending your participation in the power games of the ego and taking back your own life. You explore all of the ways that you give away your power and set the intention to stop doing it. You will then step into your own inner power and regain your self-confidence, sense of self-worth, and self-esteem. You will also take mastery over your own life.

How do we give our power away? The following list of examples can be used as a starting point for reclaiming your life.

Take Back your Power

- *Stop caring about the opinions of others.* If you care about another person's opinion of you then you become their prisoner. Be your own person in the world and ignore everything that others say about you.

- *Drop your identification with any Nation or Institution.* You give your power away to everything that you identify with. For example, if you say 'I am American' then you are giving your power away to the leaders of America. They can then use the combined power of all Americans to exert force over other nations. They can even go so far as to ask you to either kill for them or give up your life for them.

  Religious wars are another example of how the leaders of an institution can use the power that their followers have given them to use force against others.

- *Step out of Group Mind.* There is a mob mentality or 'group mind' associated with every group. If you identify yourself with being a member of a group then you take on the characteristics of that 'group mind'. For example, if I say that I am a Vancouver Canucks hockey fan then I can get lost in the energy of wanting my team to win. I may even start to dislike fans of other teams or even get involved in a riot. I have given my power away to the 'group mind' of being a Canucks fan.

  There are a myriad of examples of how you can take on a group mind. You can follow a belief system, identify with a race, become a member of a political party, call oneself a male from London, and so on. The alternative to getting lost in a 'group mind' is to simply state that you are no 'thing'. That enables you to then simply remain as the essence of who you are; Divine Love.

- *Drop your attachment to Pride*. You give your power away to anything that you are proud of. You are a prisoner of pride. You may even fall so far from Love that you would fight to defend something that you are proud of.

- *Recant all Vows and Oaths that you have made*. You give your power away every time that you make a vow or oath. Vows and oaths create a bondage. The alternative to making a vow or oath is to live in the moment and make Loving choices in present time.

- *Pay your debts, do not take on any new debts, and do not put another into debt*. Neither a borrower (give your power away to another) nor a lender (take the power of another) be.

- *End all Co-dependent Relationships*. If you are dependent on another for anything, including your happiness, then you are giving your power away to them. You can choose to relate to people from an inner space of Love rather than enter into a co-dependent relationship with them.

- *Stop wanting to be told what to Believe.* Every belief is false. If you are looking to others to tell you what to believe then you are giving your power away to them.

- *Stop allowing yourself to be Manipulated or Bullied into doing something.* If you allow others to use force or manipulation to get you to do something that you would not otherwise do then you are giving them your power.

- *Avoid Guru / Disciple relationships with anyone other than a true master*. A disciple gives their power away to a guru.

  A 'true master' is one who has integrity, is selfless, and will not abuse your power. They will not tell you what to believe and will not have you say or do anything in order to fulfill their own personal agenda or beliefs. In the Zen tradition, a true master will initially take a disciple's power and then give it back to them once they are ready.

  Beware of false gurus. Anyone who gives you a pleasant sensory experience or asks you to believe in them is likely a false guru. A false guru will use the power that you give them to further their own ego-based agenda. Avoid false gurus. I recommend that you live your life rather than someone else's.

- **Stop respecting others**. The term respect is a game of the ego. It creates expectations. The ego creates an image of what it will respect and then judges others based on that image. If I respect someone then I am typically putting them on a pedestal and am giving them my power. I may then try to emulate them and may also give their words precedence over my own inner truth. Wanting to respect another is a sign of low self-esteem.

  The alternative to respecting another is to Love oneself first and Love others second.

- **Stop becoming your Emotions**. You become your emotions when you identify with them. For example, if you say that *"I am angry"* then you have become that anger. You are then giving your power away to the emotion of anger and hence to the person who triggered that emotion. Anger, jealousy, and lust are examples of emotions that we give our power away to.

  We also give our power away to emotions such as happiness and excitement. If I seek happiness or excitement then I have given my power away to that search and to anyone who can temporarily provide it.

  Instead of becoming an emotion, you can choose to delve inside to find and remove the barrier to Love that triggered it.

These are just a few examples of the ways in which you can give away your power. I highly recommend that you take back your power from everything that you have given it to. There are two exercises at the end of this book that you can use to take back your power: '*21. Connect to your Inner Power and Retrieve your Self-Esteem*'; and, '*22. Open your Heart and Take Back your Power*'.

Is it ever appropriate to give away your power? There are a few scenarios in which it may be appropriate to *temporarily* give your power away to another.

Temporarily giving your Power Away

- **Parent and Child**. It does feel appropriate to me for a parent or guardian to take the power of a child for the early years of that child's life. A baby is not able to survive without the support of an adult and someone must initially take responsibility for its care. Ideally, the parent will always act from Love towards the child and will give the child back its power as it grows up.

- ***Spiritual seeker and Guide.*** A spiritual seeker may give their power to a spiritual guide *temporarily* while they are moving through the inner process of dissolving the ego. Ideally, the spiritual guide will be someone who is focused solely on connecting the seeker to their own inner guide and will give the seeker back their power as soon as they do. Beware of the 'False Guides' who would take your power with no intention of returning it to you.

- ***Community Member and Societal Structures.*** In order for people to gather together in community, it may be appropriate for the people in that community to give their power over to the structures of their society. Ideally, the leaders of the society would be selfless and the structures would be designed to always provide Loving service to the community.

- ***Patient and Healing Practitioner.*** A patient may choose to give their power over to a healing practitioner during a healing session. The healing practitioner would then do whatever is necessary to keep the patient's body alive while guiding the patient in healing themselves. The patient's power would be returned to them at the end of the healing session.

The qualities that I recommend you look for in anyone who you are going to temporarily give your power to are *selflessness, humility, integrity, and Love.* If your guides, societal leaders, and healing practitioners do not display ALL of these qualities then I recommend that you take your power back from them.

I would also recommend that you begin taking your power back from your parents as you move from childhood to adolescence and take it all back as you move from adolescence to adulthood.

****

Stop Trying to Take the Power of Others

The flip side of ending the game of giving your power away to others is to stop trying to take the power of others. The following list contains a few common ways in which we try to take another's power.

- **Wanting to either fix or change another.** If you are trying either to get another person to change or to fix' the way they feel then you are in your ego. You are not being Loving and you are not allowing the other person to live their own life. You are attempting to take their power away from them.

- **Blaming another for the way you feel.** If you are blaming another person for the way you feel then you are not taking responsibility for your own journey. All of your emotions are sourced from inside you. Another person can only trigger you to become emotional if you have an unhealed barrier to Love inside you. They did not create your emotional reaction. Your unhealed barrier to Love did. Blaming another person for the way you feel keeps you trapped in your ego and prevents you from healing the source of your emotions.

  By blaming another, you are essentially trying to get that other person to change rather than heal yourself. You are attempting to take their power away.

- **Manipulating another into doing what you want.** If you try and manipulate someone into doing what you want, either through the use of force or arguments, then you are attempting to take away their power.

- **Preying on another's desires, needs, or fears in order to get them to do what you want.** This is a subtle form of manipulation. You are taking advantage of the insecurities of others to get them to do what you want. This is an attempt to take the power of others in order to satisfy your ego.

- **Attempting to convince another that either you are right or they are wrong.** The desire to be right is a game of the ego. If you attempt to convince another person that you are right about anything then you are trying to take their power away. The ideas of right and wrong exist only in the world of the ego. In the words of Rumi, "*Out beyond the ideas of wrongdoing and rightdoing, there is a field. I'll meet you there.*"

- **Seeking Sympathy or solace.** If you want another to give you sympathy for the way you are feeling then you are trying to suck their energy from them. You are asking them to stop being Loving towards you and to give you their power by engaging in your story. The alternative to seeking solace is to share how you are feeling without asking for any response. You can then delve inside yourself to find and heal the source of your physical or emotional pain.

- **Imposing your Burdens on others.** If you are feeling burdened and invite another to validate your need to carry that burden then you are attempting to take their power away. The alternatives to feeling burdened are either to put down your burden or to perceive whatever you are carrying as a Loving service rather than a burden.

- **Fear mongering.** It is only the false self that feels fear. The higher self, or soul, is eternal and it cannot be harmed by anything in this physical world. There is nothing to fear. If you are afraid of something and try to get someone else to be afraid of it as well then you are attempting to take their power away. Rather than spread fear, you can choose to heal the source, inside you, of your fears.

- **Sacrificing yourself for another.** If you feel that you are sacrificing yourself for another then you are consciously or unconsciously attempting to put them under a debt of obligation. You are attempting to take their power away. You can stop playing this particular power game by ending all ideas of sacrificing yourself. Instead, you can simply be of Loving service to others.

I recommend that you bring your awareness to when you want to take the power of another. That desire for power is coming from your ego and its surfacing is an opportunity to heal yourself. Instead of acting on that desire to take the power of another, you can choose to instead delve inside to find and remove the barrier to Love that is triggering it.

****

Live Life Without Engaging in Power Games

I also recommend that you be diligent about living your life without playing the power games of the ego. One way to ensure that you avoid those power games is to follow this suggested approach for living your life.

- **Practice Mindful Awareness**

    Bring mindful awareness to everything that you do so that you can become aware of when you are about to either give your power away or try to take the power of another. Whenever you find yourself feeling drawn into the power games, stop. Do not do it. Instead, delve inside to find and remove the barrier to Love that led you to want to engage in those games.

- **Practice Self-Love**

    If you are able to Love yourself then you will be able to heal your issues of low self-esteem and low self-worth. Simply being you will then be enough, and there will be no need to give your power away. There will also be no need for you to take the power of others. You will be able to express how you are feeling without blaming others and without asking another to change in any way.

- **Maintain constant access to your own Inner Power**

    If you have access to your own inner power then there will be no need for you to indulge in the power games of the ego. I recommend that you set the intention to cultivate your ability to access your inner power.

    You do this by opening your third chakra and healing any issues that you have around self-esteem, self-worth, and self-confidence. Allow yourself to be guided to those who can support you in cultivating access to your own inner power.

- **Learn to Distinguish Truth from False**

    In this context, truth is a state of being. Truth can only be stated by the Divine within. That can only happen when the mind has fallen silent and the false self has gotten out of the way. The mind and body are then a clear vessel for Love to speak through.

    Everything said from the ego is considered to be false. Every opinion, judgment, and statement of mental knowledge is false. For example, the sky is not even blue. Once you go beyond the false self, you will see what is really in the sky.

Even a person's 'current truth' is considered to be false. The 'current truth' for a person includes both the way they feel in the present moment and their current perception of everything that they have experienced. One's 'current truth' only has validity in the present moment and will become false as soon as the person heals the source of their feelings and shifts their level of awareness.

You can learn to distinguish between when truth, 'current truth', and false are being spoken. Truth comes with an energy of Love and is being spoken by the divine within a person not by the person. If you are blessed with the opportunity to hear truth then I encourage you to simply fall silent inside and listen.

It is also possible to distinguish between when a person is speaking their 'current truth' from their heart versus when they are talking about their feelings from their ego. This distinction is very important on the self-healing journey. A person has the opportunity to heal themselves when they are speaking from their heart and are actually feeling the emotions that they are describing. There is no healing opportunity available to a person who is simply talking about their feelings from their ego.

I recommend that you cultivate the ability to feel the difference inside yourself when you are speaking from your heart versus from your ego. You can then ignore anything that your ego says. There is nothing that your ego can state that will help you on your healing journey. However, everything that you state from your heart will help you. You can then explore the way you feel deep inside and remove your deeper barriers to Love.

I also recommend that you cultivate the ability to 'hear' when another person is speaking from their heart versus their ego. That ability will enable you to be able to support them on their healing journey. You will be able to guide them out of their ego and deeper into their heart.

- **Cultivate Compassion for yourself and others**

    Compassion is love plus meditation.

Compassion for others is practiced by listening to another from a silent inner space. You are practicing the art of listening while remaining in a silent inner space. You simply listen without any judgment, opinion, desire to respond, desire to change the other, or desire to fix the other.

Compassion for yourself involves accepting the way you are currently feeling without any judgment, opinion, or denial.

- **Take responsibility for your own life**

  Choose to interact with yourself and others from an inner space of Love. You do that by:

  o   accepting yourself and others the way they are;

  o   dropping all judgments of yourself and others;

  o   taking ownership of your own emotions as being sourced from inside you;

  o   stopping blaming others for the way you feel;

  o   letting go of caring about the opinions of others; and,

  o   looking to your own inner guide, rather than others, for direction in life.

****

Heal the Source of Loneliness

I often found myself feeling lonely during the many years that I spent traveling the world seeking answers. I felt drawn to walk much of my journey alone and so I did. I didn't particularly enjoy feeling lonely and just felt that it was something I had to endure.

It was only when Osho came into my life that I discovered the possibility that loneliness may actually be something to heal rather than something to endure. He distinguished between loneliness, which is the absence of another, and aloneness, which is presence of oneself. I am missing others when I feel lonely and I am content with myself when I am alone. This distinction intrigued me and I immediately understood it. I enjoyed being by myself much of the time and only occasionally felt lonely. This distinction between alone and lonely could explain why.

I feel lonely when I miss other people. There is something that I think I need from having the companionship of people that is driving that feeling of loneliness. Loneliness stems from an unmet need. If I can find and remove that need then the feeling of loneliness will dissolve. In its place will again arise the beautiful feeling of aloneness.

This realization opened the door to my being able to heal the underlying source of loneliness rather than having to endure it. The first step was for me to accept that I was a needy man. That was difficult for me to do. Pride kicked in and my ego tried to tell me that I was not needy. After all, I had walked away from my career, my friends, and family in order to find myself. Didn't that show that I didn't need anyone? No, it simply meant that my determination to find my way home was stronger than my neediness. It didn't change the fact that the neediness was still there. I had to accept that I may not always be needy but there were times when I was. I was ready to explore the possibility that my loneliness did indeed stem from my neediness.

I began to use loneliness as a signpost indicating that there was an unmet need arising inside me. Whenever I felt lonely, I would go into a meditation and allow myself to feel the loneliness as deeply as I could. I would then ask my inner guide to show me the unmet need. It worked. I would invariably find an unmet need. That need was stemming from a barrier to Love which I would then remove and the loneliness would dissolve away. I didn't have to endure loneliness any more. I could heal it instead.

This process for healing loneliness is described in exercise '23. *Freeing Oneself from Loneliness*'.

For example, I would often feel lonely while travelling the world on my own. I explored the source of that loneliness and found that it came from a need to feel loved and appreciated by others. Underlying that need was both a desire to feel content and happy and a belief that being surrounded by people who loved me would satisfy that desire. That desire to be happy was the true source of my loneliness.

If I could let go of that desire then I would heal the source of that particular loneliness. That was a challenging journey for me. I wasn't able to simply drop that desire. I began the healing process by dropping the belief that I would be content if only I had people around me who Loved me.

I already knew that this belief was based on a lie. My friends and family had Loved me while I was working in the corporate world and I hadn't been happy. In fact, I had been miserable. I had also found numerous 'communities' of like-minded people on my travels. A number of them had welcomed me with open arms and yet I had always moved on. My sense of discontent was not satisfied by a community no matter how loving it was. The belief that being with Loving people would satisfy my desire for happiness was definitely a lie.

I was half way through the healing journey. The belief was gone. The next step was to actually let go of the desire for happiness and contentment. I knew in my heart that the discontent I was feeling stemmed from something far deeper than my simply being unhappy with my current life. It stemmed from my being disconnected from the Love that I called 'home'. I knew that the only thing that was going to alleviate the emptiness that I felt inside me was to return 'home' to Love.

It was time to drop the desire to find happiness and contentment in the external world. Dropping that desire was rather easy for me to do. I had already discovered that the only way I was going to find the contentment that I was seeking was to return 'home' and become Love. In other words, I would need to awaken. I made the choice to hang on to the desire to become Love and to let go of the false hope that I would ever be able to find happiness and contentment in the external world. I did that by renewing my intention to follow my inner guide wherever it led me and to stop chasing happiness and contentment in the world around me.

I later discovered that the desire to become Love is known as the highest desire. It is to be held onto until all other desires have been dropped. Once they have been dropped then even this highest desire is dropped too.

Feeling lonely has become increasingly rare for me. It now makes no difference to me whether I am alone or in the company of others. Either way, I feel an underlying sense of inner peace. I am essentially alone (have presence of self) at all times. Aloneness has become my inner state of being and loneliness has pretty much disappeared from my life.

****

Stop Identifying with the Roles You Play

A simple exercise revealed one of the biggest illusions that I held about myself. It shattered a part of my ego that I hadn't even known was there. The exercise was about dropping my identification with any roles that I was playing in life.

We are reinforcing the false self when we identify with the roles that we are playing. For example, if I say that I am a consultant then I am identifying myself with the role of consultant. I am then taking on a set of false beliefs based on all of the assumptions and images about what it means to be a consultant. For example, the clothes that I wear, the places that I go, the activities that I perform, and the way that I interact with potential clients are all influenced with my being identified with being a consultant. I am a prisoner of the consultant role.

The conditioning that I take on board by identifying with all of the roles that I play in life then becomes huge. For example, if I say that I am a Canadian, I am a traveler, I am a writer, I am a man, I am a brother, and I am a son then I am identified with each of those roles. Each of those identifications comes with its own set of false beliefs based on my assumptions and images of what it means to play each of those roles. Those sets of identities become a part of my false self.

I then act differently with people depending on the role that I am playing in any given moment. 'I' am putting on a different part of my false self, a different mask, depending on whether I am 'acting' as a son, a brother, a consultant, a friend, a writer, or a lover. I am a chameleon. I present a different view of myself to different people, and none of those views are real.

The alternative to taking on all of those false identities is to realize that I am not any role that I play. A simple exercise helped me to do that. The exercise involved having me walk around outside and say things to myself like 'I am a writer'. I was then to say to myself 'No I am not'. I was to do this with all of my roles and, for each one, I was to accept that the role I was playing was temporary and did not define who I really was. I was told to even include roles that were body dependent such as man, brother, and son.

This exercise was fun for me at first. I was happy to drop my identification with the roles that I had been playing throughout my life. It was easy for me to drop my identification with roles such as 'consultant' because I knew that a career was just a temporary thing. I found it a little harder to drop roles such as 'brother' and 'man' but I was also able to do that too. I knew that the body was not me. I had experienced existing outside of my body and I had relived being in many different bodies in other lifetimes. Thus, I was able to let go of identifying with any roles that were based on the body that I was currently in.

Everything was going beautifully until I said 'I am a spiritual seeker'. I stopped dead in my tracks. The feeling that came over me then was one of 'Oh shit'. I realized that I had built up a whole identity around defining myself as a spiritual seeker. The clothes I wore, the places that I went to, the books I read, and even how I perceived myself, were all based on my thinking that I was a spiritual seeker. None of it was true. None of it. Oh shit.

I stood there in a state of disgruntled shock as this realization sank in. I knew that I had messed up big time. I had trapped myself into an identity that was not me by thinking that I was a spiritual seeker. I had been strengthening my false self and blocking myself from being able to return 'home'. I was not a spiritual seeker! I was no 'thing'. It was time for me to stop defining myself as any 'thing' at all!

I felt like I had really screwed up and beat myself up over my idiocy for a little while. How could I have been so stupid as to move from being 'Corporate Bruce' to 'Spiritual Bruce'? They were both traps of the ego and all I had done was swap one jail cell for another. What an idiot!

This self-flagellation didn't last for long. It soon dawned on me that playing the role of a spiritual seeker may well have been a necessary intermediate step for me. It had allowed me to break free of the strong bonds that had kept me imprisoned within the conditioning of my society. I had stepped out of the 'Corporate Bruce' prison and into the 'Spiritual Bruce' prison but that may have been a 'good' thing. Doing so had enabled me to break free of my identification with 'Corporate Bruce'. All I had to do now was drop my identification with 'Spiritual Bruce' and I would be completely free.

Dropping that identification was easy. In fact, I had let it go the instant I realized that I had made a mistake. I was now out of both prisons. I was no longer 'Corporate Bruce' or 'Spiritual Bruce'. I was no 'thing'. I was free! I no longer had to limit what I said or did based on my having to be spiritual. I was not spiritual anymore. I simply was. This was one of the most liberating realizations of my entire journey.

I highly recommend this exercise to anyone who wishes to break free of the conditioning that keeps them locked in their own false self. The exercise is described in exercise '24. *Stop Falsely Identifying with the Roles you Play'*.

****

Identification with the Rational Mind Imposes False Limits

My rational mind was the single greatest obstacle that I had to overcome in order to become a self-healer and find my way 'home' to Love.

We have already discussed dropping our identification with the rational mind in the section above on being addicted to rational thinking. Here, we are going to expand on that discussion by briefly exploring the false limits that you impose on yourself by identifying with your rational mind.

I took a convoluted journey to discovering those limits. I spent the first forty years of my life honoring the intellect above all else. That resulted in my living a life that was not mine and did not work for me. I had then gone out in search of another way of being in the world.

I didn't find anyone in my society who knew of such a way. My friends, family, co-workers, and even a career counselor that I hired to help me were all locked into their own rational minds and were of no help to me. It was only when I came across the words of people such as Rumi, Bob Samples, and Albert Einstein that I discovered that there may be another way. These people, and many others, all seemed to be pointing at the idea that it was possible, and even highly beneficial, to go beyond the limitations of the rational mind.

Rumi hinted at the need to go beyond rational thought in his poetic way:

> *"Out beyond the ideas of wrongdoing and rightdoing, there is a field. I'll meet you there."*

The following quote from Bob Samples (which is often attributed to Albert Einstein) states it in a much more direct way:

> *"The intuitive mind is a sacred gift and the rational mind is a faithful servant. We have created a society that honors the servant and has forgotten the gift." (6)*

Lastly, Einstein suggests that the intellect cannot lead our lives, it can only serve.

> *"And certainly we should take care not to make the intellect our God; it has, of course, powerful muscles, but no personality. It cannot lead, it can only serve." (7)*

If the rational mind cannot lead our lives then what can. All of these quotes are pointing at the existence of something beyond the rational mind. Bob Samples called that something the 'intuitive mind' and I call it the 'inner guide'. The name doesn't matter to me. What is important is that there may be something beyond the rational mind that you can access.

I accessed my inner guide through a combination of meditation, dream interpretation, and automatic writing. I then followed its guidance and was pleased to discover that it both knew my way home and that it had the answers that I was looking for. I was freeing myself from my rational mind and, along the way, was discovering the false limits that came with being identified with the rational mind.

One meditation technique in particular, Dynamic Meditation (Dynamic), showed me just how limiting it was to live life with the rational mind in charge. Dynamic was created by Osho and involves five stages: chaotic breathing; catharsis; jumping up and down with one's hands in the air; freezing on the spot; and, celebratory dance. I was told that it was extremely powerful to do Dynamic for twenty-one straight days. I did it for thirty-five.

I got up at 5:30am every morning, which was hard for me, and headed off to do Dynamic. I found it to be highly beneficial but not earth shattering for the first couple of weeks. The main benefit that I received from it came during the catharsis stage where I was surfacing a great deal of the anger from my childhood. I was then able to take that anger away and work on healing it. This benefit kept me going back day after day.

It was not easy. I struggled with the third stage in particular. The third stage involves jumping up and down on the spot with your hands in the air and landing with flat feet. You are to chant 'Hoo' as you land. I was told that the intent of this stage was to get the Kundalini energy at the base of the spine moving. I found this stage to be utterly and completely exhausting.

For the first sixteen days, I hadn't come close to being able to jump up and down for the full ten minutes. On the seventeenth day, I was again struggling to jump and down when I had an 'aha' moment. I suddenly realized that my mind was telling me that this stage was too difficult for me. I wondered what would happen if I stopped telling myself that. I kept jumping and ignored my mind's thoughts about how hard it was. I then had no trouble doing it. It was actually easy for me. My body hadn't been stopping me, my mind had. My body could do it easily. Holy shit!

That was the moment when I first knew, from my own experience, that my mind was setting artificial limits on my body's capabilities. As I effortlessly jumped up and down, I felt like I was capable of almost anything as long as I stopped listening to my own mind. I did the rest of that stage with a smile on my face. I had discovered the value of listening to the body, not the mind, when it came to one's physically capabilities. The mind has no say whatsoever in setting the body's limits. This was a huge breakthrough for me.

I discussed this realization with the facilitator of a Satsang group that I was attending at the time. He verified it for me and then took it one step further. He shared this realization with the whole Satsang group. He talked about trusting the body and not allowing the mind to artificially limit the body's potential. He then added a rather amusing addendum. He told the men in the room to trust their penises when it came to selecting a sex partner. He said that the penis knows much more than the mind about the appropriate woman for us to be with. Laughter burst out all around the room but he wasn't laughing. He was serious! He went on to say that our bodies know what we need to learn through a relationship with a woman. Therefore, our body is much better at selecting a partner than our rational mind.

Really? I was intrigued by this possibility and pondered whether or not I would actually do it. Would I let my penis choose my partner? Did it really know what I needed to learn from a relationship? I had to agree that my mind had proven to be rather clueless, and had often been a huge hindrance, on this journey. I also felt that liberation from my rational mind was a key component in finding my way 'home'. However, was I willing to take that all the way to ignoring my mind's input when it came to selecting my sexual partners? Was I willing to listen to my penis?

No, I didn't feel ready to trust my erection. I still felt like I had way too many issues going on down there. I decided to make a compromise. I would be open to involving my penis as one of the factors in selecting a potential partner, just not the only one.

After this experience with the third stage of dynamic, I began to pay more attention to each stage. I found that my resistance to giving one hundred percent during any stage was pointing out ways in which my rational mind was holding me back.

Breathing Stage - Any resistance that I felt towards the rapid and chaotic breathing stage was a reflection of my *reluctance to embrace life.*

Catharsis Stage - If I didn't go absolutely crazy during catharsis then I was allowing my rational mind to *block me from accessing the way I was truly feeling.*

Freezing in Place Stage - During the fourth stage, if I allowed myself to scratch an itch, clear my throat, or move in any way then I was being shown that my mind was *trying to have me avoid myself* in some way.

Celebratory dance Stage - If I was either feeling self-conscious or 'trying' to dance in the final stage then I was in my mind and *not allowing myself to be me.*

Dynamic Meditation was extremely powerful for me. It showed me how my rational mind was imposing false limits on me by:

- blocking me from embracing life;

- preventing me from accessing how I truly felt;

- imposing artificial limits on my body;

- trying to have me avoid whatever was surfacing; and,

- stopping me from being me in the world.

These limitations have huge implications for the self-healing journey. If I could not access how I truly felt, and would not let issues surface from within, then I would not be able to heal myself. It was definitely time for me to drop my identification with my rational mind.

From that point forward, I used mindful awareness to catch myself whenever I said 'I am ......'. I knew that I was not whatever came after the words I am. I am not a writer, consultant, man, lover, or any other role. I am not even hungry or sad. Hunger or sadness can exist in the body but I am not those things. I am no 'thing'.

I recommend that you open yourself up to the possibility that your rational mind is imposing false limits on you. It is blocking you from becoming a self-healer and from living your own life.

****

Freedom is a State of Being

A simple exercise changed my perspective on what 'Freedom' was really all about.

In this exercise, we were first asked to take a few moments to meditate on what we wanted 'freedom from'. I was soon mentally rattling off a whole list of things. It included my conditioned mind, the opinions of others, my mother's voice talking in my head, a political system that did not deliver on its promises, religions that are based on fear instead of Love, the need for money, a greedy world that puts profits ahead of people, pain, suffering, disease, and much more. Eventually, I began to run out of gas and my list came to an end.

I then sat in silence for a few moments and contemplated what I really wanted 'freedom from'. I had just listed a bunch of things that I didn't want in my life. I wondered if getting rid of all of that stuff would actually bring me freedom. Was that what freedom was all about? Was it simply about getting rid of the things I didn't like? I had a feeling that there was more to freedom than that.

We then had a brief sharing circle in which people were invited to share what they wanted 'freedom from'. A few people mentioned things that were similar to my own. We then repeated the exercise except this time we were to meditate on what we wanted 'freedom for'. Aha, now that sounded good. I had the feeling that the things I wanted 'freedom from' weren't what freedom was all about; at least not for me. I thought that freedom must be about what I wanted 'freedom for'.

Again, my mind happily raced off and made another long list. I wanted freedom for having time to create, spending time with loved ones, doing whatever I felt drawn to do, being of service to others, finding the way 'home', creating a community that was based on Love instead of fear and control, and ..... I came to a sudden halt. It dawned on me that my mind was just creating a list of egotistical desires. I knew in my heart that none of those things would bring freedom either. In fact, they just created a new ego-based prison for me; one that involved the pursuit of desires.

In that moment, I knew that both 'freedom from' and 'freedom for' were games of the mind. I didn't want to play mind games any more. I just sat there and waited for the exercise to end.

The facilitator of the exercise must have seen my face drop because he asked me how the exercise had been for me. I looked up at him and said,

"I don't want freedom from anything and I don't want freedom for anything. That isn't freedom to me."

"What is?" He asked.

"I don't know", I replied.

There was a pregnant pause and then I said, *"Freedom isn't something to be gained, it is something that will arise in me when I am free from wanting anything, free from my own ego-mind. I suppose that freedom for me is simply a state of being inside me that arises when I fall completely silent inside and my inner peace cannot be disturbed by anything in the external world. I suppose that is 'freedom'."*

He simply smiled back at me. Apparently, I had nailed it. I had realized that freedom was an inner state of being. Nobody can take away my freedom except me. The only thing that can disconnect me from that inner state of being is to become identified with the false self.

I recommend that you stop trying to get away from the things that your ego wants 'freedom from' and stop trying to get what your ego wants 'freedom for'. If you do either then you will just remain stuck in the Loveless world of the false self. Your alternative is to dissolve your ego, become Love, and then follow whatever you feel divinely inspired to do. Then you will have freedom.

****

Living in The Gap is Freedom

One of my teachers in India told me that 'Living in the Gap' was freedom.

This idea of 'living in the Gap' was something that I had come across quite often during my journey. Different spiritual teachers used different words but they all seemed to be pointing at the same idea. For example, I had first read about the 'Gap' in Eckhart Tolle's book the 'The Power of Now'. I felt that the 'Now' Tolle was referring to was the same thing as the 'Gap' that my teacher in India was talking about.

I had loved Tolle's book. It strongly resonated with me. I also felt that the 'wake-up' call I received in the outback of Australian had given me a taste of what it was like to live in the 'Now'. During that call, I had fallen silent inside and a deep sense of inner peace had arisen. I had been in what I imagined to be the 'Now'.

I had also hated Tolle's book. I hated it because I didn't know how to live in the 'Now'. I had read 'The Power of Now' shortly after returning from Australia and long before discovering anything about spiritual tools, enlightened masters, and barriers to Love. I had no clue as to how to live in the 'Now'. That was one source of my frustration. There was another.

In that book, Tolle also presented the possibility that I was missing out on my whole life by not living in the 'Now'. I didn't like that possibility because I agreed with it. I felt like I had been missing out on my life by living the 'Canadian dream'. I hoped that I could resolve that problem by living in the 'Now' but I didn't know how. As a result, I came away from reading that book feeling highly frustrated.

On the positive side, that book had shown me what may be possible if I could learn to live in the 'Now'. That possibility gave me added inspiration to leave my society behind and set out on a quest to find this elusive 'Now'. The concept of the 'Now' had gradually dwindled back into the recesses of my mind. It been replaced by the determination to find my way 'home' to Love.

The idea of 'Living in the Gap' had then appeared in my life. I had come a long way since reading the 'Power of Now', and I still couldn't live in the 'Now'. I still clung to the past and worried about the future. And here I was being told that living in the equivalent of the Now (the Gap) was freedom. I strongly resonated with that possibility and desperately wanted that Freedom.

How did I learn to live in the Gap? I pondered this question very deeply. My only reference point was that experience of falling into an inner state of peace and silence in the outback of Australia. That had felt like freedom; freedom from my own monkey mind. In the years since tasting that freedom, I had gained a great deal of clarity on what that peaceful inner space was all about it. I called it 'home' and had discovered that I could return there by removing the barriers inside me that prevented me from residing there; the barriers to Love.

I then had another 'Aha!' moment. My version of 'home' was the same as the Gap and Tolle's Now. I had already discovered the way to live in the Gap! All I had to do was to continue finding my way 'home'. As my teacher in India would have said, living at 'home' is Freedom. As Tolle would have said, being at 'home' would allow me to have my life rather than to miss out on it.

This was a beautiful realization for me. I didn't need to figure out how to either be present in the Now or to live in the Gap. All I needed to do was to continue removing the barriers to Love and I would eventually end up at 'home', be in the Now, and live in the Gap. I would have freedom. Very cool.

I feel that the same applies to everyone. If you become a self-healer then the journey of healing yourself will enable you to return home to who you really are. You will be able to exist in the Now, live in the Gap, and be Love.

****

Use Imagination to Accelerate your Self-Healing Journey

I grew up believing that imagination was a bad thing. My parents would often say *"You're just imagining things"* when they wanted me to stop either feeling the way I did, behaving in a certain way, or being afraid of something. As a result, I came to believe that 'imagining things' was a 'bad' thing to do.

It came as quite a surprise to me when I later discovered that imagination is seen as the source of all creation by those of the Andean spiritual tradition. According to them, we cannot create anything until we have first imagined it. Imagination gives flight to whatever is inside us waiting to be expressed. My relationship with imagination was changed forever once I dropped my conditioned belief that it was 'bad' to imagine things. I was then able to use imagination as a powerful tool for healing myself.

It is not necessary to wait until our inner guides bring all of the situations into our lives that we need in order to find and heal our barriers to Love. We can instead use our imagination to take advantage of any emotions that arise in us. We can use the emotions that are triggered while we are watching a movie or reading a book as healing opportunities. Any emotional reaction to an external event, whether that event is happening in 'real' life or in a movie, is caused by a barrier to Love. Thus, we can use the emotions that arise inside us while we are being entertained by an imaginary story to find and heal our barriers to Love.

For example, I used this technique to great effect while watching the movie 'The Passion of Christ'. I began to cry during the crucifixion scene. I was watching the movie in a theater and crying in public definitely wasn't a regular occurrence for me. However, in this instance, I let myself cry. I felt a deep sadness flowing through me and simply allowed it to be there, while asking to be shown what inside me was really triggering it. I was soon shown that the sadness was coming from the many times during my life when I had sacrificed myself for others. At the time, I didn't know why my sacrificing myself would make me cry and I just let it happen. The tears felt deeply healing.

I then explored the world of 'sacrifice' and discovered that sacrificing myself was a non-Loving thing to do. I went into more detail on sacrificing oneself in chapter '8. *Non-Loving Motivation*'. Basically, I discovered that the tears I had shed while watching 'The Passion of Christ' stemmed from the sadness I felt for having given up on me during the many times that I had sacrificed myself. Each sacrifice was like a little emotional trauma. I was able to forgive myself for all of the times that I had sacrificed myself and that released the sadness.

In this way, imagination can be used to accelerate your healing journey. You can use your emotional reactions to imagined stories as signposts indicating that a barrier to Love has been triggered.

****

The Therapy Trap

Falling into the therapy trap is a surefire way to slow down your healing journey. What is the therapy trap?

I have used a wide variety of techniques to support me in healing myself. Those techniques were invaluable in my healing process and I feel deeply grateful to the creators and practitioners of each of them. They were also a trap. How does a therapy technique become a trap?

For example, I would turn to a therapy technique for support whenever I struggled to heal an emotional trauma on my own. I would ask my inner guide to point me towards whatever therapy was most suited to help me with that particular trauma. I would then use the indicated therapy technique to support me in healing myself. This was a highly effective process for me.

If I had stopped using the therapy at that point then I wouldn't have fallen into the therapy trap. Unfortunately, I would occasionally continue to use a therapy technique even after the emotional trauma that had drawn me to it in the first place had been healed. I would then waste my time trying to heal myself when there was nothing else for that particular therapy to support me in healing.

Thus, the therapy trap involves returning for more and more of a particular therapy after the initial trauma that took you to that type of therapy has been healed. It is a trap because there is rarely anything else surfacing from inside you that the particular therapy technique can support you in healing. Even if you have more issues surfacing, it is unlikely that the same therapy technique can support you in healing all of them. You are far better off asking your inner guide to show you the appropriate therapy technique for each subsequent issue than you are to assume that one technique can help you to heal all of your issues.

Another form of the therapy trap arises when an issue surfaces and you use a therapy technique to try and heal it because that technique worked for you in the past. I occasionally fell into this form of the therapy trap. There were a few techniques that proved invaluable for me and I couldn't help but try them on new issues. Invariably, they would not work. The technique that had worked for a past issue would not be appropriate for the new issue and I would be wasting my time.

Thus, the therapy trap involves either:

- continuing to do a type of therapy after the original trauma that took you to that therapy technique has been healed; or,

- using a type of therapy on an issue just because that therapy technique worked for a past issue.

I stopped getting caught in the therapy trap once I realized that therapy does not heal me, I do. A therapy technique can support me in moving through the final steps in healing an emotional trauma but it cannot heal me. Healing will only occur when I take action. In order to heal myself of an emotional trauma, I have to allow myself to feel the emotions associated with the original event and then use Love and forgiveness to both release those emotions and to let go of any false beliefs that I took on.

A therapy technique can guide me through the self-healing process but it cannot heal me. I have to heal myself. Once I have healed myself, with the therapy's support, then that therapy technique would have served its purpose and it would be time to move on. Returning for more therapy would be pointless. It would be a trap.

You can greatly accelerate your own healing journey by avoiding the therapy trap.

Multiple Visits to a Therapist

Despite the existence of the therapy trap, I do feel that there are times when many visits to a given therapist can be useful.

The therapy trap only applies when you have healed the issue that drew you to the therapist in the first place. It does not apply if you are still working on that issue. It may take multiple sessions to surface the underlying cause of an issue such as an addiction or depression. In those cases, I do feel that extended periods under the guidance of a given therapist can be useful.

Therapists have their own Version of the Therapy Trap

A therapist can also fall into the trap of offering therapy when there is little likelihood that their patient will benefit from it. A therapist may feel drawn to offer unnecessary therapy because of either their need for money or their pride in feeling that they have a gift to offer.

In the monetary world that we have created, a therapist is often motivated, at least partially, by the need to pay their bills. They may have every intention to be of Loving service but the need for money is still there. Thus, it can be difficult for a therapist to avoid the trap of either doing unnecessary therapy or doing therapy more slowly than is necessary. This is an all too common trap that therapists, knowingly or not, fall into.

A therapist may also do unnecessary therapy by functioning from a place of pride. It is important for a therapist to work with patients only after they have first tuned in to see if the patient is ready to heal something that their type of therapy can support. Unfortunately, it is often tempting for a therapist to skip this step and to try to support a person in their healing journey because of an ego-based desire to be a healer. That is another trap. It takes an extremely high level of integrity for a therapist to only work with people who have an issue surfacing that is both ready to be healed and is one that their therapy technique can support.

I recommend that you always tune into your own inner guide as to whether or not to continue working with a given therapist. If you feel that they have their own agenda, rather than your best interests, at heart then I recommend that you find another therapist to support you.

I wish both patients and therapists much Love in avoiding the therapy trap.

I am not describable nor definable. There is a vastness beyond the farthest reaches of the mind. That vastness is my home; that vastness is myself. And that vastness is also love." (8)

— Nisargadatta Maharaj

10. Distractions

Shortly after leaving the corporate world I read a book called 'The Spectrum of Consciousness' by Ken Wilber. In it, he referred to things such as astral travel, ESP, and Past Life Recall as "… *pernicious distractions, something that must be quickly passed through*". (9)

That quote strongly resonated with me. I had a feeling that it would be all too easy for me to get lost in playing with something like astral travel just for the sheer pleasure of it. I could see how these kinds of things could become distractions for me. I kept his warning in the back of mind throughout my journey.

The second warning regarding distractions came when a friend shared an analogy with me. He said that the journey of awakening is like climbing a mountain. There are many ledges on the mountain where one can pause to rest. However, that resting place can become a stopping point if one is not careful. It can become an obstacle to continuing all the way up to the top of the mountain. Again, this had strongly resonated with me. I didn't want to get stuck on any of those ledges. I was determined to make it all the way to the top of the mountain.

Eventually, I did begin to experience these pernicious distractions; astral travel and past life recall both came into my life. When that happened, I embraced the experience, took any lessons that the experience had for me, and moved on. I did not allow myself to get caught up in playing with them endlessly. I did allow myself to rest on the ledges for a little while but not for very long. I was determined to continue on up the mountain.

Wilbur's book and that mountain analogy had made me ever vigilant to avoid becoming trapped by any distractions on my self-healing journey. However, I could only avoid the distractions that I was aware of. If I didn't know that something was a distraction then I couldn't avoid it.

I am reminded of a Buddhist story about a monk who wanted to learn how to walk on water. The monk spent twenty-six years living by a river and dedicated all of his time and energy to learning how to walk on water. He finally accomplished this amazing feat and was excited to show his master what he could do. One day, his master rode up with his entourage. The monk greeted his master humbly and then took great joy in showing him what he had learned. The monk walked out over the river, turned around, and walked back. He was beaming as he listened expectantly for his master's comment on his achievement.

His master simply looked at him and said, *"You spent twenty-six years learning how to do that? Why didn't you just pay the ferryman to take you across the river?"*

I didn't want to waste twenty-six years of my life. I wanted to avoid all distractions. However, there were a few things that I got lost in simply because I didn't know that they were slowing down, or even threatening to derail, my journey 'home'. Basically, I was sitting on ledges without even knowing that I was doing it. Fortunately, a wise man in India pointed these oversights out to me.

This chapter contains a few of the distractions that slowed me down. Hopefully my sharing them will allow you to avoid getting stuck on your own journey. They include:

- Believing that I was 'awake' after temporarily tasting Divine Love;

- The desire to heal the world;

- Wanting to know the meaning of life;

- Using the Rational Mind to try and fulfill one's Soul Purpose.

- Wanting to become Love (which is an ego-based desire and not actually a distraction); and,

- Creating an image of what enlightenment looks like and then trying to experience that image.

I wish you much love in avoiding these distractions.

****

Being 'Awake' is a Moment to Moment Thing

Thinking you have awakened because of a temporary experience of being awake is a distraction.

You are awake when your ego is inactive and you are allowing Divine Love to function through you. Being awake will become your natural state of being once your ego has been completely dissolved. However, until then, it will be a momentary occurrence.

A person's ego can fall silent at any time. They will then experience divine Love flowing through the mind and body and out into the world. However, that does not mean that their ego has been fully dissolved. It just means that it has temporarily fallen silent. As soon as a person's ego is reactivated, and they become lost in functioning in the world through it, they fall back to sleep again. They are no longer awake.

The self-healing journey will result in your dropping your identification with the false self or ego. The ego consists of your barriers to Love and removing those barriers essentially dissolves the ego. As your ego falls away, you will experience more and more moments in which your ego is silent and Love is able to flow through you. These moments will likely change you forever. They will be full of an inexpressible sense of Love, peace, harmony, and joy. They are to be savored when they arise as they are giving you a taste of who you are. They also tend to inspire people to continue their journey until their ego has been completely dissolved and they are fully awakened.

However, I highly recommend that you do not get lost in believing that you are finished your journey just because you experience a moment of being awake. A moment of being Love (awake) simply means that your ego has temporarily fallen silent. It has not necessarily been completely dissolved.

An Indian mystic called Osho coined the term 'enlightened asshole'. It relates to this flipping back and forth between being Love and functioning from your ego. An enlightened asshole is someone who sits in a cave and achieves an inner state of bliss, harmony, and Love. He or she has become enlightened. However, if that person were to leave the cave and go down into the marketplace then they would return to being the asshole that they had always been. If someone were to cut in front of them in line then they would get angry and yell at that other person.

This is because they have not removed their barriers to Love. They have simply gone into a place, a cave, where none of their barriers to Love are being triggered.

If you are choosing to use this self-healing approach to fully awaken then you have a choice to make. Do you want to remain in the world at large or do you want to sequester yourself away in a cave, monastery, or nunnery?

If you wish to live in a cave then you do not have to remove your barriers to Love. You can sequester yourself away and become an enlightened asshole. As long as you remain in your cave, your barriers to Love will not be triggered and the energy that you then radiate out into the world will be a gift to all. On the other hand, if you wish to remain in the world of people then you will only be fully awake once you have removed all of your barriers to Love.

My journey has involved a gradual removal of my barriers to Love. I was initially gifted with a few shining moments in which I fell completely silent inside and became Love. I would then inevitably be thrown back into my ego. I soon came to realize that I could be Love as long as I was not being triggered into functioning from one of my barriers to Love. That is why the barriers to Love are so named.

Unfortunately, my Barriers to Love were not gone while I was experiencing those shining moments, they were simply dormant. Soon enough, one of them would be triggered and I would be back to functioning from my ego once again. I would no longer be Love. Over time, as I removed more and more of my barriers to Love, I have found that I am able to rest in that inner state of divine Love for ever increasing periods of time. My ego is not gone during those periods. It is simply lying dormant.

Being Love is now a much more common state of being for me than functioning from my ego. However, I do still occasionally observe my ego becoming active. Whenever that happens, emotions such as frustration, excitement, lust, and anger will flow through the body. If I identify with being those emotions then I am thrown back into my ego and I am no longer Love. On the other hand, if I can simply observe those emotions arising in the body then I can remain as Love despite their presence. Either way, I will remove whatever barrier to Love triggered them to flow through the body.

I have a feeling that many people will experience this flipping back and forth between being 'awake' and being 'asleep'. You may well face it on your own journey. Therefore, I caution you not to get caught up in believing that you are 'awake' just because of one beautiful moment. If you believe that you are 'awake' because of that one shining moment then you will only slow down, or even derail, your journey.

****

The Desire to Heal the World

The desire to heal the world is a distraction. I got lost in this distraction. I wanted to find the answers to all of the world's problems. I felt that the world was a total mess and in desperate need of help.

I had felt this way even as a fifteen-year-old boy living in Canada. At that time, the only solution that I could think of to the world's problems was to find new lands to explore so that humanity could start over in a new place. I also felt that the inhabitable parts of the planet had already been explored. There was nowhere left for us to go. In my naivety, I had then decided that I would become an astronaut and go out into space to explore. If this planet was full then we would just have to find another one. Over the next decade, I applied to the Canadian space program twice. I was rejected both times. I then gave up and had shoved this desire to solve the world's problems back down inside me.

I had turned my focus towards becoming a 'success' in the western world. I succeeded in becoming both successful and miserable. I had then given up on being 'successful' and set out on my journey of self-realization.

I travelled to many third world countries during that journey and saw firsthand what was happening in the world. I saw slums where millions of people were living in abject poverty. I saw people working in the equivalent of indentured servitude in order to feed the western appetite for material goods. I met people whose life expectancy was just thirty-five because the only way to feed their families was to do life destroying work that fed the capitalist machine. I walked through a town where the people were full of either hatred or despair because of the violence all around them. I saw many people who were missing limbs because of trying to grow food on the mine-strewn hillsides of Cambodia. I saw polluted water, garbage strewn across otherwise pristine landscapes, and plastic from across the seas washing up on beaches.

On and on it went. The devastation to people's lives and to the environment because of humanity's thirst for consumption was almost unbelievable. I was shocked.

It was impossible for me to ignore what I was being exposed to and my heart broke. I felt ashamed to be from the western world. What were we, as humans, doing to each other and to the planet? I felt that people all over the world were suffering terribly, and that the environment was being destroyed, all in the name of rampant consumerism and greed.

And it wasn't just in the third world where I saw suffering. I saw haggard and drawn faces in cities all across both North America and Europe. Where had the joy in life gone? I felt like corporations were making people prisoners of debt and sucking the life out of them. I felt that governments had their own, or lobbyists, interests at heart rather than the interests of the people they were supposed to be 'serving'. I walked through two civil war zones and yet the most dangerous and violent places that I saw were the inner cities of the USA.

I felt like the people of the West were prisoners of the fear-based conditioning that bombarded them from the moment they took their first breath. I also remember feeling hated by those around me simply for being inside a white man's body. I felt that religious fervor and nationalistic pride were inspiring hatred and separatism. What a mess.

My desire to 'heal the world' surfaced with a vengeance after being exposed to all of this. I did not like the world that I was seeing and I wanted to change it. I was ready to help the world but what could I do?

I pondered that question many times over. I did help a few people along the way and I did give money to those most in need wherever I went. However, my efforts felt like a drop in the ocean compared to what was needed to alleviate the suffering of so many. I badly wanted to do more, much more.

My internal question soon became, '*how can I end the suffering for everyone in the world once and for all?*' As you may have noticed, I have a tendency to think big.

I searched for an answer to that question and found myself agreeing with the words of Einstein:

> "*The significant problems we face cannot be solved at the same level of thinking we were at when we created them.*" (10)

I felt that this quote applied to the world as a whole. In order to clean up the mess we had made of the world, we were going to have to find a new level of thinking.

So, the question became, what level of thinking had created the world's problem? It was clear to me that the prevailing mode of thinking for the past few centuries has been rational thinking. I had already come to feel that rational thoughts are inherently violent (as they are sourced from the intention to defend and strengthen the false self). It then resonated with me that the destruction and suffering that I saw all over the world would be a natural result of using rational thoughts to create the religions, corporations, and social structures that ruled the world. To me, rational thinking was the level of thinking that had created the world's problems.

I then reflected on the effectiveness of using rational thinking to solve the world's problems. I had met many beautiful people all over the world who were trying to solve problems using rational thinking. Their solutions had struck me as being neither effective nor long lasting.

One of my favorite examples of this came from a friend of mine who had been a Belgian ambassador in Africa for twenty-six years. During that time, he approved the building of twenty hospitals by Belgian charities. The charities would study a region in order to determine which areas were economically viable and could support the running of a hospital. The intent was to build a hospital, staff it for two years, and then turn the running of the hospital over to the local people. Of those twenty hospitals that were built, not one is still functioning.

To me, this was an example of a group of people observing a problem, a lack of health care, and then using rational thinking to come up with a solution. In this case, their 'solution' did not work primarily because the local people did not want the kind of health care that they were offering. However, that hadn't stopped the charities from doing what they 'thought' was best.

I had many other examples of the failure of rational thinking to solve the world's problems just from looking at what has been going on around the world during my lifetime. Environmental organizations have been working for decades to help the environment yet we, as a race, continue to destroy our planet. There have been a wide variety of peace movements going on throughout my life yet peace does not appear to be any closer to flourishing in the world. I also haven't seen a lasting solution be found for either the violence in the Middle East or for the violence that exists between faiths and ethnicities. If anything, religious wars seem to be escalating rather than diminishing.

On a smaller scale, I had talked to the head of an NGO who had been trying for ten years to bring fresh water to the remote villages of Nepal. He had been able to dig just one well in those ten years because of what he referred to as 'red tape'. Another example was a pottery studio that was built by a well-meaning group of Japanese people in a remote Peruvian village that was known for its pottery. The studio remains unused because the people in the village did not want it. Doing pottery was part of the culture and families did it together. Going to a modern studio would separate the family unit. The examples are endless.

I did know of a few beautiful 'success' stories but, in general, the world seemed to be no better off now than it had been thirty-five years ago; when a fifteen-year-old boy had begun to worry about it. I felt like the well-meaning efforts of rational people all over the world were failing to make inroads into solving the world's problems. That left me feeling that, just as Einstein had indicated, rational thinking was not the answer.

I felt that the only way to truly solve the world's problems was going to be to find an alternative level of thinking to rational thought. That is quite a statement for an engineer, with an MBA, who had become a strategic planner within the IBM organization to make. I had thrived on rational thinking during the first half of my life and now I was feeling that rational thought was not going to help the world. I had come a long way since walking away from a 'successful' career.

This exploration of rational thinking, and the world it had created, actually left me feeling optimistic. For a long time, I had felt like it was hopeless to think that we could find answers to the world's problem and I felt that the earth was doomed. No longer. I began to feel that there was a possible solution. All we had to do was find a new level of thinking; one that was not inherently violent.

Rather than try to use my rational mind to try and solve the many problems that I encountered on my journey, I chose to search for that new level of thinking. I felt absolutely determined to find it and to then show people how to access it. If Einstein was right, and I felt he was, those people would then use that level of thinking to solve our problems.

Unfortunately, my quest was being triggered partially from my desire to 'fix' the world. As a result, my efforts were coming from my ego and were infused with violence. I often found myself becoming righteously angry whenever I saw suffering in the world. I knew that anger was not a part of a new level of thinking that was going to resolve anything. My anger was simply an indicator of a problem inside me.

I knew in my heart that I could not help anyone, let alone the world, as long as I still had anger, lust, frustration, righteousness, and so many other sources of violent thoughts floating around inside me. How could I contribute to healing the world when I was still full of fear, anger, and pain?

I couldn't, and I knew it. I was going to have to heal myself before I worried about healing the world.

When this issue first arose for me, I was spending most of my waking hours functioning from my ego and not from Love. I also knew that I was operating from the very level of thinking that had created the world's problems in the first place. This was my obstacle. As long as I continued to function from my ego, I would not be able to contribute anything to help the world.

It did not matter how well-meaning I 'thought' I was. I knew in my heart that I was going to have to heal myself before I could find a level of thinking that could help the world. Until then, I would constantly be triggered into functioning from my rational mind and no Love would come from me.

I was going to have to help myself first before I could help anyone else. I reluctantly set aside my search for a new level of thinking that could help the world and instead focused on my own inner healing journey.

You are here to make a difference in the world

I say 'reluctantly' because the desire to help the world was very strong in me. It had been floating around inside me from a very young age and it was constantly being reinforced. Throughout my journey, I kept receiving messages from people that I was here to make a difference in the world. Examples of those messages included:

- my being told by a clairvoyant that I was here to 'end mankind's inhumanity to mankind';

- an enlightened master telling a friend of mine that I had 'potential'; and,

- the wife of a famous Thai 'seer' foretelling that I would start a spiritual movement soon.

Bloody hell! Those kinds of messages were driving me crazy. It felt so overwhelmingly daunting to think about what they were hinting at.

To top that off, I also felt like my inner guide was pointing me in the direction of finding a way to solve the world's problems. During some of my mediations, I was having the first inklings of a 'dream' for a more Loving form of community, one that would shape the world to come, emerging from within me.

All of this felt like one hell of a burden. I didn't know what to do about any of it. I was just doing my best to remain open to the possibility that I was here to help the world in some way. I was also doing my best to let go of any desire to actually help the world. This was all very confusing.

The icing on the cake came when I began to feel like I may even have found a new level of thinking. The thoughts that arose from beyond my mind, when I was resting in a silent inner space, were infused with Love rather than violence. I began to wonder what would happen to the world if more and more people began to interact from that inner state of peace and silence. Would their thoughts be infused with Love and would they provide the answers to the world's problems? Would the world then become a more peaceful and loving place?

I felt that it would and I became excited about this possibility. However, I also knew that I was not even close to being able to consistently function from the inner space that allowed Loving thoughts to emerge from within me. I was still spending a great deal of my time functioning from my ego.

Where did that leave me? Why was all of this stuff about my contributing to '*ending mankind's inhumanity to mankind*', having '*potential*', and '*creating a new spiritual movement*' coming at me? I hadn't asked for any of it. What was it all about? I was confused.

What to do? Do I continue to pursue my desire to help the world or do I just focus on myself for the time being and ignore that desire?

I felt like I was faced with an inner conundrum between the guidance I was receiving to be of service to the world and the guidance I was receiving to heal myself first. I also felt like there was 'truth' to both sides of this conundrum.

It then dawned on me that it may actually be possible to do both. Perhaps the '*potential*' that His Holiness saw in me, and the '*spiritual movement*' that I was supposedly going to start, would both manifest after I had healed myself. I felt like I was on to something. Maybe 'I' could be involved in healing the world but only after my false self had been completely dissolved. I loved this possibility.

I eventually came to accept that 'my' wanting to change the world was indeed a distraction. There was nothing that I could do to help the world until I had first healed myself and become Love. Only then would I be functioning from the level of thinking that allowed Loving, rather than rational, thoughts to flow through me.

In the words of Nisargadatta Maharaj,

> *"Only the people who have gone beyond the world can change the world. It never happened otherwise. The few whose impact was long lasting were all knowers of reality. Reach their level and then only talk of helping the world." (11)*

I decided to make the healing of myself be my primary focus. However, I didn't completely ignore the world around me. I also set the intention to remain open to the possibility of receiving inspiration from within that would show me a way to help the world. I actively worked on removing my barriers to Love while trusting that I would be shown how to be of service to the world if I was meant to be.

I was then able to let go of my ego's desire to help the world. I knew that, no matter how badly my ego wanted to help solve the world's problems, it was not going to be able to. I felt myself relaxing at a very deep level as I let that desire go. It felt like a huge burden had been lifted from me.

A selfish motivation for wanting to change the world

I later realized that I had been harboring a highly selfish motivation for wanting to help the world.

If the world changed then I wouldn't have to. If the world was a peaceful and Loving place then I wouldn't get emotionally triggered and wouldn't have to heal myself. I could simply rest in that inner space of Love. Unwittingly, my ego had been fantasizing about helping the world rather than having to endure its own destruction.

****

Wanting to Know the 'Meaning of Life'

There is no meaning to 'my' life.

When someone is asking 'What is the meaning of life?', they are typically asking, 'What is the meaning of MY life?'. The 'my' is false. As long as 'I' believe that 'I' am the false self then my life has no meaning. How can the false have meaning? The ego is a set of false beliefs. How can there be any meaning to a life lived believing that the ego and body is who you are?

Thus, wanting to know the meaning of your life is a distraction. There is no meaning to 'your' life. I got caught up in this distraction. My inner journey was often a challenging one and, at times, I found myself looking for some kind of justification for putting myself through it. My mind wanted to have a meaning for constantly looking in the mirror and destroying my false self. Unfortunately, the desire to find that meaning was actually reinforcing the false self rather than enabling me to move beyond it. I was actually building up my ego by looking for a meaning to its existence. As soon as I realized this contradiction, I dropped the desire to find a meaning to my life.

All the pressure that I had been feeling to 'accomplish' something with my life then fell away. I felt freer than I had in years. In the words of Confucius,

> *"Everyone knows how useful it is to be useful. No one seems to know how useful it is to be useless."*

I had come to realize that 'I' was useless.

The Meaning of Life in General

I have come to feel that the true meaning of life, for those who are caught up in identifying with the false, is to learn their soul lessons and break free of that false identification.

After a being has freed themselves from the illusion of being a person then something else shines through. They have become Love and an inspiration arises from that space of Love. That inspiration contains their soul purpose. However, a soul purpose cannot be fulfilled by a person who is operating from their mind. It is a soul purpose after all, not a mind purpose.

A person has to go beyond this world of identifying with the ego-mind before worrying about having any meaning or purpose to their existence. Until they do that, their life has no meaning.

****

The Rational Mind Cannot Fulfill your Soul Purpose

Any attempt to fulfill your soul purpose with your rational mind is a waste of time. It is a distraction.

So, what is a soul purpose?

There is something beyond the mind. I call it my inner guide, Soul, or Higher Self. When you go beyond your mind, and become Love, an inspiration will then emerge from within. That inspiration will be your soul purpose.

I first started to sense the existence of 'inspiration' when thoughts began to arise from within me when I was resting in a silent inner space of Love. Those thoughts had a different feel to them than my rational thoughts. There was a gentleness to them that my rational thoughts did not have. They also held a wisdom that my ego did not have access to. I began to refer to these thoughts as 'Loving thoughts', rather than rational ones, because they carried the energy of Love.

These Loving thoughts began to appear long before I completely dropped my identification with the false. It was through these thoughts that I began to get glimpses of a new kind of 'community' that would supposedly usher in a golden age for humanity. Those glimpses had me wondering if I had incarnated in order to play a part, however small, in ushering in that age. That possibility seemed very much aligned with the external guidance that I was receiving about being a part of *'ending mankind's inhumanity to mankind'* and *'creating a new spiritual movement'*. I began to refer to those glimpses as my 'dream'.

I enjoyed receiving these glimpses as they came when I was abiding in a deep sense of inner peace and joy. However, my rational mind would then kick back in and I would begin to get scared. My ego found the very idea of my being involved in something like that to be incredibly daunting. *"No way, there is no way that I can start a spiritual movement or create new forms of community. I know nothing about spirituality. I am just a lost and confused engineer."*

I would then go into denial and hide away from the world. I would focus on my own inner journey and try to pretend that no one had ever said that I had 'potential'.

I didn't know it at the time but I was being gifted with glimpses of my soul purpose. A soul purpose is a 'task' that your soul has incarnated to perform. I feel that every soul incarnates with both a set of soul lessons to learn and a soul purpose to fulfill. The soul lessons are related to learning how to remain as the essence of who you really are, divine Love, in every situation that arises in this world of form. A soul purpose is something that a soul will have the opportunity to fulfill once a person has awakened to Love.

Again, please don't believe anything that you read in this book. Instead, I invite you to be open to the possibility that all of this is true for you. You can then explore it for yourself.

Your soul purpose belongs to your soul and not to your rational mind. Your rational mind cannot fulfill your soul purpose. Any effort that you make with your mind to fulfill it is only going to lead to frustration and failure. In order to fulfill your soul purpose, you will need to drop all identification with the false self and turn your life over to your higher self. You can then act, moment by moment, on the divine inspiration that emerges from within, and trust that your soul purpose will be fulfilled.

It can be a tremendous distraction to have glimpses of your soul purpose before you are ready. If you learn your soul purpose while you are still identified with your false self then you will likely make the futile attempt to 'try' and fulfill that purpose. You will be wasting your time and you will inevitably fail.

I know this from my own personal experience. I was given glimpses of my soul purpose long before I had gone beyond my mind. I wasted years 'trying' to fulfill my soul purpose using my mind. At the time, 'I' actually thought that 'I' could accomplish my soul purpose. Silly me. My efforts to fulfill it simply reinforced my ego and distracted me from the journey of becoming Love.

Eventually, 'I' gave up on trying to fulfill my soul purpose. Magically, I then began to have events be drawn into my life that seemed to be moving me towards actually fulfilling it. I wasn't doing anything to make those events occur yet they were happening. That was when I began to realize that I could only fulfill my soul purpose by keeping my rational mind out of the way and acting only on the divine inspiration that I was receiving from within.

I then began to turn my life over to what I refer to as 'Divine Will'; the divine guidance that I receive from my inner guide. I now trust that my soul purpose will be fulfilled by my remaining silent inside and acting, moment by moment, on the inspiration that emerges from within. I do not need to rationalize what will happen if I act on that inspiration. I simply need to act. How, or even if, my soul purpose will be fulfilled is of no concern to 'me'.

That said, until my soul purpose is fulfilled, I will remain locked in this world of form. In essence, having a soul purpose is a form of bondage. Nisargadatta Maharaj uses the word 'destiny' to refer to what I call soul purpose. He described the issue of attaining freedom from one's soul purpose in the book 'I am That'.

> *"Accept your destiny and fulfill it – this is the shortest way to freedom from destiny, though not from love and its compulsions."* *(12)*

What does that mean?

Nisargadatta is alluding to the idea that you can only become free of your soul purpose by fulfilling it. Until then, you are imprisoned in this world of form and will continue to incarnate until it is fulfilled. Once fulfilled, you will be free of it but not from *"love and its compulsions"*.

In order to fulfill your soul purpose, you must turn your life over to the essence of who you really are, Divine Love, and allow Love to function through you. You are then acting solely on Love and its compulsions.

In summary, any attempt to fulfill your soul purpose with your rational mind is a waste of time. It is a distraction. Your soul purpose belongs to your soul not to your rational mind. Drop your identification with the false and turn your life over to Divine Will. You will then be acting solely from Love and its compulsions, and your soul purpose will be fulfilled.

****

Communities of the Future

Any attempt by the rational mind to create Loving communities is a distraction and is destined to fail.

I felt that I had removed most of my barriers to Love once I had reached the point of spending the majority of my time as Love. I was at peace and was content. I was allowing Love to flow through me and had turned my life over to my Higher Self. I felt that 'I' was close to being done in this world.

I couldn't have been more wrong. All I had really done was to remove the first layer of my barriers to Love. That first layer was composed of the barriers related to my being identified with the false self. They included:

- every desire that I had to enhance the experience of being a person;

- all of my emotional traumas;

- all of my beliefs around what it meant to both be a person and have a successful life; and,

- every fear that stemmed from the core fears of either the death of the body or the death of the ego.

I had worked diligently on removing those barriers to Love. I had then begun to spend more and more of my time as Love rather than as the false self. Everything was moving along beautifully for me. I had a deep sense of inner peace and was allowing Love to flow through me.

And then I had a vision of what communities of the future were going to look like. This vision was much more detailed and complete than anything I had received before. It came the night after I had what is referred to in the shamanic world as the 'Divine Masculine' experience. During that experience, I had allowed my awareness to leave the body and enter into light. I was then everywhere at once and was observing this world of form from many different perspectives. It was an intensely blissful experience which I will describe in detail in a future book.

The evening after having that experience, I woke up in the middle of the night with a vision flowing into my mind. It was a vision of communities of the future. I later shared the vision with a shaman that I was working with in Baja, Mexico. He told me that he had received the same vision in the 1980's. He called it the 'Universal Download' and said that many others had received it. I was pleasantly surprised by this news. It seems that I wasn't going crazy and was actually tapping into something that many others had seen. Very cool.

The shaman then told me that he had tried to create a community modeled on that vision in the 1980's but it had failed. He asked me where it was going to start and when. I didn't know. I still don't.

I will be writing a booklet soon that will provide a full description of what these communities look like. In summary, they will be initiated by three to four people who have all reached the point of being Love. Those people will form the core of the community and will create an energetic field of Love that will be felt, knowingly or not, by all members of the community. Additional individuals will then be drawn to live near the vibration of Love that this core group is holding. Those individuals would hold the intention to become Love themselves. The families of those individuals would join them and the community would begin to grow.

The core values of these communities will be harmony, Love, peace, unity, and balance. The members of the community will be learning to live in harmony with all living beings; including people, animals, plants, rocks, and spirits. The communities will also be based on co-creation. There will be co-creation between men and women, between people and nature, and between people and spirits.

The physical make-up of the communities will not be defined in advance. That will depend on both the natural environment in which the community is created and the inspiration that each member of the community receives.

The maximum size of a community will be 5,000. The core group can only hold the vibration of Love effectively for up to that number of people. When a community reaches that maximum size, a few individuals, who have become Love themselves, will leave the community to seed a new one. In this way, new communities will constantly be forming and will spread out across the world.

The societal structures that exist in the world today will be ignored. These new communities will be created outside of those structures. Gradually, more and more people will gravitate away from the existing societal structures and into these new communities. The existing structures will eventually fade away.

After receiving this vision, I felt hopeful that these communities would have a profound effect on the world. If they did exist then their leaders would be putting Loving thoughts out into the world rather than rational ones. The new level of thinking that Einstein had alluded to, and that I had been searching for, would then be guiding the communities of the future. New societal structures would be created from Love rather than from violence. We could actually move into a world of harmony, Love peace, unity, and balance.

I was excited by this vision and my desire to heal the world returned with a vengeance. I knew that these communities could only be seeded by people who had become Love and I badly wanted to find people who were internally driven to do so. Unfortunately, my wants and desires were coming from my ego. I then began to surface my second layer of barriers to Love; the barriers related to my being of service to others.

I had not yet fully grasped the idea that 'I' could only be of service to the world by turning my life over to my higher self. I wasn't ready to completely trust life and hence to trust Love. I wanted to help people awaken and I wanted to do so now. Those desires resulted in my occasionally falling from grace and becoming rational rather than remaining Loving.

For example, I began to guide people in returning 'home' to who they really were. I was able to Lovingly guide many people and most of the feedback that I received was highly positive. However, I also fell from grace a number of times. My desire to have people wake up from the dream of thought resulted in my occasionally trying to push people farther than they were ready to go. I also become frustrated when people didn't 'get' it. I was going back into my ego and becoming non-Loving. I was falling from grace.

At times, I felt like I was starting my journey all over again. In a way, I was. I was surfacing a whole new layer of barriers to Love that were related to being of service to others and to the world. I hadn't discovered them earlier in my journey because I had been focused on healing myself and not on being of service to others. These barriers came flooding to the surface once I began guiding others, and I worked diligently to remove them.

For example, I dropped the desire to have people wake up. I did that by honoring that each person was 'exactly where they needed to be'. They had their own journey to follow at their own pace. I also accepted that the world needed to be the way it was so that more and more people would feel inspired to begin their own inner journey. I let go of any desires to have people wake up and to have the world be different than it was.

That was not as easy as it sounds. How could I accept that a perfect world could include children starving to death, women being raped, wars flourishing, and the environment being destroyed? That was a journey unto itself. I had to heal a great deal of anger before being able to accept that.

My soul still cries out at the level of suffering that so many people in the world are facing. However, I also feel that the world needs to be this way in order to push people out of their comfort zones. A life lived from the mind is a wasted life but it is also a safe life. People need something to inspire them to step out of their safe existence and to begin waking up. Perhaps that something is a world of so much suffering that people become disillusioned and look for an alternative.

I don't know if the state of the world today will be enough to inspire you to wake up. All I do know is that it is not up to me decide when it is time for you to begin your journey home. It is up to you. I cannot make you wake up and any effort on my part to do so is non-Loving.

Thus, I no longer push anyone. Instead, I provide people with opportunities but I do not interfere with their journey. I constantly invite people to embark upon their inner journey and then I accept whatever choice they make. If they accept the invitation then I support them on their journey. If they decline the invitation then I simply send them Love and move on.

I am continuing to be of service to others to this day and I am ever vigilant to catch myself when I fall from grace. Whenever I do fall, I apologize to those affected and delve inside to remove the barrier to Love that was triggered. I am now able to, more often than not, be Love even while being of service to others. I have learned that 'I' cannot be of service to anyone. Only Love can. All 'I' can do is get out of the way and allow Love to flow through me.

Receiving that vision of communities of the future triggered another ego-based desire in me. I felt like I had been shown how humanity could move into a golden age of harmony, Love, peace, unity, and balance. That was like manna from heaven for me. It was what I wanted more than anything else, and I wanted to see it happen sooner rather than later. I wanted to see these new communities start to form right away.

Thus, I made multiple attempts to create one. Every attempt failed for one ego-based reason or another. I was not successful in creating a community of the future but I did learn a tremendous amount about myself. Every failed attempt unearthed more barriers to Love from the second layer of my ego. Those barriers were related to my trying both to control the formation of the community and to get people to become more Loving so that they could help create those communities. Frustration and disappointment often arose from inside me during those days.

Eventually, I realized that 'I' cannot create these communities of the future. Only Love can do that. Any attempt by 'me' to create them is a distraction because it causes me to interact from my ego rather than from Love. This realization allowed me to let go of my desire to create a community. I was then able to return to being Love.

My intention now is to allow Love to flow through me and to trust that Love will create these communities, if they are meant to form. I will simply allow inspiration to guide my words and actions. If that inspiration leads me towards participating in the creation of these communities then so be it. If it doesn't then so be that too.

****

A Golden Age for Humanity

Is humanity on the cusp of a golden age?

I don't know but I do know that any effort by the ego to create a golden age is a distraction.

That said, I do feel that humanity has the opportunity to move into a golden age. I have been working on my own self-healing journey for many years now. Along the way, I have spent time in spiritual communities, and with spiritual leaders, all around the world. I have been pleasantly surprised to discover that I am not alone in doing the inner work necessary to become Love. There are literally thousands upon thousands, perhaps even millions, of us who are making the journey 'home'. That gives me hope that we, as a race, may well be on the cusp of a golden age.

I feel that this golden age will not be heralded by any one person or group. It will happen only when enough people heal themselves, come together, and create from an inner space of Love. That is the dream.

Will that golden age emerge?

I do not know. I do know that any attempt to use the rational mind to create it will fail. Only Love can create it and Love can only do that when we get our egos out of the way. My hope is that the level of suffering in the world does not have to increase much more before enough people become ready to turn inwards and become Love.

At this point, I feel that humanity could go either way. We could continue to harm the planet by remaining identified with our rational minds or we could create a golden age by turning inwards and becoming Love. It is up to us.

Which way will we go? We will see.

****

Wanting to Become Enlightened

The desire to achieve enlightenment is an obstacle to actually achieving enlightenment but having that desire is a blessing not a distraction.

I was not trying to become enlightened through my inner journey. I was focused on both discovering a form of Love that resonated with me and finding my way back to the peaceful and silent inner space that I had felt in the outback of Australia. I refer to the latter as finding my way 'home'. I was also trusting that, if enlightenment was meant to be a part of my journey then it would appear. It did.

My first exposure to the term enlightenment came when I worked with an 'enlightened master' in a Tibetan monastery. He did not refer to himself as enlightened, others did. He was possibly the most insightful man that I have met. He seemed to know everything that was going on inside me without me having to tell him. He also came across as being solely concerned with guiding me on my journey without any self-interest and without any judgment whatsoever. Receiving his guidance was a life changing experience for me. I remain deeply grateful to him for his time and guidance.

Was he enlightened? I don't know. There was definitely something unique about him. However, I couldn't really describe what that was in words that would do it justice. The best that I can do would be to say that he was selfless, Loving, insightful, and stern. He was supposedly enlightened but I didn't know what that meant.

My second exposure to the term enlightenment occurred when I visited the ashram of another 'enlightened master' in northern India. His energy was completely different from His Holiness (the first enlightened master that I met). This master exuded an energy that literally blew my mind. All I could say after receiving a hug from him was "Wow, wow, wow."

He spent one Christmas morning sitting down with me and giving me insights into my life and my soul's journey. That was one of the most amazing gifts that I have ever received. His words touched a place deep inside me. That is when the possibility of my becoming enlightened arose and, although I didn't know what that really meant, it scared me. That fear piqued my curiosity even more. Why would even the idea of becoming enlightened leave me feeling so afraid?

I then began to wonder what enlightenment was and if it fit into my journey. I had a feeling that I was going to have to overcome my fear of it one day, but first I needed to find out what it was.

These two supposedly enlightened masters exuded a very different energy from each other. They were both deeply insightful and both seemed selfless. However, that is where the similarity ended. One had a strong and penetrating energy while the other had an amazingly beautiful and gentle energy. Meeting these two enlightened masters was not enough for me to understand what enlightenment was. I gave up trying to figure it out. I just trusted that I would be shown what enlightenment was if and when I was meant to know.

It next came up during a Satsang that I attended in Pune, India. The facilitator of that Satsang described the desire to achieve enlightenment as being an obstacle to actually doing so. He talked about how the seeking of anything, including enlightenment, kept a person locked in their mind and blocked enlightenment. That idea very much resonated with me. I knew that all of my desires were barriers to Love and so it only made sense to me that the desire to achieve enlightenment would prevent it from happening.

I had been struggling with this issue. I didn't have the desire to achieve enlightenment but I did have the desire to find my way 'home'. I had been wondering if that desire was just another game of the ego. Was my desire to return 'home' blocking me from actually getting there? I remember listening intently as the facilitator of that Satsang broached this subject.

He went on to say that it is the false self that has the desire to seek enlightenment and that enlightenment can only be achieved by going beyond the false self. If a person holds onto the desire for enlightenment, or any other desire for that matter, then they will remain identified with the false and will not achieve enlightenment. Again, this very much resonated with me, and my heart sank. I 'knew' that it was indeed my false self, my ego in particular, that wanted to find the way 'home', and that 'home' lay beyond the false self.

What to do? Do I stop trying to find the way 'home'? Won't I then just spin my wheels and waste another life?

I felt like I was caught in a catch-22. It was my ego that wanted to find the way home and my ego couldn't go there. I was pouring all of my energy into removing the barriers to Love so that I could see through the illusions of the ego, and the effort to do so was coming from that same ego. I felt deeply confused.

Do I keep going or do I stop? Does my desire to find the way home prevent me from returning there? This was not good.

Fortunately, I wasn't left hanging for long. The facilitator of that Satsang then began to talk about how it is actually a blessing to have the desire for enlightenment arise. Until that happens, a person will remain trapped in their illusion of a separate self; possibly for many lifetimes. He added that the desire for enlightenment is considered to be the highest desire. It opens the door for a person to be able to break free of the illusory world and become enlightened.

I felt myself starting to relax as this sank in. I felt that my desire to find the way 'home' was doing the same thing for me as the desire for enlightenment would be doing. It was opening the door to my going beyond the false self and was giving me the motivation to return 'home' to Love. I had always felt that my having this desire was a blessing and I felt more than a little relieved to receive confirmation that it was.

I also felt like I was missing something. If the desire to find my way 'home' was preventing me from getting there then how could I both have that desire and return 'home'?

I couldn't. The last piece of the puzzle fell into place when the conversation moved on to talk about letting go of even the highest desire. The desire for enlightenment was to be held onto until all of the lesser desires had been discarded and then it was to be dropped as well. A person could then rest in their natural state of being and invite enlightenment to enter in.

Okay, that worked for me. I didn't need to drop my desire to find the way 'home'; at least not yet. I actually needed to hold onto it until I had let go of all other desires and then I could let it go too.

I enjoyed this discussion. It had thrown me for a loop initially and had then given me a clearer understanding of my journey. I had been feeling that my desire to find the way 'home' was an obstacle to my getting there and had received confirmation that it was. However, I had also learned that holding onto that desire was going to allow me to remove all of my other barriers to Love. Once they were all gone then I could drop the desire to find my way 'home' and actually return there.

This was huge for me. I had been concerned about what this desire meant for my going beyond the mind and now I got it. The desire to find my way 'home' was an obstacle to returning 'home' but it was not a distraction. It was a blessing.

****

What is Enlightenment?

Using the mind to envision what enlightenment is and then trying to achieve that vision is a distraction.

I still wasn't clear on what the word enlightenment meant. We had talked about the desire for enlightenment being a blessing during that satsang but we had not explored the actual meaning of enlightenment. I remained a tad clueless and that was okay by me. If I needed to know more about it then I trusted that, when the time was right, I would be shown.

I didn't have to wait long. I was living in Pune, India while attending that Satsang and was in the habit of also attending what was called 'white robe' at the Osho ashram every evening. 'White robe' is an event that includes a brief celebratory dance, watching a video of an Osho discourse, and then a brief meditation.

During one of those evening discourses, Osho brought up the topic of enlightenment. He did that shortly after I had been exposed to it in Satsang. I smiled to myself when this happened. I feel that there are no coincidences in the world and I felt like I was being invited to explore this topic more deeply. I listened attentively to Osho speak about enlightenment.

The part of his discourse that jumped out at me was when he said that three things were needed for enlightenment:

- *"relax the body;*

- *bring thoughtlessness to the mind; and,*

- *silence to the heart."*

He didn't actually say what enlightenment was. He just stated that three things were needed in order to achieve it. Enlightenment seemed to be quite an important subject and my curiosity was now going through the roof. I had finally reached the point of actually feeling drawn to look into it.

I recalled having read a book by Osho a couple of years earlier that had included a description of enlightenment. The description had gone over my head at the time and I wondered if I might be able to grasp it now. I was in the habit of writing notes from the books that I read in the back of my journals and it was possible that I had the appropriate journal with me. After that evening's 'white robe', I returned to my room and found the journal with my notes on Osho's book. The book was called 'Maturity'. In that book, Osho defined enlightenment as follows.

> *"... to become so nonexistent as ego that the whole oceanic existence becomes part of you."* (13)

I had not been able to relate to this description of enlightenment when I had first read it. I still wasn't absolutely clear on what it meant. I had tasted what it felt like to go beyond the ego but had not had the oceanic experience of existence becoming part of me.

I reflected deeply on what it could possibly mean to be "*nonexistent as ego*". During the brief moments when my ego had fallen silent, I had temporarily fallen into a silent and peaceful inner state of being that I called 'home'. I had a burning desire to find my way back to that 'home'. Was abiding in that peaceful inner state what Osho meant by being nonexistent as ego?

I was pondering that possibility when it dawned on me that the three things Osho described as being necessary for enlightenment provided a fairly accurate description of 'home'. The deeply peaceful inner state that I fell into when my mind fell silent was a lot like having a relaxed body, a thoughtless mind, and a silent heart! Whoa. Could the inner state of being that I called 'Home' be the inner state of being that invited in enlightenment?

I let this sink in for a moment and had a strong feeling that this was the case. I felt like I had been pursuing enlightenment without even knowing it. I felt overawed by this realization. My mind then leapt off to imagine what it would be like to have the whole oceanic experience become a part of me. I found myself smiling inside as my imagination took over.

I then shook myself out of it. I didn't want to get caught up in the mind game of trying to experience whatever I imagined enlightenment to be. Enlightenment was beyond the ego and I knew that it was a distraction to use my ego to try and experience something that was beyond it. Any effort by my mind to experience enlightenment would take me away from it not towards it. I brought myself back down to earth.

All that I had realized was that my returning 'home' would create the inner state of being that invited in enlightenment, nothing more. I still didn't know what enlightenment was and I didn't need to know. I felt myself relaxing at a very deep level. This was wonderful news for me. I felt like I had just been given confirmation that finding my way 'home' was the most appropriate thing for me to be doing with my life.

I had often felt like I was flying blind on my journey. I didn't have a guru or a master by my side to constantly guide me. All I had was a fierce determination to return 'home' and a trust that my inner guide knew how to get me there. I sometimes wondered if I was either off my rocker or on a wild goose chase.

I wasn't! I was heading towards an inner state of being that invited in enlightenment. All I had to do was to keep going; to continue healing myself by removing the barriers to Love. That confirmation felt wonderful to me.

I still had the nagging feeling that I was going to have to face my fear of enlightenment one day. I knew that fear was a barrier to Love and that I was going to have to face that fear before I could return 'home' and invite in enlightenment. However, I didn't know how to face that fear. How does one face a fear of something that one does not understand? I decided to simply trust that I would be shown how to overcome this fear when the time was right. The day for facing it did eventually arrive but that is a story for another day.

I ended my exploration of enlightenment at that point. I had not discovered what enlightenment was. All I had was Osho's words that it was to *"become so nonexistent as ego that the whole oceanic existence becomes part of you"*. However, I didn't want to use my ego to try and understand what the oceanic experience would be like. Any effort to do so would be a game of the ego and would distract me from the journey of dissolving the ego and becoming Love.

I had received confirmation that returning 'home' was a beautiful thing to be doing with my life. That was enough for me. I was content to let go of worrying about enlightenment.

I returned to focusing on healing myself so that I could return 'home'. Whatever happened after that was of no concern to my ego.

Instead of seeing through the eyes of illusion, see through the eyes of the Divine.

11. In Closing

You now have everything you need to become a self-healer. You have been invited to open up to the possibility that pain and disease stem from energetic disturbances in your being. Those disturbances are created either by your barriers to love or by a misalignment between the life you are choosing to live and the life you incarnated to live. You can heal yourself by removing both your barriers to Love and any misalignments in your life. We have discussed the following process for healing yourself.

- Look in the mirror that is your life in order to observe when the signposts that healing is needed arise.

- Use the three pillars to find and remove the barriers to Love and misalignments underlying those signposts.

- Trust that the body will then heal itself.

The journey of becoming a self-healer is not for the faint of heart. It requires you to be absolutely honest with yourself about the way you feel. It also asks you to shine the light of awareness into the darkest corners of your ego. Shining that light is done through self-Love. Self-Love is referred to as the flame of transformation because it will burn away all of the illusions that you hold about yourself and your life.

Healing yourself is a spiritual journey. You will be removing the barriers to Love from inside you that lead to disease. The barriers to Love are the set of fears, beliefs, emotional traumas, and desires that make up your ego. Removing those barriers effectively dissolves your ego. As your ego falls away, you will awaken to who you really are.

Embarking upon the journey of becoming a self-healer is arguably the greatest adventure that you can undertake. You will connect to your own inner guide and find your own answers to all of the questions that you may have. You will discover that Love, peace, freedom, and joy are all states of being that arise from inside you as you remove your barriers to Love.

You will also find that your own rational mind will be your greatest obstacle in becoming a self-healer. While you are identified with the false, your rational mind is in control of your life. It is going to think that it can find and remove your barriers to Love but it can't. It will only get in the way of your self-healing journey. You will have to cultivate trust in your inner guide and turn to it for guidance in removing your barriers to Love.

On this journey, your rational mind will also be losing its place as the ruler of your life. As you dissolve your ego, by removing your barriers to Love, you will gradually be turning control of your life over to your inner guide. Your rational mind is not going to like being moved from its role as master of your life to its place as the servant of your inner guide. It will fight you. However, if you can cultivate trust in your inner guide then you will be able to overcome your rational mind's illusion of control.

Your self-healing journey will accelerate exponentially once your inner guide takes the reins of your life. You will be able to remove the barriers to Love much more rapidly and be able to spend more and more time in that silent inner space that allows Love to flow through you. You will then be free of being a prisoner of the false. You will have become Love.

I invite you to embark upon your own journey of becoming a self-healer. There will be challenges and pitfalls along the way but the rewards are immeasurable; healing yourself and awakening to who you are.

You do have to walk your own healing path. No one can walk it for you. However, you do not have to walk it alone. Others can guide and support you along the way. This book is intended to be a starting point for providing you with that guidance and support.

Those of you who decide to embark upon your own inner journey will be the ones who herald a golden age for humanity. I wish you much ease, grace, and Love on your journey.

Glossary

Words often have different meanings to different people. These are the definitions of some of the key words and phrases that are used in this book. The definitions of these words may not match either the dictionary definition or your definition.

Barriers to Love – The barriers to Love are the four components of the ego; fears, desires, beliefs, and emotional traumas. They are called barriers to Love because a human being cannot be functioning from one of these barriers and be Love.

Divine Love (a.k.a. Love) – Divine Love is the energy of pure Source awareness and of the soul. Love will only flow through a human being when they have fallen silent inside and have gone beyond their ego-mind. This form of Love is healing.

Ego (a.k.a. ego-mind) – The ego is a person's set of fears, beliefs, desires, and emotional traumas. Functioning from any one of these four components of the ego results in a person becoming completely disconnected from Love.

Ego-Mind (a.k.a. ego) – See Ego.

False Self – The false self includes the ego-mind and the physical body. It is so-called because identifying oneself with the false self prevents a human being from knowing who they really are.

Heart-based love – Heart-based love is other centered. It is about imposing your ego's beliefs of what is best for another person onto them. It is a game of the ego and there is no healing power in this form of love.

Higher Self (a.k.a. Inner Guide and Soul) – The Higher Self is the eternal aspect of your being that resides beyond the ego-mind and body. It is seeded from pure Source Awareness and carries the energy of divine Love. It is also called your soul or inner guide.

Home – Home is an inner state of being that is silent, peaceful, and joyful. It is attained through cultivating a relaxed body, a silent mind, and a quiet heart. It is the state of being that enables the energy of divine Love to flow through a person and out in to the world.

Inner Guide (a.k.a. Higher Self and Soul) – Your Inner Guide is the eternal aspect of your being that resides beyond the ego-mind and body. It is seeded from pure Source Awareness and carries the energy of divine Love. It is also called your soul or higher self.

Insight Meditation – Insight Meditation is a technique for having your inner guide provide you with insights on a specific question or intention. It is performed by focusing on the question you would like to ask and then using any meditation practice to enter into a meditative state. You then simply wait for your inner guide to provide the answer.

Looking in the Mirror – Looking in the Mirror is to use mindful awareness to observe your inner reaction to life's events. You observe when any fear, anger (and any other emotion), or pain arises inside you. You also observe when you are triggered into reacting from a non-Loving motivation such as wanting to be right or espousing a belief. Fear, anger, pain, and a non-Loving motivation are the signposts indicating that a barrier to Love inside you has been triggered and that you have some self-healing to do.

Love (a.k.a. Divine Love) - – (Upper case) Love is the energy of pure Source awareness and of the soul. Love can flow through a human being when they have fallen silent inside and have gone beyond their ego-mind. This form of Love is healing.

love – (Lower case) love is ego-based. The two types of love that have been created by the ego are mind-based love and heart-based love. These forms of love are games of the ego and have no Love in them whatsoever. There is no healing power in love.

Meditation – Meditation is a state of being. Meditation is the art of shifting your awareness to ever subtler levels of awareness while remaining aware of the previous levels.

Meditative Practices – Meditative Practices are various processes that are used to achieve the inner state of meditation. Examples include Vipassana, guided, insight, kundalini, Dynamic, and silent meditation. Any activity that enables your ego-mind to fall silent and for you to move to subtler levels of awareness can be considered a meditative practice. Even surfing, skiing, and chopping vegetables can be meditative.

Mind-based love – Mind-Based love is what we are referring to when we say things such as 'I love chocolate because it tastes good' or 'I love you because you make me happy'. Mind-based love is all about what your ego gains from getting what it wants. It is a game of the ego and there is no healing power in this form of love.

Mindful Awareness – Mindful Awareness is to be aware of everything going on, both inside you and outside of you, without reacting to it. You simply observe it.

Pure Source Awareness (a.k.a. Source) – Pure Source Awareness is a field of awareness that suffuses everything in this world of form. It is the One that we all return to when we let go of identification with both the false self and the higher self. It has been referred to by many belief systems with terms such as the Holy Spirit, Source, Tao, Universal Consciousness, God, and the Supreme Self.

Self-Healer – A Self-Healer is a person who is able to find and remove the energetic disturbances inside themselves that have led to an illness or disease. Once those energetic disturbances are removed, the body will heal itself.

Self-Love – Self-Love is to accept yourself exactly as you are without judgment. You accept the way you feel, the motivation for your thoughts, words, and actions, your inner emotions and demons, your ailments, and your body. Accepting yourself does not mean that you have to stay the same way forever. It just means that you are accepting yourself as you are today. Self-Love opens the door to healing. Unless you can accept something, you cannot heal it.

Soul (a.k.a. Higher Self and Inner Guide) - The soul is the eternal aspect of your being that resides beyond the ego-mind and body. It is seeded from pure Source Awareness and carries the energy of divine Love. It is also called your higher self or inner guide

Source (a.k.a. pure Source awareness) – a field of awareness that suffuses everything in this world of form. It is the One that we all return to when we let go of identification with both the false self and the higher self. It has been referred to by many belief systems with terms such as the Holy Spirit, Tao, Universal Consciousness, God, and the Supreme Self.

Trust – Trust is to trust in your inner guide only. Do not trust your ego-mind, anyone else's ego-mind, nor any form of external God. Your inner guide will bring the situations into your life that you need in order to learn your soul lessons and it will guide you towards the life you incarnated to live. It will also enable you to find and remove your barriers to Love.

Appendix A: Exercises

1. Healing the Source of a Pain or Illness.

This exercise describes a process for finding and healing the root cause of a pain or illness. The root cause will either be a barrier to Love or a misalignment between your chosen life and the life you incarnated to live.

1. Accept that pain and illness are messengers and that the body is a self-healing mechanism (i and ii).

2. Find a quiet space where you can sit in silence (iii).

3. Bring your awareness to the pain or illness and allow yourself to feel it.

4. Feel gratitude to the pain or illness for bringing you its message.

5. Enter into a meditative space and ask to be shown the true source, inside you, of the pain or illness (iv).   If the root cause is a misalignment between the life that you are currently living and the life you are meant to live then go to step 6. If the root cause is a barrier to Love then go to step 7.

6. Use exercise '*5. Bringing your Life into alignment with your Soul*' to heal the barriers to Love underlying the misalignment and to then bring your life into alignment with the life that you incarnated to live. Go to step 8.

7. Heal the barrier to Love using the appropriate exercise for that type of barrier: '*6. Letting go of a Particular Fear*'; '*7. Removing a Belief*'; '*8. Healing an Emotional Trauma*'; or, '*9. Letting go of a Desire*'.

8. Give the body time to begin healing itself. If the body heals then you are finished with this exercise. If the body does not heal then there is another layer of healing to be done (v). Return to step 1.

Notes:

i.   It may take you some time to find and heal the energetic source of the pain or illness. Take whatever steps are necessary to physically or mentally treat the pain or illness prior to undertaking this exercise. For example, if you have put your hand on a hot burner then remove your hand from the burner! If your body needs medical attention to keep it alive and functioning while you focus on finding and healing the true source of the pain or illness then get that medical attention. Do whatever you need to do for the body before beginning this exercise.

ii.   This exercise is based on a perspective of healing that involves accepting that all pain and illness are messengers. They indicate that there is an energetic disturbance in your energy body caused by either your taking on a barrier to Love or having a misalignment between your chosen life and the life that you are meant to be living. In order to heal the pain or illness, you will need to either remove the underlying barrier to Love or bring your life into alignment with the life you are meant to live. The energetic disturbance will then be released and the body will heal itself.

iii.   Invite a friend to be there if you feel that their support will be beneficial. Choose a friend that you know will support you in feeling deeper into the pain or illness without trying to pull you out of it.

iv.   It may take time and a number of attempts before you see either the barrier to Love or misalignment that triggered the pain or illness. Be patient.

v.   There are often multiple layers of healing to be done for a particular pain or illness. You will need to repeat this exercise for each layer before the body will heal itself.

2. Healing the Source of an Emotional Reaction (such as Anger)

This exercise describes a process that can be used to heal the source, inside oneself, of any emotion that arises in the body (i and ii). The exercise is described using anger as the emotion that has arisen. If anger is not the emotion that you are dealing with then simply substitute your emotion for anger in the following steps.

1.   Find a quiet space where you can sit in silence (iii).

2.   Visualize the scenario that created the anger (or other emotional

reaction) and allow yourself to feel the anger arising in your body.

3. Enter into a meditative space, focus on where in the body you feel the anger, and ask to be shown the true source, inside you, of the anger (iv). If the root cause is a misalignment between the life that you are currently living and the life you are meant to live then go to step 4. If the root cause is a barrier to Love then go to step 5.

4. Use exercise '*5. Bringing your Life into alignment with your Soul*' to heal the barriers to Love underlying the misalignment and to then bring your life into alignment with the life that you incarnated to live. Go to step 6.

5. Heal the barrier to Love using the appropriate exercise for that type of barrier: '*6. Letting go of a Particular Fear*'; '*7. Removing a Belief*'; '*8. Healing an Emotional Trauma*'; or, '*9. Letting go of a Desire*'.

6. Recall the scenario that triggered the anger in the first place. If you no longer feel angry then you are finished with this exercise. If you still feel anger then there is another layer of healing to be done (v). Return to step 1.

Notes:

i. All emotions are sourced from inside oneself. External events can only trigger an emotion in you if you have either an unresolved barrier to Love or a misalignment in your life. There is no one to blame for your feeling angry or for your feeling any other way. Own your emotions as being sourced from inside you and heal yourself. If someone triggers you to become angry, or to feel any other emotion, then they are giving you a gift. They are showing you that you have something inside you that needs to be healed.

ii. The source of all of your emotional reactions, including anger, will be either a barrier to Love or a misalignment between your chosen life and the life that you are meant to live. You can heal yourself by either removing the underlying barrier to Love or rectifying the misalignment. Doing that will remove the source of your emotional reaction.

iii. Invite a friend to be with you if you feel that their support will be beneficial. Choose a friend that you know will support you in feeling deeper into the anger without trying to pull you out of it.

iv.   It may take time, and a number of attempts, before you see the root cause of your anger. Be patient.

v.   There are often multiple emotional layers underlying an emotional reaction such as anger. You will need to repeat this exercise for each layer before the anger will be completely released.

3. Healing the Source of Fear

This exercise provides a way to heal the feeling of fear when it arises in the body (i).

1.   Find a quiet space where you can sit in silence (ii).

2.   Visualize the scenario that created the fear and allow the fear to grow stronger.

3.   Fall into a meditative state, focus on where in the body you feel the fear, and ask to be shown the root cause, inside you, of the fear (iii). If the root cause is a misalignment between the life that you are currently living and the life you are meant to live then go to step 4. If the root cause is a barrier to Love then go to step 5.

4.   Use exercise '5. *Bringing your Life into alignment with your Soul*' to heal the barriers to Love underlying the misalignment and to then bring your life into alignment with the life that you incarnated to live. Go to step 6.

5.   Heal the barrier to Love using the appropriate exercise for that type of barrier: '6. *Letting go of a Particular Fear*'; '7. *Removing a Belief*'; '8. *Healing an Emotional Trauma*'; or, '9. *Letting go of a Desire*'.

6.   Recall the scenario that triggered the fear in the first place. If you no longer feel fear then you are finished with this exercise. If you still feel fear then there is another layer of healing to be done (iv). Return to step 1.

Notes:

i.   Fear arising in the body is showing you that you have either a barrier to Love that needs to be healed or a misalignment between your chosen life and the life you incarnated to live. Fear can be triggered by any one of the four barriers to Love. It can be arising from: a fear of something in particular; feeling afraid of having a conditioned belief be proved false, feeling afraid of having an emotional trauma recur; or, feeling afraid having satisfaction of a desire be blocked.

ii.   Invite a friend to be there if you feel that their support will be beneficial. Choose a friend that you know will support you in feeling deeper into the fear without trying to pull you out of it.

iii. It may take time and a number of attempts before you see the root cause of your fear. Be patient.

iv.   There are often multiple emotional layers underlying a fear. You will need to repeat this exercise for each layer before the fear will be completely removed.

4. Healing the Source of a Non-Loving Motivation

This exercise provides a way to remove the source of what caused you to have a non-Loving motivation behind your thoughts, words, or deeds (i).

1.   Find a quiet space where you can sit in silence (ii).

2.   Visualize the scenario in which the non-Loving motivation arose and allow yourself to feel that motivation.

3.   Fall into a meditative state and ask to be shown the root cause, inside you, of that non-Loving motivation (iii). If the root cause is a misalignment between the life that you are currently living and the life you are meant to live then go to step 4. If the root cause is a barrier to Love then go to step 5.

4.   Use exercise '5. *Bringing your Life into alignment with your Soul*' to heal the barriers to Love underlying the misalignment and to then bring your life into alignment with the life that you incarnated to live. Go to step 6.

5.   Heal the barrier to Love using the appropriate exercise for that type of barrier: '6. *Letting go of a Particular Fear*'; '7. *Removing a Belief*'; '8. *Healing an Emotional Trauma*'; or, '9. *Letting go of a Desire*'.

6. Recall the scenario that triggered the non-Loving motivation in the first place. If you no longer feel that motivation then you are finished with this exercise. If you still feel the non-Loving motivation then there is another layer of healing to be done (iv). Return to step 1.

Notes:

i. If you have a non-Loving motivation then you are being shown that you have either a barrier to Love that needs to be healed or a misalignment between your chosen life and the life you incarnated to live.

ii. Invite a friend to be there if you feel that their support will be beneficial. Choose a friend that you know will support you in feeling deeper into the non-loving motivation without trying to explain it and without attempting to marginalize it.

iii. It may take time and a number of attempts before you see the root cause of your non-Loving motivation. Be patient.

iv. There are rarely multiple barriers to Love underlying a non-Loving motivation but it can happen. You will need to repeat this exercise for each barrier before the non-Loving motivation will be completely removed.

5. *Bringing your Life into Alignment with your Soul*

This exercise provides a way to bring your life into alignment with the life you incarnated to live (i and ii).

1. Find a quiet space where you can sit in silence.

2. Allow yourself to ponder the misalignment that you have discovered between your chosen life and the life you incarnated to live.

3. Sit in meditation and ask to be shown the steps that you need to take in order to bring your life into alignment with your soul's journey.

4. Consider the possibility that you are going to make the changes necessary to bring your life into alignment (iii). If you feel any fear at that possibility then go to step 5. If you feel any resistance

then go to step 6. If you feel neither then go to step 7.

5. Sit in meditation and ask to be shown what you are afraid of. Use exercise '*3. Healing the Source of Fear*' to remove the fear from your being. Return to step 4.

6. Use exercise '*16. Freeing yourself from Feeling Stuck*' to remove the resistance that you are feeling. Return to Step 4.

7. Make the necessary changes to your life in order to bring it into alignment with the life that you incarnated to live. If you find yourself feeling confused about the next step to take in your life then return to step 3.

8. Recall the scenario that triggered the signpost that pointed you at the misalignment in the first place. If you no longer feel that signpost then you are finished with this exercise. If you still feel it then there is another layer of healing to be done (iv). Return to exercise 1, 2, 3, or 4 depending on which signpost is involved.

Notes:

i.   This exercise is intended to be used after you have followed a signpost and discovered that you have a misalignment between the life you are choosing to live and the life that your soul incarnated to live.

ii. This exercise allows you to change your life in order to bring it into alignment with your soul. There are two primary reasons why it is important for you to live the life that you incarnated to live rather than the life that your ego wants you to live. First, the only way to learn the soul lessons that you incarnated to learn is to listen to your soul rather than your ego. Second, the only way to free yourself of the pain, anger, fear, or non-Loving motivation that triggered you to find the misalignment is to bring your life into alignment with your soul's journey.

iii. There is often a feeling of fear or resistance involved in leaving your existing life and moving into a life that is in alignment with the one that you incarnated to live. You will need to remove that fear or resistance before making the necessary changes to your life.

iv. There may be multiple misalignments or multiple barriers to Love underlying a signpost. You will need to repeat the exercise for the signpost until each misalignment and each barrier to Love has been removed.

6. *Letting Go of a Particular Fear*

This exercise provides a way to let go of a particular fear (i and ii).

1. Choose whether you wish to either face the fear directly or use meditation to find the lie underlying the fear (iii and iv). If you are choosing to face a fear directly then go to step 2 otherwise go to step 3.

2. Face your fear. Take whatever action is necessary for you to either say or do whatever it is that frightens you. If the fear then dissolves away then you are finished with this exercise. If it does not dissolve away then go to step 3 (v).

3. Find a quiet space where you can sit in silence (vi.)

4. Visualize a scenario that creates the fear and then allow the fear to grow stronger.

5. Fall into a meditative state, focus on where in the body you feel the fear, and ask to be shown the lie underlying the fear (vii).

6. Choose to stop believing that lie (viii). The feeling of fear will then dissolve away (ix).

Notes:

i. This exercise is intended to be used after you have discovered that a barrier to Love inside you is a fear of something in particular. The earlier exercise from this appendix, '3. *Healing the Source of fear*', is the one to use when you feel fear arising in the body and want to find the source of that feeling of fear. That other exercise will show you which of the four barriers to Love is triggering that fear to arise. If the source of the feeling of fear is a fear of something in particular then this exercise is intended to be used to remove that specific fear.

ii. Beneath every fear is a false belief; a lie. When you are able to let go of the lie underlying a fear then the fear will dissolve away.

iii. There are two approaches to freeing oneself from a fear. The first is to simply face the fear head on and, when the fear does not materialize, it dissolves away. The second is to use meditation to find and release the lie underlying the fear.

iv. Do not face a fear head on if doing so would cause physical harm. Use the meditative approach to deal with those types of fears.

v. Facing a fear head on does not always work. We often create circumstances in our lives that make sure that our fears do come to fruition. If we believe in a fear strongly enough then we will subconsciously do everything in our power to prove ourselves right. Fear then becomes a self-fulfilling prophecy. The only way to free ourselves from this type of fear is to go inside and find the lie on which it is based.

vi. Invite a friend to be there if you feel that their support will be beneficial. Choose a friend that you know will support you in feeling deeper into the fear without trying to pull you out of it.

vii. This may take some time and a number of attempts before you are shown the lie. Be patient.

viii. There are rare cases when you may not be able to let go of the lie. For example, the fear of death is based on the lie that 'I am the body' and that fear can be dropped only by letting go of any identification with the body. Letting go of that identification may be difficult for you. If you are unable to let go of the lie underlying a fear then set the intention to do so and trust that your inner guide will eventually show you how to do it. In the meantime, you will remain afraid of that particular thing.

ix. The feeling of fear may not dissolve away if there are multiple lies associated with that particular fear. This does not happen very often as there is typically only one lie associated with a particular fear. However, if the fear does not dissolve away then return to step 3 and remove the next lie. Repeat the process until all of the lies are removed and the fear is gone from your being.

7. Removing a Belief

This exercise is to be used for removing a conditioned belief (i and ii).

1. Find a space where you can sit quietly.

2. Enter into a meditative state and ask to be shown the lie underlying the belief (iii).

3. Choose to let go of the lie and the belief will fall away (iv).

Notes:

i. This exercise is intended to be used after you have discovered that a barrier to Love inside you is a conditioned belief. You will have found the belief when you were following a signpost (fear, an emotional, pain, or a non-Loving motivation) down inside yourself and discovered that the root cause of the signpost was a belief.

ii. Every belief is false. They are games of the false self. You will have to drop every belief that the false self holds in order to become Love.

iii. Every belief has an underlying lie on which it is based. If you can find the lie and let it go then the belief will fall away.

iv. You may find yourself struggling to accept that the lie is indeed a lie. Remember, everything that the false self believes is a lie. If you are not willing to let go of the lie then the belief will keep you imprisoned in the false self.

8. Healing an Emotional Trauma

This exercise describes a process that can be used to heal an emotional trauma (i, ii, and iii).

1. Decide on whether you wish to heal the emotional trauma on your own or with the support of a therapist. If you decide to use a therapist then go to step 2 else go to step 5.

2. Select a therapy technique and a therapist that you feel are appropriate for supporting you in healing this particular emotional trauma (iv and v).

3. Have the therapist support you in recalling the memory of the original traumatic event and feeling the emotions that you felt at that time (vi and vii).

4. Have the therapist then guide you in using a combination of Love,

learning your lessons, and forgiveness to heal yourself (viii and ix).
Go to step 8.

5. Find a quiet space where you can sit in silence (x).

6. Allow yourself to recall the memory of the original traumatic event
    and to feel the emotions that you felt at that time (xi).

7. While feeling those emotions, use a combination of Love, learning
    your lessons, and forgiveness to heal yourself (viii).

8. If the memory of the emotional trauma had surfaced simply
    through living your life then go to step 14. If you discovered the
    emotional trauma by following a signpost down inside yourself
    then go to step 9.

9. If the signpost was a fear, emotional reaction such as anger, desire,
    or non-Loving motivation then go to step 10. If the signpost was a
    pain or illness then go to step 12.

10. Visualize the scenario from your life that triggered the signpost
    (the fear, emotional reaction, desire, or non-Loving motivation)
    and feel whether or not it is gone. If it is gone then you have
    released the emotional pain and can move on to step 16. If you can
    still feel the signpost then there are more emotional layers that
    need to be healed (xii). Go to step 11.

11. Follow the signpost back down inside yourself and allow yourself
    to feel each emotional layer that is still present. Use exercise '2.
    Healing the Source of an Emotional Reaction (such as Anger)'
    from this appendix to heal each of those emotional layers. Return
    to step 10.

12. In the case of the signpost being a pain or illness, you may choose
    to find out if the healing is complete by simply giving the body
    time to heal itself. However, we recommend that you proactively
    explore the pain and illness that led you to the emotional trauma in
    order to see if there are any more emotional layers that need to be
    healed (xii). Allow yourself to feel the pain or illness and follow it
    down inside yourself to feel if there are any emotional layers still
    present. If you do feel an emotional reaction then go to step 13
    else go to step 16.

13. Use exercise '*2. Healing the Source of an Emotional Reaction (such as Anger)*' from this appendix to heal all of the emotional layers that you find. Return to step 12.

14. In the case of the memory of the emotional trauma having surface while living your life, allow yourself to recall the memory of the original event. If you can recall the event without becoming emotional then go to step 16. If you still feel any emotions at all then there are additional emotional layers that need to be healed (xii). Move on to the next step.

15. Allow yourself to recall the original event and to feel whatever emotions arise. Use exercise '*2. Healing the Source of an Emotional Reaction (such as Anger)*' from this appendix to heal the emotional layer that you have found. Return to step 14.

16. The final step in healing an emotional wound is to release the false beliefs that were taken on when the original traumatic event occurred (xiii). Visualize yourself as the person that you were when the original trauma occurred. Visualize yourself telling that traumatized part of you that you will look after it now and that it no longer needs to be afraid. If that part of you is receptive to your presence then go to step 18 else go to step 17.

17. You have found that the traumatized part of you is not receptive to you. Simply reassure that part of you that you Love it and that you are there for it whenever it needs you. Sit with it for a few minutes and then tell it that you will return to see it again soon. Take a break from this healing process for a few hours, or a few days, and then return to step 16.

18. Ask the traumatized part of you if it is okay for you to give it a hug. If that part of you allows you to give it a hug then go to step 19. If it does not allow you to hug it then sit with it for a few minutes before telling it that you will return to see it again soon. Take a break from this healing process for a few hours, or a few days, and then return to step 16.

19. Invite that traumatized part of you to merge back into you and become a part of you once again. If it merges back into you then go to step 20. If it does not merge back into you then sit with it for a few minutes before telling it that you will return to see it again

soon. Take a break from this healing process for a few hours, or a few days, and then return to step 16.

20. Having the traumatized part of you merge back into you signals that it has let go of the false beliefs that it needs to be protected in some way. The healing journey is complete (xiv). You will still have the memory of the original traumatic event but the associated emotions and the false beliefs will both be gone. If a pain or illness had manifested because of the emotional trauma then the body will begin to heal itself.

Notes:

i.   This exercise is intended to be used after you have discovered that a barrier to Love inside you is an emotional trauma. You will have found the emotional trauma through having a traumatic memory surface. That memory may have surfaced either during day to day life or when you were following one of the signposts (fear, an emotional reaction, pain, or a non-Loving motivation) down inside yourself and discovered that the root cause of the signpost was an emotional trauma.

ii. An emotional trauma is created when the original event is too emotionally painful for a person to be able to handle at the time. That person's psyche then creates a false belief that 'it' had been threatened and that 'it' has to be protected from a recurrence of that event. That false belief creates a disturbance in the person's life force energy; a wound. That false belief is then stored, along with both the memory of the event and the emotions that arose at the time of the event. That memory is then typically buried away and forgotten.

iii. The person will then act in the world from the false belief that they took on. They may have no recollection of having taken on the false belief and may not even be aware that they are reacting from it. They may react to external events with fear or with an emotion such as anger or sadness. If the false belief is left in place long enough then it can manifest physically as a pain or illness.

iv. Allow yourself to be drawn to the appropriate technique for supporting you in healing this specific emotional trauma. It is quite likely that you will use a number of different therapy techniques on your healing journey. You will likely have multiple emotional traumas surface and each one may require a different technique. Trust that your inner guide will direct you to the technique, and therapist, that can support you in healing the particular emotional trauma that has surfaced.

v.   A therapist does not heal you, you do. They can only guide you through the self-healing process. They can guide you in recalling the original traumatic event and into feeling the emotions that you felt at the time of the event. They can then guide you through the healing process of your using Love, visualizations, learning your lessons, and forgiveness to heal yourself. If your therapist thinks that they can heal you, rather than simply support you in healing yourself, then I recommend that you find another therapist.

vi.   As outlined in this book, you have to feel it to heal it. You have to feel the way you did at the time of the original trauma before you can heal yourself. A therapy technique cannot heal you. It can only support you in healing yourself. You must feel the emotions from the time of the original wound and then use Love, learning your lessons, and forgiveness to heal. When you do that, the false beliefs will be let go and the emotions that were stored along with the original memory will be released. Only then will you have healed the emotional trauma.

vii.   If the therapist does not ask you to feel the emotions associated with the original event then you will not be able to heal yourself while working with them. I recommend that you find another therapist.

viii.   You will have healed yourself when the false beliefs that you took on at the time of the original event have been let go and the emotions that were stored along with the memory of that original event have been released. Letting go of the false beliefs happens when the wounded part of you lets go of its need to feel protected. Releasing the stored emotions occurs when you forgive all those involved in the event (including yourself) from the depth of those emotions. No healing occurs if you mentally forgive. You have to feel it to heal it.

ix.   Forgiving another person heals you not them. Forgiveness frees you from your inner trauma. It does not matter how the other person responds to your forgiveness. That is their journey not yours.

x. Invite a friend to be there if you feel that their support will be beneficial. Choose a friend that you know will support you in feeling deeper into the emotional trauma without trying to pull you out of it and without trying to tell you what to do. The other person is there solely as a Loving presence.

xi. You have to feel it to heal it. You must feel the emotions from the time of the original wound and then use Love, learning your lessons, and forgiveness to heal. When you do that, the emotions that were stored along with the original memory will have been released.

xii. At this point you will have healed an emotional layer. However, there may have been multiple emotional layers (wounds) created by the one traumatic event. For example, a person who has been abused as a child may need to first heal the wound that was created by the abuser. They may then need to heal a wound that was created by any anger that they feel towards a parent or guardian for not protecting them. You will know if there is another emotional layer (wound) to be healed if you still feel emotional when you recall the original memory of the emotional trauma. Another way to know if there are multiple emotional layers (wounds) associated with an emotional trauma is to recall the journey that you took from feeling the original signpost (fear, emotional reaction, pain, or non-Loving motivation) to finding the memory of the underlying traumatic event. If you passed through a number of emotional layers on that journey then each one of them will need to be healed.

xiii. The final step in healing an emotional trauma is to release the false beliefs that were taken on because of the traumatic event. It is the traumatized part of you that took on those false beliefs and it is only that part of you that can let them go.

xiv. Both the emotions stored with the memory of the traumatic event and the false beliefs that the traumatized part of you took on will have been released.

9. *Letting Go of a Desire.*

This exercise is to be used for letting go of a desire (i, ii, and iii).

1. Find a space where you can sit quietly.

2. Ask to be shown the false belief about how you think you will benefit from satisfying the desire (iv and v). If you think you will gain something that you feel you are lacking then go to step 3. If you think that you will benefit by being able to avoid the way you are feeling then go to step 4. If you think that you will benefit by gaining relief from a pain or illness then go to step 5.

3. Enter into meditation and ask to be shown the barrier to Love that is causing you to seek outside yourself for something that can only be found inside you (vi and viii). Go to step 6.

4. Enter into meditation and ask to be shown the feeling that you are trying to avoid (vii). Remain in meditation and ask to be shown the barrier to Love that is triggering that feeling (viii). Go to step 6.

5. You can only gain permanent relief from a pain or illness by healing the barrier to Love that is underlying it (ix). Heal the source of your pain or illness using exercise '*1. Healing the source of a pain or illness*'. Once the pain or illness has been healed then go to step 7.

6. Heal the barrier to Love using the appropriate exercise for that type of barrier: '*6. Letting go of a Particular Fear*'; '*7. Removing a Belief*'; '*8. Healing an Emotional Trauma*'; or, '*9. Letting go of a Desire*'.

7. You will have then removed a false belief about how you thought you could benefit from that desire. Allow yourself to feel whether or not you still have the desire. If it is gone then you are finished with this exercise. If you still feel the desire then return to step 1 and remove the next false belief about how you think you will benefit from satisfying this desire (x).

Notes:

i. This exercise is intended to be used after you have discovered that a barrier to Love inside you is a desire. You will have either simply become aware that you are holding onto a desire or you will have followed one of the signposts (fear, an emotional, pain, or non-Loving motivation) down inside and discovered that the root cause of the signpost was a desire.

ii.   Every desire comes from the ego and is based on the false belief that you will benefit in some way from satisfying that desire.

iii.   You must free yourself from all desires in order to become Love. Every desire must be dropped. That said, the desire to find your way 'home' and the desire to achieve enlightenment are called the highest desires. Having one of them appear in your life is considered to be a blessing because it will give you the determination to either find your way 'home' or achieve enlightenment. The highest desires are still desires of the ego, and they will prevent you from actually returning 'home' or achieving enlightenment, but they are to be held onto until all other desires have been dropped. At that point, they will need to be dropped as well.

iv.   Every desire is based on the false belief that 'you' will gain something by satisfying that desire. The false self may gain something but the essence of who you are will not. Chasing after desires of the false self will only prevent you from healing yourself and returning home to Love.

v.   The benefit that you think you will get from satisfying a desire will be either to gain something that your false self thinks it lacks, to avoid the way you are feeling, or to gain relief from a pain or illness. For example, one of the most common desires that people have is to find a man or woman with whom to have a relationship. This desire is sourced from that person either wanting to avoid a feeling (e.g. depression or loneliness) or having a belief that they will gain something from the relationship that that they feel they are lacking inside themselves (e.g. self-worth, Love, or happiness).

vi.   You cannot gain self-worth, Love, happiness, or anything else from outside of yourself. Everything that you need is inside you. If you have a desire to seek something outside of yourself then that desire is being triggered by a barrier to Love.

vii.   Your feelings are signposts indicating that something inside you needs to be healed. If you try to avoid your feelings then you will not be able to heal your barriers to Love and will not become a self-healer.

viii.   This may take some time and a number of attempts before you are shown the barrier to Love. Be patient.

ix.   It is important for you to get whatever medical attention is required to keep your body alive. Once the body is being taken of then you can work on healing yourself by allowing yourself to feel the pain and asking to be shown the message that it is bringing you. If you try to avoid the pain then you will not be able to receive the message.

x.   It is possible to have multiple false beliefs underlying one desire. This happens when you falsely believe that you will benefit in many ways from satisfying it. If that is the case you will need to repeat this exercise for each one of those false beliefs.

10. Learning to Feel Again.

This exercise is intended to give you practice in experiencing how different emotions feel inside your body (i). You can do this exercise on your own or with a group of people.

1.   Select one emotion, perhaps anger, to begin the exercise with.

2.   Recall a situation in your life that led to your feeling angry. Visualize that situation and allow yourself to feel the anger.

3.   Bring your awareness to how the energy of anger feels inside your body.

4.   Pick another emotion (such as sadness, happiness, shame, frustration, jealousy, hatred, excitement, or guilt) and repeat steps 1 through 3 for that emotion. Repeat steps 1 through 3 for all of the emotions that you can think of (ii).

Notes:

i.   This exercise is for those people who have difficulty in knowing how they actually feel. Many of us, myself included, were raised in a way that teaches us to repress the way we feel. For example, I was told that "big boys don't cry" and that I shouldn't get angry. As a result, I became very good at suppressing my emotions. My answer to "how are you?" was always to say either "good" or "fine". In fact, I had buried my emotions so deep that I couldn't have told someone how I felt even if I had wanted to. I no longer knew. If you also struggle to feel your own emotions then this exercise is a way to learn how to feel again.

ii. With practice, you will be able to feel the subtle difference between how each different emotion feels energetically within your body. You will then be able to tell someone how you actually feel.

11. Expressing the Way You Feel

This exercise is intended to give you practice in expressing the way you feel out loud (i, ii, and iii). It is to be done in a group setting and ideally involves between six and twelve people (iv).

1. Select one question that every person is going to answer during this exercise (v).

2. Have one person stand up while everyone else remains seated.

3. The person standing then begins to express how they feel by answering the selected question.

4. The people sitting are to stand up when they feel that the person speaking is expressing how they truly feel from their heart not from their mind (vi).

5. The person speaking will continue talking until everyone else in the room has stood up (vii and viii).

6. Once everyone is standing, the speaker will stop talking and everyone will sit down. If everyone has had a turn standing up to speak then the exercise is over. If there are people who have not yet answered the question then have the next person stand up to speak and return to step 3.

Notes:

i. This exercise gives you an opportunity to both practice expressing your feelings openly and honestly, and to listen to how other people sound when they are expressing the way they feel.

ii.   Love is acceptance. If you are able to accept yourself exactly as you are in any given moment then you are Loving yourself. That includes accepting the way you feel.

iii.   Accepting the way you currently feel does not mean that you will have to feel that same way always. It just means that you feel that way in this moment. You then have the opportunity to find and heal any barriers to Love that may underlie those feelings. You can only become a self-healer by Loving yourself through accepting the way you truly feel.

iv.   I would recommend a minimum of three people for this exercise.

v.   Pick a question that asks you to express how you feel about something. For example, 'How do you feel in this moment', 'How do you feel about the opposite sex', or 'How do you feel about your body'. Use your imagination to come up with a question that is relevant to the group of people that has gathered together for this exercise.

vi.   The people listening are given the opportunity to practice listening to the energy behind the words being spoken not just to the words themselves. It is possible to feel when a person is speaking from their heart versus from their mind. With practice, you will learn to hear what it sounds like when a person is expressing the way they truly feel from the depths of their being.

vii.   The person speaking will have the opportunity to become aware of what it feels like to speak from their heart versus from their mind. It is only when they are able to speak from their heart that they will be able to discover how they truly feel.

viii.   Most people have a 'controller' of some kind inside themselves that blocks them from speaking about how they truly feel. This exercise provides a way to go beyond that 'controller' and discover how you truly feel. It provides a way to experience self-Love.

12. Dyading

A dyad is an exercise in which two people sit opposite each other and express the way they truly feel about a selected topic. It is an opportunity to practice Loving yourself by expressing the way you feel. It is also an opportunity to practice the art of listening (i and ii).

1. Have each pair of people sit facing each other. Have them position themselves close together so that they you do not have to strain to hear what the other person is saying.

2. Have each person select a question that they would like to answer during the dyad (iii).

3. Agree on which one of you will begin by talking. The other person will begin by listening.

4. Begin the exercise by having the one who is to listen ask the one who is to talk the question that the speaker has selected.

5. The speaker then answers that question for 5 minutes (iv and v).

6. The person listening does so with a neutral expression. They do not comment on what they are hearing and they do not otherwise react in any way. They simply rest in a silent inner space and listen to the other person share their feelings (vi).

7. After five minutes, the person speaking stops talking and says 'thank you' to the listener. The two people now swap roles. The person who was speaking now becomes the listener and the person who was listening becomes the speaker.

8. The new listener then asks the new speaker the question that the new speaker had selected.

9. The new speaker then expresses the way they feel for 5 minutes. The new listener simply listens without responding or reacting in any way.

10. Repeat steps 4 through 10 three more times so that each person has the opportunity to speak four times and to listen four times. Each person is to answer the same question for all four cycles of the exercise (vii).

Notes:

i. The art of listening involves listening to another person speak from a silent inner space. There is no desire to formulate a reply or to otherwise respond in any way. The listener is simply holding a silent space of Love in which the speaker is able to explore the way they truly feel.

ii.   This exercise requires an even number of people. It can be done in groups of 2, 4, 6, 8, 10, and so on. Simply have everyone pair off and then have each set of two people sit facing each other for the duration of the exercise.

iii.   Pick a question that invites you to express how you feel about something. For example, 'How do you feel in this moment', 'How do you feel about the opposite sex', or 'How do you feel about your body'. Use your imagination to come up with a question that is relevant to the way you are feeling in the moment. You do not have to pick the same question as your partner.

iv.   Start ever sentence with the words 'I feel' rather than 'I think'.

v.   Have a timer available to you for this exercise. Set it to five minutes whenever someone begins their turn to talk. The timer could either be a device or a third party who provides this function for you.

vi.   The person listening has the opportunity to practice listening to someone share their feelings without responding in any way to what is being said. Listening without the desire to reply is a major component of the art of listening. It allows the listener to create a space of Love for the speaker.

vii.   The two people do not have to answer the same question. However, they do need to keep answering their own chosen question for all four cycles of the exercise. That gives them the opportunity to delve deeper and deeper into the way they truly feel about the question.

13. Ground Yourself

This exercise describes a way for you to ground yourself. This exercise works well in conjunction with the next exercise '*14. Center Yourself*' (i, ii, and iii).

1. If you are familiar with the seven main chakras in the body then go to step 4 otherwise go to step 2 (iv).

2. Visualize a metallic hoop going around your upper thighs at the level of your groin area. Visualize that hoop as being tight around your hips so that you cannot slip through it.

3. Visualize chains connected to this hoop and going down to the very center of the earth and hooking into the earth's core. You are grounded and this exercise is over.

4. Visualize an energetic cord attached to your first chakra and going down into the core of the earth. Visualize it hooking into the core of the planet and anchoring you. You are then grounded.

Notes:

i. If you can maintain your grounding and centering regardless of what is happening around you then you are able to remain calm in the face of life's events. You will not get lost in any emotions, thoughts, or pains that arise in the body. You are then able to choose how you wish to respond to life rather than be a prisoner of the barriers to Love that trigger your inner reactions.

ii. Grounding yourself involves anchoring your energy down into the earth. You are then able to stand firmly rooted no matter what comes your way.

iii. You can do this exercise in a group or on your own.

iv. The seven main chakras that this step is referring are from the Hindu Chakra System. They are energy centers that are located in: the groin area (first chakra); a couple of inches below the belly button (second chakra); the upper abdomen (third chakra); the center of the chest (fourth chakra); the throat (fifth chakra); the third eye (sixth); and, the top of the head (seventh chakra).

14. Center Yourself

This exercise describes a way for you to center yourself. This exercise works well in conjunction with the previous exercise '*13. Ground Yourself*' (i, ii, and iii).

1. Bring your attention to whatever thoughts are running through your mind. The focus of your awareness will now be inside your head just behind your forehead. You will not be centered (iv).

Note how this feels for you.

2. Bring your attention to the center of your chest. The focus of your awareness will now be in your heart chakra and you will be heart-centered not centered (v). Note how this feels for you.

3. Bring your attention to the very center of your head (between the temples and half way up your head) simply by intending to do so. The focus of your awareness will then be in the center of your head and you will be centered (vi). Note how this feels for you.

Notes:

i.   If you can maintain your grounding and centering regardless of what is happening around you then you are able to remain calm in the face of life's events. You will not get lost in any emotions, thoughts, or pains that arise in the body. You are then able to choose how you wish to respond to life rather than be a prisoner of the barriers to Love that trigger your inner reactions.

ii. Everyone has a focus of awareness. The focus of your awareness will reside in whatever place you bring your attention to. You can move the focus of your awareness by simply intending to do it and then moving your attention to the place where you want the focus of your awareness to be.

iii. You can do this exercise in a group or on your own.

iv. You will typically become 'lost' in your thoughts when you put the focus of your awareness inside your forehead in this way. You will be functioning in the world from the thoughts generated from your ego.

v.   You will typically be focused on doing what you 'think' is best for others when you are heart centered. You will be functioning from your conditioning around love and around how people 'should' act in the world. You will still be functioning from the ego.

vi. Remaining centered in this way allows you to maintain a calm and peaceful inner state of being regardless of any external events that life brings your way. You then have the opportunity to be Loving towards yourself and others.

15. *Performing an Insight Meditation*

This exercise describes the process for performing an insight meditation on any question about yourself that you would like to have answered by your own inner guide.

1. Find a quiet space where you can sit in silence.

2. Focus your awareness on the question you would like to ask.

3. Enter into a meditative space and ask to be shown the answer to your question (i and ii). Be patient and trust that your inner guide will show you the answer (iii).

4. Once you have the answer then take action based on that answer.

Notes:

i.   It may take you some time to find and hear the answer. Your rational mind will likely jump in and try to provide you with an answer. Whatever your rational mind provides is a guess and will invariably be wrong. Be patient. Wait until you hear the answer from your inner guide rather than from your rational mind.

ii. It can be difficult at first to distinguish between when your inner guide is answering the question and when your rational mind is jumping in with its guesses. You may find that you think it is your inner guide speaking when it is actually your rational mind. You will then listen to that answer and it will temporarily lead you astray. Be patient with yourself. You will learn how to distinguish between your inner guide's answers and those of your rational mind. There is a feeling of knowingness that comes with the answers from your inner guide. That feeling is far different than the mental knowing that comes from your rational mind. It comes with a deep sense of truth.

iii. Trust is one of the three pillars of becoming a self-healer. It is an invaluable tool on your healing journey and it is absolutely necessary for doing insight meditations. You will be trusting your own inner guide rather than your mind, another person's mind, or any form of external God. Your inner guide is the only 'one' that knows your answers.

16. *Freeing Yourself from Feeling 'Stuck'.*

This exercise is intended to show you a way to free yourself from feeling 'stuck'. The feeling of being 'stuck' invariably stems from your being afraid to either face a barrier to Love (usually an emotional trauma) that is surfacing or to follow the guidance of your inner guide (i).

1. Find a space where you can sit quietly.

2. Enter into meditation and ask to be shown the fear underlying your feeling of being stuck (ii).

3. Use exercise '*6. Letting go of a Particular fear*' to heal the fear.

4. If the fear that you have just healed was a fear of facing either an emotional trauma or one of the other three barriers to Love then go to step 5. If the fear was of following the guidance of your inner guide then go to step 6.

5. Heal the barrier to Love using the appropriate exercise for that type of barrier: '*6. Letting go of a Particular Fear*'; '*7. Removing a Belief*'; '*8. Healing an Emotional Trauma*'; or, '*9. Letting go of a Desire*'. Go to step 7.

6. Follow the guidance that you are receiving from your inner guide.

7. You will have healed a source of your feeling stuck. Allow yourself to tune into the feeling of being stuck and see if it has dissolved away. If it has then you have completed this exercise. If it has not then you have another fear that is keeping you stuck (iii). Return to step 1 and repeat this exercise for the next fear that has you feeling stuck.

Notes:

i. The feeling of being 'stuck' invariably stems from your being afraid to either face a barrier to Love (usually an emotional trauma) that is surfacing or to follow the guidance of your inner guide. To free yourself of feeling stuck, you need to first find and release that fear. You can then either heal the barrier to Love that is surfacing or do whatever your inner guide is asking you to do. The feeling of being 'stuck' will then dissolve away.

ii. This may take some time and a number of attempts before you are shown the fear. Be patient.

iii.   It is possible that there will be more than one fear underlying your feeling of being stuck. If this is the case then you will need to repeat this exercise for each fear.

17. Healing Depression

This exercise is to be used for healing the source of depression. The source of depression is invariably a failure to accept something about yourself or your life. Depression occurs when you want things to be different than they actually are.

WARNING: This exercise for healing depression can be emotionally painful. It is recommended that you only do this exercise when you are in a 'safe' space and have developed the ability to remain in mindful awareness regardless of any emotions that are running through your body. In this case, a 'safe' space is a physical environment in which the people around you are proficient in this process and are available 24 hours a day to support you

1. Accept that the source of the depression is a failure to accept something about yourself or your life.

2. Find a space where you can sit quietly and invite a friend to join you in that space (i).

3. Enter into meditation and allow yourself to feel the depression as strongly as you are able. Ask your inner guide to show you what it is about yourself or your life that you are failing to accept (ii, iii, and iv).

4. Once you see what it is that you are failing to accept then the next step is to accept it. If you are able to do so immediately then do it and the depression will lift. In that case, go to step 9. If you are unable to accept it immediately then go to the next step.

5. Accept that life is perfect exactly as it is (v).

6. The scenario that came into your life and triggered your depression has a lesson to teach you. Go into meditation and ask to be shown that lesson (vi).

7. Embrace the lesson. If you are struggling to embrace the lesson then there is a barrier to Love that must be removed before you can

embrace it. Enter into meditation and ask to be shown the barrier to Love that is blocking you (vii). Heal the barrier to Love and then embrace the lesson (viii).

8. Accept whatever it was about yourself or your life that you were resisting.

9. The depression will then lift (ix and x). If the depression does not lift then there is something else about yourself or your life that you are also not accepting. Go back to step 1 and repeat this exercise to find and accept the next thing that you are resisting.

Notes:

i. It is recommended that you invite a friend to support you through this process. Choose a friend that you know will support you in falling deeper into the depression without trying to pull you out of it.

ii. It often requires you to go deep into the depression and feel it at its strongest before you will actually see what it is that you are failing to accept. You may need to return to this process a few times before you are shown the source of your depression. Be patient.

iii. Your mind cannot help you with this process. It is your inner guide that will show you what you are resisting not your mind. If you think that you know the source of your depression, and you are still depressed, then you don't know. If you heal what you thought was the source of your depression and you are still depressed then it was not the source. It was just your mind jumping in with something that it thought was the answer. Your mind does not know the answer. If it happens to guess right then that would be luck not insight.

iv. It is only your inner guide that knows what it is that you are resisting. Wait until you hear the answer from your inner guide before attempting to heal whatever it is that you are not accepting. With practice, you will learn to distinguish between your mind making things up and your inner guide providing you with the answer. One helpful tip to use when trying to distinguish between your mind and your inner guide is that the answer to what it is that you are resisting will almost always be a surprise.

v.   Life is perfect exactly as it is. This is 'true' in the context that life is bringing the experiences into your life that you need in order to learn the lessons that you incarnated to learn. It does not mean that you have to spend your life living with any pain and suffering that arise. It only means that pain and suffering are coming into your life in order for you to learn your lessons. The scenario that is triggering your current depression has a life lesson for you. By accepting 'what is', you then have the opportunity to learn that lesson.

vi.   It may take time and repeated attempts before you are shown the lesson. Be patient. You may find yourself not wanting to admit to yourself that there is a lesson in this scenario for you. It is important that you be honest with yourself about what the lesson may be.

vii.   It may take time and repeated attempts before you are shown the barrier to Love. Be patient.

viii.   Use the appropriate exercise from this book for healing the barrier to Love that you have found: '6. *Letting go of a Particular Fear'*; '7. *Removing a Belief'*; '8. *Healing an Emotional Trauma'*; or, '9. *Letting go of a Desire'*.

ix.   It is possible that your depression is stemming from your not accepting more than one thing about yourself or your life. If that is the case then you will need to repeat this exercise for everything that you are not accepting.

x.   One of the beautiful things about learning the lessons underlying your depression is that your life then tends to go in a new direction. You will have opened the door to having new life experiences that will bring you your next set of lessons. Your life will then change in unforeseen ways. The benefit of having your life change in this way is that you would not have used your mind in a fruitless struggle to try and make it change. That only leads to depression.

18. *Expressing Guilt Out Loud*

This exercise provides you with the opportunity to express out loud everything from your past that you feel guilty about (i and ii).

1. Count the number of women in the group and then create a circle of chairs for that many women. Have all of the women sit in a circle using those chairs.

2. Count the number of men in the group and then create a circle of chairs for that many men. Create a distance between the two circles so that what is whispered in one circle cannot be heard in the other circle. Have all of the men sit in a circle using those chairs.

3. Have all of the women lean forward in their chairs until their foreheads are almost touching and they are looking down at the floor.

4. Have all of the men lean forward in their chairs until their foreheads are almost touching and they are looking down at the floor.

5. Tell everyone that these are sacred circles and that nothing that is said in these circles is to be repeated outside of them. Ask everyone to agree to this.

6. Select one man and one woman to begin the exercise. Have the selected man and woman begin the exercise by whispering one thing that they feel guilty about. They are to whisper loud enough for everyone in their circle to hear them but not loud enough for anyone outside their circle to hear them (iii).

7. Have the person to their right then whisper one thing that they feel guilty about. Keep going around the circles until everyone has had a chance to express something they feel guilty about. Then keep going around the circles again and again until everyone has expressed everything that they feel guilty about.

8. Once everyone has finished expressing the things they feel guilty about, have everyone stand up and hug the others from their circle.

9. This exercise is over. However, each person may choose, at a later date, to take each item that they still feel guilty about into exercise '*19. Letting go of Guilt over a Past Action*'.

Notes:

i.   This exercise is to be done with a group of people. The group can be done with all men, all women, or with a mixed group. There needs to be a minimum of three people of a given sex to make this exercise effective.

ii.   You will be expressing out loud everything from your past that you feel guilty about. Expressing these items out loud has the cathartic effect of shining the light of awareness on the items you feel guilty about. For many of the items, that awareness will often be enough to dissolve the guilt away. However, there will likely be some past actions where the guilt is so deeply held that expressing it out loud does not heal it.

iii.   When one person is speaking, everyone else in the circle is to listen to them without judgment. The listeners are to remain silent and not comment on anything that is said in the circle. They may acknowledge the speaker by simply saying 'Ho' if they share a similar feeling of guilt.

19. *Letting go of Guilt Over a Past Action*

This exercise is intended to free you of any feelings of guilt that you are carrying because of a specific event from your past.

1. Accept that you do indeed feeling guilty. You cannot let go of guilt until you first admit to yourself that you are feeling guilty.

2. Enter into a meditative state.

3. Recall the event that you feel guilty about and allow the feelings of guilt to grow inside you. Bring your attention to wherever in your body you feel the guilt the strongest and allow the feeling to grow as strong as it can become.

4. Once you feel that you have reached the depths of the guilt that you feel for whatever you did then send whomever you hurt a heartfelt apology. Visualize the person and apologize to them either out loud or silently in your head (i).

5. You will know that you have truly said sorry from the depths of your emotional pain when you feel that pain starting to dissipate from inside you. The release of that pain is often accompanied by tears. Allow yourself to cry until the tears cease flowing.

6. Continue to sit in meditation and tune in to see if you are feeling angry towards yourself for what you did. If you are not feeling angry then your healing is complete and you can skip the remaining steps.

7. Stay in meditation and allow yourself to feel the anger that you have towards yourself. Ask to be shown the barrier to Love underlying that anger (ii).

8. Heal the barrier to Love using the appropriate exercise for that type of barrier: '6. *Letting go of a Particular Fear*'; '7. *Removing a Belief*'; '8. *Healing an Emotional Trauma*'; or, '9. *Letting go of a Desire*'.

9. Go back into meditation, recall the scenario, and ask to be shown the soul lesson that you are to learn from this event. The lesson will be related to whatever barrier to Love inside you caused you to fall from grace (iii).

10. Embrace the lesson. Make a commitment to yourself to own the lesson and to do your best not to repeat the action that caused you to feel guilty.

11. Forgive yourself for your fall from grace. Allow yourself to feel the anger towards yourself for your actions and forgive yourself (iv). You will know that you have managed to actually forgive yourself when the anger dissolves away.

Notes:

i. You do not need to say sorry in person. The apology will free you from your emotional pain and is not intended to do anything for the other person. If you choose to apologize in person then please remember that how they react to your apology is none of your business.

ii. When the original event occurred, you were not able to remain in a Loving inner space and reacted from your ego instead of responding from Love. Reacting from ego is to fall from grace. If you had been able to remain Loving then you would not be feeling guilty. It will have been a barrier to Love that triggered you into functioning from your ego. You will need to find and heal that barrier to Love in order to ensure that you do not fall from grace again when a similar situation arises in your life.

iii.   The lesson will be directly related to the barrier to Love that triggered you into falling from grace. For example, the lesson may be something like allowing sexual desire to disconnect you from Love can result in your doing things that are harmful to yourself and others. The lesson would then be to remain connected to the inner space of Love even when sexual desire is present in the body.

iv.   It is important to feel the anger towards yourself before attempting to forgive yourself. Mental forgiveness accomplishes no healing. It is the part of you that is angry at yourself that must forgive you.

20. Freeing Yourself from Feeling Obligated to do Anything

This exercise is intended to support you in finding and healing the barriers to Love underlying any feelings of obligation (i).

1. Allow yourself to be honest with yourself about the true motivation behind everything that you say and do.

2. When you find that your motivation for doing something is coming from a feeling that you 'should' do it then don't do it. Do not do anything that you think you 'should' do. In other words, do not do anything out of obligation.

3. Enter a meditative state and visualize the event that is causing you to feel obligated. Allow the feeling of obligation to grow stronger in you and ask to be shown the barrier to Love that is underlying that feeling.

4. Heal the barrier to Love using the appropriate exercise for that type of barrier: '*6. Letting go of a Particular Fear*'; '*7. Removing a Belief*'; '*8. Healing an Emotional Trauma*'; or, '*9. Letting go of a Desire*'.

5. Visualize the original event that caused you to feel obligated. If you no longer feel obligated to do it then go to step 6. If you still feel obligated then you have another barrier to Love underlying that feeling of obligation. Return to step 3.

6. The feeling of obligation will be gone. You can now revisit your decision not to do the thing that you originally felt obligated to do.

If you now feel drawn to do it then you are free to do whatever it was from a Loving inner space. If you don't feel drawn to do it then don't do it.

Notes:

i.   There is a part of you that will resent the things that you do out of obligation. That resentment will then be present inside you throughout any subsequent interaction and will prevent you from being Loving towards yourself and others. If you want to become Love then it is necessary for you to stop doing anything out of obligation. All feelings of obligation are coming from barriers to Love inside you. Instead of acting from obligation, you can choose to find the barrier to Love inside you that is causing you to feel obligated and heal it. You will no longer feel obligated. You can then do whatever it was from an inner space of Love.

21. Connect to Your Inner Power and Retrieve Your Self-Esteem

This exercise provides a way to connect to your own inner power and retrieve your self-esteem. It is intended to be used for situations in which you have felt bullied or humiliated in some way.

Connect to your inner Power

1.   Ground and center yourself (i).

2.   Bring energy from mother earth up through the chakras in the base of your feet (ii). Bring the energy up through your legs and into the root chakra at the base of your spine (iii). Mix that energy with your own energy in the root chakra and have part of that mixture flow down your grounding.

3.   Bring the energy of the cosmos, of father sun, down through the top of the spine (at the back of the neck). Bring that energy down your spine and into the root chakra (iii). Mix the energy with the energy of mother earth and with your own energy in the root chakra. Have part of that mixture flow down your grounding.

4.   Visualize bringing some of the mixture of energy from your root chakra up through your second chakra and into the third chakra in your upper abdomen (iii and iv). Visualize the energy in your third chakra as a ball of golden yellow light.

5. Visualize the golden yellow energy flowing out from the ball of light in your third chakra and infusing every cell of your being. You will have then accessed your inner power.

Take back your Power – Retrieve Self-Esteem

6. Pick a memory of being bullied or humiliated in some way.

7. Visualize a red rose in front of you. Visualize all of the energy from the incident flowing out of you and into the rose. Visualize the rose blowing up.

8. Repeat step 7 until you feel that all of the strong emotions associated with the incident have been released.

Take back your Power – Stepping into Personal Power

9. Bring your awareness to the golden yellow light in your third chakra (v).

10. Visualize the incident and the other people involved. Visualize yourself standing in front of them and state (either out loud or in silence): *"This is me!"*. Repeat that statement until you feel that you have taken your power back (vi).

Notes:

i.   Use exercises '*13. Ground Yourself*' and '*14. Center Yourself*'.

ii.   There is a foot chakra in center of the base of each of your feet. These chakras allow the energy of mother earth to enter your body.

iii. You may not initially be able to feel the energy that you are visualizing. Begin by simply trusting that it is flowing and, with practice, you will be able to feel it.

iv.   The third chakra is your power center. It is where you can access your inner power. It is also where any issues that you have with self-esteem, self-confidence, and self-worth are stored.

v.   Bringing your awareness to your third chakra enables you to step fully into your inner power.

vi.   You will know that you have taken your power back when you feel that you are able to say the words 'This is me!' with no hesitation. You will be saying them without holding anything back.

22. *Open Your Heart and Take Back Your Power*

This exercise provides a way to open your heart and then take back your power. It is intended to be used for any situation in which you have given away your power to a person or institution (i).

Open your heart chakra (ii)

1. Ground and center yourself (iii).

2. Visualize a ball of emerald green light in your heart chakra (iv and v). Allow that energy to expand inside your heart chakra.

3. Visualize the green energy flowing out of that ball of light and flowing into every cell of your body.

4. Visualize this energy of Love flowing out of the ball and flowing to your Loved ones and to anyone else that you like.

Take back your Power

5. Think of a scenario in which you have given away your power (i).

6. Bring your awareness to your third chakra (your power center in your upper abdomen).

7. Visualize the scenario in which you gave away your power and send the other players in the scenario the emerald green energy of Love.

8. Consciously terminate any agreements that were made as part of giving away your power (vi).

9. Visualize how you could have interacted from a Loving space in that scenario (vii).

10. Visualize your energy flowing back from the other players (or from any institutions) and into your third chakra.

11. Set the intention to both retain your power and come from Love (for yourself and others) in the future.

Notes:

i. Examples of situations in which you may have given away your power include: caring about the opinions of others; identifying with something; making a vow or oath; taking pride in something;

wanting to be told what to believe; becoming a disciple; and, becoming your emotions.

ii.   The heart chakra is located in the center of your chest and is the fourth of the seven main chakras in your body. Issues to do with Loving yourself and Loving others will be stored in this chakra.

iii.   Use exercises '*13. Ground Yourself*' and '*14. Center Yourself*'.

iv.   Emerald green is the color of Love.

v.   You may not initially be able to feel the energy that you are visualizing. Begin by simply trusting that it is flowing and, with practice, you will be able to feel it.

vi.   An agreement will have been made if you either took a vow or oath, or became subservient to a person or institution in some way. You can terminate the agreements by either intending to reverse the vow or oath, or intending to no longer be subservient to anyone or anything.

vii.   Replay the scenario in your imagination with your acting differently than what actually occurred. Replay it in different ways until you feel that you are playing it out in a way that enables you to stay in a Loving space for yourself and the others involved.

23. *Freeing Oneself from Loneliness*

Loneliness stems from neediness. If you are feeling lonely then you actually have an unmet need inside you that you want to fill. It may be a need for a beloved to return or a need to talk to someone about whatever is going on for you. This exercise provides a way to heal loneliness by finding and releasing the ego-based need(s) that are causing it (i).

1. Find a quiet space in which to explore the feeling of loneliness that has arisen.

2. Enter into meditation and allow the feeling of loneliness to grow stronger inside you. Ask your inner guide to show you the ego-based need that is at the root of your loneliness (ii).

3. The ego-based need is a desire. Take the need into exercise '*9. Letting go of a Desire*'.

4. If the need that you released in the previous step was stemming from the absence of another person then go on to step 5 otherwise go to step 8.

5. You will only prolong your suffering by hanging on to the other person. Clear the energy of the person from your being using exercise '31. *Clearing the Energy between yourself and another'*.

6. Send them Love. Visualize a ball of emerald green light in the center of your chest (in your heart chakra). Visualize sending that green light (Love) to the other person.

7. Let them go by first performing a good-bye ceremony (iii). After the ceremony, cut any energetic cords that may exist between you and that person using exercise '32. *Cutting Cords'* (iv).

8. You will have cleared an ego-based need from your being. Allow yourself to tune into the feeling of loneliness and see if it has gone. If it is gone then you have finished this exercise. If it is still there then there is another need underlying your loneliness (v). Return to step 1 and repeat this exercise for the next need.

Notes:

i. Aloneness is presence of self. Once you release the needs that underlie your loneliness, you will find yourself feeling much more comfortable, and even happy, being alone. You will have presence.

ii. Every ego-based need is a desire. There is a false belief underlying every desire that you will somehow benefit from satisfying that desire.

iii. A good-bye ceremony is any ceremony that you do by yourself to express gratitude to the person and to say good-bye to them with Love. For example, you can write down everything that you feel grateful to that person for and everything related to them that you want to let go. You then sit in front a fire and state each item out loud one by one as you put the paper on which it is written into the fire. The fire will then burn away all of the energy that is left between the two of you. When you are finished burning all of the items, send the other person Love and say a silent good-bye.

iv.   We create energetic cords between ourselves and others whenever we enter into a co-dependent relationship with them. For example, you can have cords with your friends, co-workers, parents, institutional leaders, and lovers. It is beneficial to cut all of your cords. You do not create cords with those that you enter into unconditionally Loving relationships with.

v.   There may be multiple unmet needs underlying one feeling of loneliness. If, after removing an unmet need, the feeling of loneliness has not disappeared then there are additional needs to be removed. The feeling of loneliness will disappear only when all of the unmet needs underlying the feeling have been released.

24. *Stop Falsely Identifying with the Roles that you Play.*

Every role that you play in life is temporary. Your roles do not define who you are (i and ii). This exercise is intended to break you free from falsely identifying with the roles that you play.

1. Find a quiet area where you can walk around in silence without having anyone disturb you.

2. Walk slowly through that space and say to yourself *"I am a consultant (for example)"* and then say *"No, I am not"* (iii). Accept the possibility that the label that you are putting on yourself is just a temporary role that you are playing and that it is not who you are (iv).

3. Repeat step 2 for every role that you play in life.

Notes:

i.   The roles that you play are things like lawyer, consultant, spiritual seeker, retailer, mother, man, sister, and so on. If you then say something like 'I am a lawyer' then you are making a false statement. The role that you play does not define who you are. Unfortunately, if you define yourself by your roles then you lock yourself into having to live by the assumptions and images that come with those roles.

ii.   You are not the career that you choose. It is simply a temporary role that you are playing. You are not even a father, daughter, mother, man, or woman. Those are simply roles that you are playing in this lifetime. The roles you play are not who you are. You are no 'thing'.

iii. The word consultant is inserted here solely as an example. Please replace that word with anything that you label yourself as.

iv. Roles are played by the false self (mind and body) not by you. By accepting that you are not the roles that you play, you open yourself to the possibility of dropping your identification with the false.

25. Healing Your Judgments of Others

This exercise is designed to enable you to find and remove the barriers to Love that underlie your judgments of others (i).

1. Bring mindful awareness to your thoughts and observe when you have a judgmental thought of another.

2. Own the judgment as having nothing to do with the other person and being a reflection of you not them.

3. Apologize to anyone that you may have treated in a judgmental way.

4. Find a quiet space where you can be alone.

5. Enter into meditation and hold the judgmental thought in your mind. Ask to be shown the barrier to Love (fear, belief, emotional trauma, or desire) that triggered the judgmental thought (ii).

6. Heal the barrier to Love using the appropriate exercise for that type of barrier: '6. *Letting go of a Particular Fear*'; '7. *Removing a Belief*'; '8. *Healing an Emotional Trauma*'; or, '9. *Letting go of a Desire*'.

Notes:

i. Every judgment is false. Every judgment of another is a judgment of yourself. Your judgments are being created by your conditioned mind. The source of each judgment is a barrier to Love (a fear, belief, emotional trauma, or desire) that you can heal.

ii. It may take some time, and repeated attempts, before you are shown the barrier to Love. Be patient.

26. Healing Your Judgments of Self

This exercise is to be used for healing the source of a judgmental thought about yourself (i and ii).

1. Accept that judging yourself is non-Loving. Make the choice to Love yourself instead of judging yourself (iii).

2. Bring mindful awareness to your thoughts and observe when you have a judgmental thought about yourself (iv).

3. Find a quiet space where you can be alone.

4. Enter into a meditative state and hold the judgmental thought in your mind. Ask to be shown the barrier to Love (fear, belief, emotional trauma, or desire) that triggered that thought (v).

5. Heal the barrier to Love using the appropriate exercise for that type of barrier: '*6. Letting go of a Particular Fear*'; '*7. Removing a Belief*'; '*8. Healing an Emotional Trauma*'; or, '*9. Letting go of a Desire*'.

Notes:

i. Judging yourself is non-Loving. Every judgmental thought (negative or positive) about yourself is being created by a barrier to Love.

ii. You can heal the source of a judgmental thought by finding and removing the barrier to Love that is triggering it.

iii. Loving yourself begins by accepting the way you currently feel. If you are holding onto a judgment about yourself then accepting that you hold that judgment is the Loving thing to do for yourself. You can then find and remove the barrier to Love underlying that judgment.

iv. You can replace step 2 with a proactive initiative to find and remove all of the judgmental thoughts that you currently hold about yourself. Make a list of every way in which you judge yourself. You can do this by asking yourself questions such as '*What do I like or dislike about the way I treat others?*' and '*What do I like or dislike about my body?*'. You may also choose to include everything that you say after making the statement, '*I wish that I wasn't so ... dumb, ugly, self-conscious, unlovable, and so on'.* You can then perform the remaining steps in this exercise for every item on your list.

v.   It may take some time, and repeated attempts, before you are shown the barrier to Love. Be patient.

27. *Letting Go of Playing the Victim Role*

The Victim role is the ego seeking attention. Playing the victim role leads to your having negative thoughts about yourself and drains your life force energy. It is a non-Loving way to treat yourself. Instead of playing the victim role, you can be loving towards yourself and heal the barrier to Love that is triggering you into playing that role. This exercise is to be used for letting go of the non-Loving action of playing the victim role.

1. Choose to stop playing the victim role (i).

2. Use mindful awareness to observe when you are feeling like a victim.

3. Find a silent space where you can be alone.

4. Enter into meditation and allow yourself to feel like a victim. Let the feeling grow stronger inside you. Ask to be shown the barrier to Love that is causing you to crave attention by playing the victim role (ii).

5. Heal the barrier to Love using the appropriate exercise for that type of barrier: '*6. Letting go of a Particular Fear*'; '*7. Removing a Belief*'; '*8. Healing an Emotional Trauma*'; or, '*9. Letting go of a Desire*'.

6. You will have healed one of the barriers to Love underlying your feeling of being a victim. It is possible that there are multiple barriers to Love underlying that feeling. Go back into meditation and observe whether or not you are still feeling like a victim. If you are then return to step 4. If you are not then you have completed this exercise.

Notes:

i.   The biggest obstacle that many people face in letting go of playing the victim role is that being a victim has become a part of their identity. They don't want to let it go. They are afraid that they won't get any attention at all if they stop receiving attention for their being a victim. That fear keeps them stuck in the victim mentality. If this is the case for you then heal that fear using exercise '3. *Healing the Source of Fear*' and then choose to stop playing the victim role.

ii.   It may take some time, and repeated attempts, before you are shown the barrier to Love. Be patient.

28. *Freeing Oneself from Addictive Cravings*

Addictions do not provide you with what you really want. What you really want is to be free of the feelings that you are trying to avoid by succumbing to that craving. Giving in to the craving will provide temporary relief at best and will often leave you feeling worse afterwards. The Loving thing to do for yourself is to not succumb to an addictive craving. Instead, find the feelings that you are trying to avoid and then remove the barriers to Love underlying those feelings. You will then be free of that particular instance of the addictive craving. This exercise is intended to provide a way to free yourself from an addictive craving (i).

1.   Use mindful awareness to observe when you are craving something (ii).

2.   If you find that your desire to either do something or consume something is coming from an addictive craving then do not do it (iii).

3.   Find a quiet space and invite a friend to join you in that space (iv). Talk about the way you feel about the addictive craving and also talk about what you feel it is that you are trying to avoid (v). It is important to talk only about the way you feel and not to talk about what you think (vi).

4.   Enter into meditation, allow yourself to feel the addictive craving, and ask to be shown the feelings about yourself or your life that you are trying to avoid (vii).

5.   Remain in meditation and ask to be shown the barrier to Love underlying the feelings that you are trying to avoid (viii).

6.   Heal the barrier to Love using the appropriate exercise for that type

of barrier: '*6. Letting go of a Particular Fear*'; '*7. Removing a Belief*'; '*8. Healing an Emotional Trauma*'; or, '*9. Letting go of a Desire*'.

7. There may be multiple feelings that you are trying to avoid through succumbing to an addictive craving. Co back into mediation and observe whether or not the addictive craving is gone. If it is gone then you are finished with this exercise. If it is not gone then you have another feeling to find and heal. Return to step 4.

Notes:

i.   There is a difference between feeling drawn to do something and craving it. When you feel drawn to do something, such as watch a movie, then there is usually going to be an insight gained from doing that activity. There is nothing long term to be gained from succumbing to a craving. You may receive temporary relief from an emotional or physical pain but succumbing to a craving is simply delaying the inevitable; the need to face yourself.

ii. Be absolutely honest with yourself about your true motivation for wanting to do something. Are you feeling drawn to it or are you wanting to do it in order to avoid the way you are feeling? It is only by being honest with yourself that you can find and heal your addictions.

iii. It can be difficult to choose not to give in to temptation. If you do give in to temptation then you can do this exercise the following day; after you have 'sobered' up. It is not too late to remove the barrier to Love that caused you to have the craving in the first place.

iv. You can do this exercise alone but we recommend that you invite a friend to join you. Choose a friend who is capable of supporting you from a Loving space.

v.   It may help for you to talk about your feelings about this addictive craving in order to gain some clarity on them. In that case, the friend is there to listen to you speak without replying or commenting on what you are saying in any way. They are there solely to guide you in speaking from your heart about your true feelings on the topic. You may wish to skip the step of talking about your feelings and go straight into the meditation. If that is the case for you then go on to the next step.

vi.   It does not matter what you think. The mind cannot help you to heal an addictive craving. It is only by following your feelings down inside yourself that you can find the deeper feelings that you are trying to avoid through an addiction. Begin each sentence with 'I feel' rather than 'I think'.

vii.   It may take some time, and repeated attempts, before you are shown the feeling that you are trying to avoid. Be patient.

viii.   It may take some time, and repeated attempts, before you are shown the barrier to Love. Be patient.

29. *Breaking the Addiction to Rational Thinking*

We become addicted to rational thinking by identifying with being the false self (the mind and body). We are then disconnected from who we really are and believe that our rational thoughts are actually true. Rational thoughts are inherently violent. They are generated by the ego and are all about defending and strengthening the false self. When we are addicted to rational thinking, our friends are the ones whose rational minds agree with ours and our enemies are those whose minds do not. Conflict is never far away. Rational thoughts and Love cannot co-exist inside you. This exercise is intended to provide you with a way to free yourself from your addiction to rational thinking (i).

1. Use mindful awareness to observe when you are identified with being rational (ii).

2. As soon as you become aware that you are being rational, stop sharing your rational thoughts with anyone.

3. Find a quiet space to sit in silence.

4. Replay the rational thought stream in your head and ask your inner guide to show you the barrier to Love that triggered those thoughts (iii).

5. Heal the barrier to Love using the appropriate exercise for that type of barrier: '6. *Letting go of a Particular Fear'; '7. Removing a Belief'; '8. Healing an Emotional Trauma'; or, '9. Letting go of a*

Desire'.

Notes:

i.   The alternative to rational thoughts is Loving thoughts. Loving thoughts, also known as divine inspiration, arise from inside you when you cultivate peace within and allow your rational mind to fall silent. Once the rational mind is silent, Loving thoughts will arise from your higher self. Loving thoughts are infused with the energy of Divine Love. When you allow Loving thoughts to flow through you and out into the world, you create a Loving space that invites others to become more Loving.

ii.   You are being rational when you have rational thoughts and believe that they are true. Be absolutely honest with yourself about whether or not you believe what your rational mind is stating. It is only the false self that believes rational thoughts have credence. You cannot be rational and Loving at the same time. When you are being rational, you are functioning from a barrier to Love. You can choose to remove that barrier to Love and become Loving rather than remain rational.

iii. It may take some time, and repeated attempts, before you are shown the barrier to Love. Be patient.

30. Creating Loving Relationships

Creating a Loving relationship with others in your life means that you hold the intention to interact with the other person from an inner space of Love. The relationship is an opportunity to learn about yourself not the other person. You are learning about what causes you to fail to interact with the other from Love. Those failures are caused by your barriers to Love which you can then remove. This exercise is intended to provide you with a way to create Loving relationships in your life (i and ii).

1.   Set the intention to interact with the other person in a relationship from an inner space of Love.

2.   Accept that the relationship is an opportunity to learn about yourself not the other person.

3.   Bring awareness to your true motivation for every interaction that you have with that person (iii). Is your motivation Loving (coming

from a silent inner space) or non-Loving (coming from ego)? Be honest with yourself about when you are being non-Loving in your motivation.

4. If you become aware that you are being non-Loving then a barrier to Love inside you has been triggered. Go on to step 5. If your motivation is Loving then return to step 3.

5. Apologize for being non-Loving towards the other person.

6. Find a quiet space to be alone.

7. Enter into meditation and replay the non-Loving interaction in your mind. Ask to be shown the barrier to Love that triggered you into being non-Loving (iv).

8. Heal the barrier to Love using the appropriate exercise for that type of barrier: '*6. Letting go of a Particular Fear*'; '*7. Removing a Belief*'; '*8. Healing an Emotional Trauma*'; or, '*9. Letting go of a Desire*'.

9. Return to step 3.

Notes:

i. It is possible to have a Loving relationship with a person who is not being Loving in return. You simply focus on the way you are being in the relationship and remove any barriers to Love that you find inside you. You do not take anything that the other person says or does personally, and you do not try to change them in any way. You simply Love them by accepting them exactly as they are.

ii. If the other party in the relationship also holds the intention to interact with you from an inner space of Love then the two of you can create a mutually Loving relationship. In these relationships, there is an acceptance that you are both learning and that no one is perfect. If you fall from grace in your ability to remain Loving then you own your emotions and you do not blame the other party for how you feel. Instead, you delve inside to find and remove the barrier to Love that triggered you into become non-Loving. Similarly, if the other party becomes non-Loving then you are not to take anything they say personally. You are simply to Love them by accepting them exactly as they are. You remain connected to the inner space of Love. From that space of Love, you can also support them in healing their barrier to Love at their own pace.

iii. This exercise does not end until the relationship itself ends. Once you choose to enter into a Loving relationship then you are committing yourself to bringing mindful awareness to every moment of that relationship. You will continue to do so until the other person is no longer in your life.

iv. It may take some time, and repeated attempts, before you are shown the barrier to Love. Be patient.

31. Clearing the Energy Between Yourself and Another

This exercise is intended to both remove another person's energy from your being and to reclaim your energy from their being.

1. Sit comfortably either on a chair or in the lotus position.

2. Visualize the other person sitting in front of you in the same posture.

3. Go into meditation.

4. Hold your hands next to your first chakra, palms outward, and state the following out loud: *"I give your energy back to you"*. Wave your arms away from your body, as though you are pushing their energy away from you, when you say this.

5. With your arms fully extended, turn your palms back to face you and say out loud: *"I take my energy back from you"*. Move your hands back towards your own first chakra, as though you are bringing your energy back to you, when you say this.

6. Repeat the above two steps two more times for the first chakra. You will then have done both steps three times for that chakra.

7. Repeat the above three steps for each of the seven main chakras.

32. Cutting Cords

This exercise is intended to provide you with a way to cut the energetic cords that you create with people (i and ii).

1. Sit on a chair with the soles of your feet on the floor.

2. Ground and center yourself (iii).

3. Scan your energy body in order to detect any cords that are attached to you (iv).

4. Visualize an energetic sword slicing through all of your cords (v).

5. Visualize the end of the cords that are then dangling from you dissolving away (vi).

Notes:

i. We create energetic cords between ourselves and others whenever we enter into a co-dependent relationship with them. For example, you can have cords with your friends, family members, co-workers, institutional leaders, and lovers. You do not create cords with those that you enter into unconditionally Loving relationships with.

ii. It is beneficial to cut all of your cords. Cutting cords enables you to clear away any residual energy from relationships that are no longer active. It also allows you to let go of outdated patterns of behavior with relationships that are still active. Letting go of those patterns enables to have current time interactions with people rather than interactions based on those old patterns.

iii. Use exercises '*13. Ground yourself*' and '*14. Center Yourself*'.

iv. You may not be able to detect your cords when you first do this exercise. Initially, you can simply set the intention to detect the cords and then sit in silence to see if you can. With practice and trust, you will be able to either sense or visualize the cords between yourself and other people. Move on to the next step regardless of whether or not you can sense your cords.

v. Until you have learned to detect the cords yourself, you can simply visualize a sword passing all around your body and severing every cord that may be there.

vi. If you are unable to detect the ends of the cords dangling from your body then you can simply set the intention to have them dissolve away and then visualize it happening.

Bibliography

1. Chinmoy, Sri, "9. Love is a thing to become", *srichinmoylibrary.com*, Agni Press, 1975. Web. Accessed February 27, 2015. <http://www.srichinmoylibrary.com/when-god-love-descends/9-love-thing-become>

2. Maharaj, Nisargadatta, I am That, Page #495, Acorn Press, Durham, North Carolina, 1st American Edition (December 1, 1997), © 1973.

3. Ibid, Page 413.

4. Tolle, Eckhart, "Don't Take Your Thoughts Too Seriously", *Mind Power News*, Article excerpted from Stillness Speaks by Eckhart Tolle, new World Library, 2003. Web. Accessed on February 27, 2015 <http://www.mindpowernews.com/BeyondThinking.htm>

5. Estes, Clarissa Pinkola, "You Were Made for This", *Awakin.org*, Jan. 28, 2008. Web. Accessed on February 27, 2015, <http://www.awakin.org/read/view.php?tid=548>

6. Samples, Bob, "Bob Samples Quotes", *goodreads.com*. Web. Accessed on February 27, 2015, <http://www.goodreads.com/author/quotes/84371.Bob_Samples>

7. Einstein, Albert, "The Theosophy of Albert Einstein", *www.filosofiaesoterica.com*, Wing Books, New York, 1996. Web. Accessed on April 28, 2017, <http://www.filosofiaesoterica.com/the-theosophy-of-albert-einstein/>

8. Maharaj, Nisargadatta, I am That, Page #531, Acorn Press, Durham, North Carolina, 1st American Edition (December 1, 1997), © 1973.

9. Wilbur, ken, The Spectrum of Consciousness, Page #108, Quest books, Wheaton, IL, second Quest Edition (1993), © 1977, 1993.

10. Einstein, Albert, "Albert Einstein Quotes", *goodreads.com*. Web. Accessed on February 27, 2015, <http://www.goodreads.com/quotes/272021-the-significant-problems-we-have-cannot-be-solved-at-the>

11. Maharaj, Nisargadatta, I am That, Page #326, Acorn Press, Durham, North Carolina, 1st American Edition (December 1, 1997), © 1973.

12. Ibid, Page 495.

13. Osho, <u>Maturity: The Responsibility of Being Oneself</u>, Page #95, St. Martin's Griffin, New York, NY, 1st Edition (1999), © 1999.

ABOUT THE AUTHOR

Bruce currently lives on Cortes Island in British Columbia with his wife and son. He provides service to others through acting as a spiritual guide. A spiritual guide is one who has connected to his or her own inner guide and can support others in connecting to their own inner guide. He offers one on one guidance, facilitated discussions, and awareness retreats.

Bruce lived in a Tibetan Bon monastery in India where he studied under a Dzogchen master and has combined what he learned there with Peruvian Shamanism and Zen principles to create a program for awakening people from the western mind. The program is called 'The Way Home' and it provides people with guidance in both remembering the essence of who they truly are and removing the barriers inside themselves to being Love.

He has also been gifted with a vision of how communities of the future are going to be formed. This vision is one that has been received by many people all over the world. His passion is to guide and support people in becoming a part of creating those communities and thereby heralding a Golden Age for humanity.

Bruce can be contacted at brucejtaylor@yahoo.com.

www.ingramcontent.com/pod-product-compliance
Lightning Source LLC
LaVergne TN
LVHW051357080426
835508LV00022B/2871